CU00543607

Christian Human Rights

Intellectual History of the Modern Age

Series Editors
Angus Burgin
Peter E. Gordon
Joel Isaac
Karuna Mantena
Samuel Moyn
Jennifer Ratner-Rosenhagen
Camille Robcis
Sophia Rosenfeld

*A complete list of books in the series
is available from the publisher.*

Christian Human Rights

Samuel Moyn

PENN

UNIVERSITY OF PENNSYLVANIA PRESS

PHILADELPHIA

Publication of this volume was aided by a generous grant from the Andrew W. Mellon Foundation.

Copyright © 2015 University of Pennsylvania Press

All rights reserved. Except for brief quotations used for purposes of review or scholarly citation, none of this book may be reproduced in any form by any means without written permission from the publisher.

Published by
University of Pennsylvania Press
Philadelphia, Pennsylvania 19104–4112

www.upenn.edu/pennpress
Printed in the United States of America

A Cataloging-in-Publication record is available from the Library of Congress

Cover design by John Hubbard

ISBN 978-0-8122-4818-0 hardcover
ISBN 978-0-8122-9277-0 ebook

For Julian and Paul

[T]o reaffirm faith in fundamental human rights, in the dignity
and worth of the human person . . .

—United Nations Charter, 1945

Contents

Introduction

Christmas Day, 1942. The outcome of World War II was undecided. A month before, the tide at Stalingrad had turned against the Germans; just two days before, General Erich von Manstein had abandoned his efforts to relieve the Wehrmacht's doomed Sixth Army. Still, there was no telling that the extraordinary German strength in the war on display so far would now ebb quickly. Nonetheless, the Roman Catholic pontiff, Pius XII, had something new to say.

The Americans had formally entered the war a year before, but the Allies would not reach mainland Italy for another nine months, or make it to Rome for a year and a half. The pope felt himself in dire straits. His relationship with Benito Mussolini had long since soured, and he was a prisoner in his own tiny Roman domain. As for the Jews, the worst victims of the conflict, millions were dead already; the victims at Babi Yar had lain in their ravine for more than a year; Treblinka, the most infernal death camp, had begun killing operations six months before and much of its grim work was already complete.

Officially, of course, the papacy and its leader were neutral in the war and did not play politics. Many of Pius's flock, however, were to be found on all sides of the war. To the extent recent observers have revisited Pius's Christmas message, it has been to argue about whether he could or should have said more about the Holocaust than he did. But the real interest in the message is what the pope was for, not what he was against. In this fight, Christianity stood for values, and in the perspective of world history, Pius XII had some new ones.

On that day, the appeal to reaffirm faith in the dignity of the human person, and in the rights that follow from that dignity, reached unprecedented heights of public visibility. The very first of the five peace points that Pius XII offered that day ran as follows:

> *Dignity of the Human Person.* He who would have the Star of Peace shine out and stand over society should cooperate, for his part, in giving back to the human person the dignity given to it by God from the very beginning. . . . *He should uphold respect for and the practical realization of . . . fundamental personal rights* . . . . The cure of this situation becomes feasible when we awaken again the consciousness of a juridical order resting on the supreme dominion of God, and safeguarded from all human whims; a consciousness of an order which stretches forth its arm, in protection or punishment, over *the unforgettable rights of man* and protects them against the attacks of every human power.[1]

It was a critical turning point, one that has defined history since, if not exactly in ways that Pius XII intended.

People now treat such affirmations, and especially the notion that human dignity provides the foundation for universal human rights, as a set of conventional and enduring truths. Yet it was all rather new at the time. The

Roman Catholic Church had previously rejected the hitherto secular and liberal language of human rights. But now the pope turned to it, making human dignity its new basis. Around the same time, ecumenical formations of transatlantic Protestant elites proclaimed human rights to be the key to future world order. The communion between human rights and Christianity was therefore a novel and fateful departure in the history of political discourse.

Undoubtedly, the pope's first peace point was the supreme, influential, and most publicly prominent invocation of human dignity during World War II proper and likely in the whole history of political claim-making to that date. It gave Christian "personalism" a broad hearing, attaching supreme ethical significance to human beings agonizingly caught between individualist atomism without community and "totalitarian" statehood without freedom. Alongside novel Protestant discussion, it was also at or near the top of the list of prominent wartime invocations of the basic idea of universal human rights, especially when understood as a framework—as Pius XII would express it very clearly two years later in his 1944 Christmas message—of world and not merely state order.[2] But what did such conceptions mean as they made their way into, and did much to define, democratic and international ideals after the war?

The history of human rights in the 1940s was not just a matter of Christians adopting long-standing rhetoric or even commitments, in spite of the long prior history of rights in various forms and settings. Amplifying the importance of human rights before a vast public, Pius's statement also recrafted the meaning of the principles it merely claimed to recall to importance. It made what had been secular and liberal into a set of values that were now religious and conservative. And it provided an inkling of how Christians would come to defend the postwar democracies they later founded in Western Europe, which were also religious and conservative in nature. This book tells the story of how this became possible.

The ideological association of Christianity and human rights depended on contingent and time-bound circumstance no later than the 1940s and shortly before. Far from teaching us simply about the Christian invention of human rights in the 1940s, interesting and important as that development was, the history of this crystallizing moment casts light on the fortunes of the concept as a whole. Not the least of the reasons is that it turns out to be quite difficult to find non-Christians who enthused about human rights, and more especially their basis in human dignity, in the age. The history of Christian human rights in the 1940s is the major part of the history of human rights generally at the time, before the principles inspired the slogans of mass movements and became central elements of contemporary international law.

Mainstream observers are generally unaware of—for their secular historians have nervously bypassed—the Christian incarnation of human rights, which interferes with their preferred understandings of today's highest principles. Meanwhile, those interested in Christian sources, overwhelmingly Christians themselves, are prone to misinterpret them. The proposition that human rights arose with profound connections to Christian contexts is normally defended, in both public discourse and scholarly arguments, in a highly abstract way and about long ago events.[3] It was from "the biblical conception of man," Pope John Paul II noted in 2003, that "Europe drew the best of its humanistic culture, and, not least, advanced the dignity of the person as the subject of inalienable rights."[4] Preference for classic sources that supposedly cast the die for Christianity's advocacy of human rights across the millennia is especially evident among certain Christians who most want to take credit for what have become the premier values of the day, precisely in view of their contemporary prestige. According to such views, it is rather old Christian lineages—stretching from the Annunciation to the Reformation—that help explain the existence, shape, and prestige of the idea of human rights today.[5]

Looking back that far is not a mere distraction. No one could plausibly claim—and no one ever has—that the history of human rights is one of wholly discontinuous novelty, whether in the 1940s or after.[6] But radical departures nonetheless occurred very late in Christian history, even if they were unfailingly represented as consistent with what came before: this is how "the invention of tradition" most frequently works.[7] Christian human rights were injected into tradition by pretending they had always been there, and on the basis of minor antecedents now treated as fonts of enduring commitments. Novelty always comes about not ex nihilo but from a fragmentary past that is coaxed into a more robust form. Even partial continuity across time often proceeds through rediscovery and reactivation of lost possibilities and underemphasized realities. Many of those who want the ideological association of Christianity and human rights to be deep and lasting are participants in such inventions rather than analysts of them, for they play down or pass over the fact that Christianity had mostly stood for values inimical to those we now associate with human rights.[8] It took a set of wrenching experiences for Christianity to come to seem favorable to them. This book tries to understand how large an impact those experiences made—and how much continuity they left behind.

The truth is that Europe and therefore the modern world drew nearly everything from Christianity in the long term. It would be fictitious to retrospectively edit the long and tumultuous history of Europe, as if everything we liked about the outcomes were due to its hegemonic religion, while the rest was an unfortunate accident or someone else's fault. And to the extent this is true, the challenge of isolating the crucial period for a strong ideological link of Christianity with human rights changes. It means looking not so much at Jesus (or even at the Reformation), but at novel mid-twentieth-century interpretations of what his teachings demand, to understand how the huge set of possibilities the Christian legacy bequeathed was winnowed down.

The trouble, after all, is not so much that Christianity accounts for nothing, as that it accounts for everything. Without Christianity, our commitment to the moral equality of human beings is unlikely to have come about, but by itself this had no bearing on most forms of political equality—whether between Christians and Jews, whites and blacks, civilized and savage, or men and women. That had been true for millennia, and it was mostly still true on Christmas Day, 1942.[9] If the winnowing of Christian values was not complete (and never is, since traditions are never set), it was above all because the war was undecided. Pius's peace points are fascinating because they introduce human dignity and rights before the war's outcome was clear.

It was not just that over its long trajectory, Christianity had stood for the star of peace but also the dogs of war when their violence was thought to serve justice; that its members had powered abolitionism in the nineteenth century but also that slavery's defenders relied on Christianity's long tolerance and support for the institution; that Christians stood for the spiritual kingdom but also had served worldly empires, from Rome to modern global ones; and that, whatever the fervency of their commitment to the equality of souls, patriarchy in so many forms was perhaps their fundamental commitment. Most relevant to our purposes, Christians and Christian thought were deeply entangled in the collapse of liberal democracy on the European continent between the wars. Catholicism in particular had celebrated victories for its social teachings in the fall of liberal democracy in authoritarian Austria, Spain, and Portugal in the 1930s, and Vichy France during the war, even as a Catholic priest was the titular head of Nazi Germany's most subservient client state, Slovakia. Christians even had truck with fascism. From the pinnacle of the churches to the rank and file, only a few Christians denounced it in these years, and normally then in the name of strictly Christian ideals and interests; more acquiesced to fascism, or fervently served it, including in Nazi Germany, which some were calling "the holy reich."[10]

And yet it is also Christians who did much and perhaps most to welcome and define the idea of human rights in the 1940s, as well as some of its core notions such as the importance of human dignity, which nobody else was yet making central in 1942. How was this possible? Perhaps it was because, to a rather disturbing extent, human rights and especially human dignity had no necessary correlation with liberal democracy. Certainly not in 1942, when Christian leaders such as the pope were not yet (to the extent he ever became) friendly toward that regime. It would be tempting to argue that its flirtation with far-right politics and the horror of totalitarianism summoned Christianity back to its true essence, but this argument only works so long as it is recalled that the fundamental truths its partisans wanted most to honor were morally constraining and that human rights entered the equation as a belated discovery about how to achieve enduring ends. And so when liberal democracy later came in Western Europe, it was in a conservative and religious form graced by a commitment to human dignity that signaled enormous continuity with the past, not simply learning from mistakes.

Almost unfailingly, the annunciation of human rights in the 1940s is now viewed by the general public and professional scholars as the uncomplicated triumph of liberal democracy. But the general thesis of *Christian Human Rights* is that through this lost and misremembered transwar era, it is equally if not more viable to regard human rights as a project of the Christian right, not the secular left. Their creation brought about a break with the revolutionary tradition and its *droits de l'homme*, or—better put—a successful capture of that language by forces reformulating their conservatism.

For this reason, the central question about Christian human rights in the 1940s is whether the Christian and conservative encounter with human rights—the embrace of liberal principle by forces once inimical to it—is plausibly seen as a victory for liberalism. Conservatism, to be sure, was updated through affiliation with historically liberal norms and a historically liberal language. Authoritarian solutions to crisis were taken off the table—with the very large exception of the Iberian peninsula, where they survived for several more decades. But in reviewing this process, it behooves one to ask whether Christianity and conservatism were able to change liberalism more than they were changed by it. In this period, perhaps the most durable and fateful transformation was the start of a new era in liberalism—specifically, the ideological origins of religiously inflected Cold War liberalism in the face of the specter of "totalitarianism."[11] It was a new liberalism that substantially overlapped with conservatism, suitably corrected, after the purgation of the extreme right and for the sake of standing down the left, extreme and not so extreme. In many respects, that conservative vision of liberalism remains alive and well.

This book on the origins of Christian human rights therefore focuses most of all on the extent to which, across the 1930s and 1940s, the language of rights was extricated from the legacy of the French Revolution, the secularist mantle of which the Soviet leaders were now widely seen to have assumed. And thanks to the championship of rights within a new political formation—constitutionally organized religious democracy governed by Christian parties—a compromise between Christianity and democracy became not only palatable but a precious resource for the future of religious values.

In the nineteenth century, what Pius XII in 1942 called the "unforgettable rights of man" were precepts that

9

his predecessors had tried very hard to forget, because their success or failure was very closely correlated with the success or failure of secular liberalism in the wake of the French Revolution (though the latter's own Declaration of the Rights of Man and Citizen had celebrated rights as "sacred"). Thanks to events across the 1930s and 1940s, this was no longer true. Indeed, Christians redefined and went a long way toward capturing these precepts. They were able to do so because of their confidence—a rather impressive epistemic confidence that many might like to have about their values—that they knew the moral truth and that it ought to be imposed everywhere. Christian human rights were part and parcel of a reformulation of conservatism in the name of a vision of moral constraint, not human emancipation or individual liberation. Jesus's truth had been intended to set men free, but not for the sake of their creative autonomy or the satisfaction of their preferences. This liberation was for the sake of subjugation: so that men and (perhaps especially) women could conform to God's will and moral order.

Much of the shift that led to the centrality of rights as part of the defense of religiously oriented conservative democracy was due to hard experiences. It was not just that older flirtations with far-right regimes increasingly failed, inciting unsavory episodes of destruction and slaughter more than they served to advance Christian values. The year 1939 seized the mind. After Adolf Hitler allied with hated Joseph Stalin—the most fearsome enemy of Christianity, even if he did the most to put Hitler down—the emerging theory of "totalitarianism" emphasized the risk that states could snuff out their civil society seemed deeply pertinent. As a result, rights could appear a formidable antidote to a new syndrome of state hypertrophy inimical to religious values. Once World War II exploded, Christian suffering in war and under occupation was tremendous and could provide further credibility to something like human rights. There was persecution of the churches, deportation of enemies, and forced labor that understandably drew attention to the excesses of the state run amok. Recent observers have learned to insist that Christian suffering was nowhere near the worst of the era—and that Christians overwhelmingly ignored Jewish suffering to the extent they knew about it or were not participating in causing it. Moreover, for all the exile, imprisonment, and occupation that many Western European Christians underwent, the worst of Christian suffering (like the worst of Jewish suffering) occurred in the East. But Eastern European Christians played little role in the genesis of human rights. Nevertheless, there is no reason to dispute that what Westerners saw was a contributing factor in a new rights consciousness. A commitment to moral order now incorporated personal rights after a learning process about where that commitment could lead. Not just the individualist anarchy of "modernity," paranoid responses to which had once driven reactionary political affiliations, but also now the state terror of right-wing as well as left-wing government had to be avoided.

"Human rights" came to figure because, in the crucible of reaction before and during World War II when they flirted with authoritarian states (or built their own), Christians learned that the cultivation of moral constraint depended on keeping the spiritual communities that offered their vision of ethical life a home partly free from the state. Frequently, this learning occurred in the name of fidelity to many inherited hierarches, especially of gender but also of class. Christian social morality had also pushed early and insistently for moral limits on capitalist immiseration and some response to free-market outcomes, though it preferred local and nonstate solutions unless Christian ideology directed the state, as occurred in different ways before, during, and after World War II.[12] Yet by 1944, it was clear to most that it would not do for churches to fully capture Caesar's power when spiritual life was beyond his ken. It was also for this reason that, in the 1940s, human rights for Christians were a communitarian project, and not only or so much a liberal one.

There are four conventional opinions about human rights in the 1940s that, in view of these arguments, will have to be abandoned or corrected. First, there is the claim that institutions such as the United Nations, which allowed for the birth of the Universal Declaration of Human Rights (1948), deserve most scrutiny. With that understandable emphasis, however, historians have routinely ignored broader culture and ideology, in which Christianity loomed largest in early human rights discourse.[13] Self-consciously Christian historians such as Mary Ann Glendon and John Nurser, in their pioneering works, have rightly emphasized the prominence of Christian thinking in the United Nations processes that led to the Universal Declaration, even while soft-pedalling how divisive and partisan this provenance made the efforts they chronicled. This book builds on theirs but also insists on the need for a broader view of the scene as a whole, including in other locales and in circles not specifically directed at United

Nations outcomes.[14] Similarly, Mark Mazower has provocatively argued that human rights emerged in hydraulic replacement for earlier intergovernmental schemes of minority protection.[15] Yet only a very few thought about the point of human rights in this way, and indeed the primary sites of dignity, personalism, and rights were ideological sloganeering and local politics, rather than a mostly sterile attempt to change international order or even to give entitlements legal effect within the Western European zone. Mazower's claim is genuinely helpful in seeing how religious freedom was reconceived in the era, after a long period of collective protection that was now individualized. A regional treaty known as the European Convention of Human Rights certainly emerged; as a later chapter will show, however, its real significance at the time and for decades was a statement of values—often frankly Christian ones—rather than any genuine transformation of regional governance. (That has awaited our time.) Thus attention to public discourse shows that the birth of human rights was not so much about new individualist schemes of protection as communitarian investment in moral order.

Second, historians have followed the general public in treating human rights as a response to the Holocaust. Yet few who said they cared about human dignity and rights in the 1940s said so because of the Jewish fate, and the pope is a good example of this broader truth. Christmas 1942 was the darkest hour of what one historian called "Christian Europe's darkest night," but the initial flickering of Christian human rights was not intended to illuminate the plight of the Jewish people and did not occur for their sake.[16] Pius's much disputed priorities never fell making the Holocaust ethically central, when it was occurring or after.[17] The same was to be true when rights and dignity became important to the political ideology of early postwar Western Europe under Christian Democratic rule. And if so, it was in part because of Christianity's recoil at Nazism more generally, and its ultimate consequences for the churches, but also because Christians were more intent on advancing their ideals and interests in new schemes of achieving order. Past atrocities mattered far less than future ascendancy. For them, human rights were a moralizing project, not simply a moral reaction.

Third, historians treat human rights as the fruit of a multicultural communion. But this notion fails to do justice to the fact that the sole abstentions to the Universal Declaration in the United Nations General Assembly reflected the sway of organized Christianity's greatest enemies, old and new: Islam and communism. Above all, it fails to reckon with the fact that Western Europe became the initial homeland of human rights (and especially human dignity, since Western European constitutions were almost the sole ones to cite that principle for a long time). In the 1940s, Western Europe initiated its long age of the political hegemony of the Christian Democratic movement: no doubt the truly crucial fact that a sober return to the history of human rights in the era must stress.

Fourth, there is the widespread belief that human rights arose on the ruins of prior mistakes and in a total break with those political experiments—fascism, notably— undertaken by Europeans shortly before. Human rights promised a "world made new," in Glendon's phrase, which has disguised how much of the old world survived, in part because Christians who had chosen a different politics shortly before wanted continuity and not only change. Their most cherished projects, from moral community at home to missionary activity abroad, were now reformulated in terms of "human rights." For this reason, this book contends, the only way to come to grips with Christian human rights is by recognizing their short-term origins in and through the 1930s, without truncating Christian politics as if they began after 1942, when more had become apparent about what the postwar world would look like.[18] There has been a recent call for the study of so-called transwar continuities, and it is clear that the story of Christian human rights demands such an approach.[19]

Christian Human Rights begins with 1937: probably the most crucial date in the story, for it is when the discourse reached the heights of Christianity. This was because, on the basis of newly popular notions of the centrality of the "human person" to Christian political thought, it was also at this date that the expiring pope Pius XI and his soon to be successor Pius XII realized that totalitarian states of the left and even of the right threatened the moral community for which Jesus had long ago called. It was at this date that human dignity became a major item of Christian political discourse and—thanks to the coincidence that Catholic Ireland scuttled its first constitution and wrote a new one then—was embedded for the first time in constitutional history. Still, as the constitutional outcome showed, human dignity and the rights it grounded were not only compatible with conservative moral governance—such governance was their aim. A new sort of constitutionalism was born with which religious conservatism made peace and which became a powerful tool of order.

After the guns of World War II allowed this solution to become popular—and eliminated the partisans of rival ones—a minority tendency became general. As recent work by scholars such as Martin Conway and Wolfram Kaiser illustrates, in Western Europe, conservative rule took root, and ideological slogans that had been marginal before won out, judging by the spectacular rise of Christian Democratic politics and the belief systems of many of Europeanization's most influential advocates.[20] In striking respects, this Christian-conservative complex defined the putatively global efflorescence of human rights far more generally than has been recognized. For much of the rhetoric that mushroomed in response to the period's wrenching upheaval, and certainly the enthusiasm for human rights in particular, the Catholic publicist Jacques Maritain was the most prominent expositor. In 1942, Maritain suddenly realized that human rights were not only central to Christian teaching; they were to be its salvation after interwar and wartime error. Taking up his transwar trajectory in the context of Christian political thought generally, *Christian Human Rights* examines the popular notion of "the human person" that surged in the 1930s and was embedded in early post–World War II human rights discourse, in the Universal Declaration, Western European politics, and beyond. Maritain's case does not of itself, of course, explain the eventual association of human rights with postwar Christian conservatism. For example, Maritain himself was unconvinced of the extent to which mere party politics could usher in the new kind of Christian civilization, based on human dignity, for which he called.[21] As a proxy for intellectual historians for a far fuller and more complicated reconstruction of the transformation of Christian politics, however, Maritain is easily the best choice.

That the first half of this book focuses more on Catholics should not imply that transatlantic Protestantism was unimportant in the invention of Christian human rights. Though the case of Catholicism provides an especially vivid example because of its drastic reassessment of rights and its creative incorporation of liberalism to save conservatism, many Protestants offered a parallel trajectory. The summer of 1937 was also when the epoch-making Oxford Conference took place, the major event in the crystallization of transatlantic Protestant "ecumenism," which laid the foundation for the World Council of Churches after World War II. It was thanks to this event that the rhetoric of "the human person" as a moral alternative to power politics—and likewise defined against the totalitarian specter—was matched in some transatlantic Protestant thinking. It found resonance from high politics to modest enterprises. Writing his senior thesis at Princeton University in the midst of World War II, then Protestant theologian John Rawls—long before he became renowned as a philosophical standard-bearer of secular liberals—could affirm that "an individual is not merely an individual, but a person, and . . . a society is not a group of individuals but a community."[22] Neo-orthodox Protestant theologians such as Emil Brunner had convinced him—much as Maritain convinced so many others—that personhood and community were mutually entailed rather than mutually exclusive.

Thus personalism and the rise of rights as a bulwark against totalitarianism also burgeoned within Protestant networks across the same period, and to examine some of their stakes *Christian Human Rights* turns to the work of Gerhard Ritter, the dean of German historians of the period. If Maritain was the leading theoretician of human rights then, Ritter was their preeminent historian. His Lutheran understanding of where human rights had come from illustrates the cultural politics of a conservative Christian, once American ascendancy was clear and as the Soviet ally that had been so crucial to putting down National Socialism now threatened a new totalitarian outcome.

In Ritter's Germany, Protestantism was so compromised by its recent nationalist temptation that its representatives rushed to forge a new and enlarged notion of "the Occident" (*Abendland*) that embraced Catholics, as well as Protestants across the English channel and even across the Atlantic ocean. The whole geography of Protestantism was shattered due to World War II, with ancestral territories under Soviet occupation and soon communist rule. Locally, the division of Germany fundamentally reshaped the confessional balance, allowing Catholicism unprecedented importance in the politics of the new federal republic, led by former Cologne mayor and pious Roman Catholic Konrad Adenauer. Globally, the same events, alongside the prestige of their victory, gave Anglo-Americans newfound priority as the geopolitical leadership of Protestantism that Germans had been loath to relinquish as recently as the prior decade. Ritter's narrative of how human rights might help Germany (so long as their secularist implications were avoided) was intended to acknowledge the sudden importance of Catholics whose thought and politics appeared more central for Protestants across old confessional lines (not least in the new Christian Democratic Union that came to rule West Germany for decades).[23] Even more, it showcased Anglo-American Protestants, not only because they had saved the West from self-imposed ruin but also because they now were the new guarantors against external threats. For this was the last reason that Christianity came to define human rights so deeply: after World War II, whose ending saw communism reach so far west, Anglo-American Protestants were regarded as the last hope to keep its secular evil from striking ever deeper into the so-called Occident—the age-old Christian homeland.

As a transnational intellectual and political entity after World War II, however, Protestantism is underresearched relative to its Catholic companion, even though it featured its own versions of Christian human rights and indeed some of the earliest, especially when understood as potentially global principles of a new order. It is certainly clear that Anglo-American Protestantism offered preeminent spokesmen for human rights as such principles during wartime, when continental Europeans were still unsure about how the war should turn out. And later, when it came to the most important human right for Christians, religious freedom, Anglo-American Protestantism had to become the source of fundamental change for long-standing Catholic assumptions. After World War II, there occurred a historic compromise between the camps of Catholics and Protestants that had often been adverse before. The compromise defined Christian human rights to the core, and one of their most interesting contemporary legacies was also due to it.

To illustrate both facts, the book concludes with a chapter that offers some indication of the legacy of Christian human rights today, in European Court of Human Rights cases about the Muslim headscarf and the meaning of religious freedom. The reason to study the past is its legacies, and this chapter expands the frame of the inquiry to include transatlantic Protestant calls for human rights and a new age of religious freedom in particular. Liberty of conscience had always been the dearest right to Protestants, but after World War II, it came into its own; the driving factors were the anticommunist fight and the cause of missionary Christianity, and a surprising conversion of Catholic politics to incorporate this right that popes had long anathematized even occurred. Many of the headscarf cases today originate in France, where the culprit in the discrimination against Muslims surely has been the secularist opprobrium that republicanism has always cast on religion—Christianity long before Islam. Yet at the European level, there were ideological and doctrinal sources of the approval of the headscarf bans that paradoxically originated in the opprobrium that Christianity has historically cast on secularism. The uses of the right to religious freedom to police Muslims in the present "secular" age of a de-Christianized Europe, the book ends by suggesting, is not only a cautionary tale, showing that the historical avatar of the persecuted Muslim today is not so much the former Christian as the once feared communist enemy. It exposes how even across the vast changes separating then and now, including the ruin of organized Christianity in its onetime citadel, there are troubling if unsuspected legacies to be found.

Never—or almost never—is religion merely politics, and one of the deepest aspirations of many of those reinterpreting Christianity across the 1930s and 1940s was to put the "established disorder" of the world of politics (as one of them called it) in its place for the sake of suprapolitical truth. Often, the goal was not to move rightward (or, for that matter, leftward) as upward—and thus orthogonally to politics as a whole. And yet such aspirations had inevitably this-worldly implications, especially when they found their ways into such documents as national constitutions and international declarations or came to be mobilized by parties and publicists pursuing agendas with definite implications for the terms of collective life here and now. There are thus two equal and opposite errors to be avoided: if the first is to treat the spiritual as just the ideological mystification of the political, the second is to forget that the most otherworldly claims are ultimately significant—certainly for the secular historian—for how they affect this world.

All history, of course, is selective, and this set of soundings is no different, covering neither the totality of human rights talk in the era (much of which has been assayed in earlier scholarship) nor even of religious versions of it, and notably that of an evanescent Christian left. The sheer anarchy of the Christian response to the confusing events of the era was pronounced, even once the war wound down and options became clearer. Recently, indeed, historians have stressed how fluid the immediate aftermath of 1945 really was, before conservative political rule triumphed over its competition in continental Europe and many experiments failed to reach durable form or were forcefully contained.[24] The emphasis on volatility most definitely applies to the Christian sector of politics in 1945, where no one foresaw the triumph of Christian Democracy coming and contingency predominated, not necessity. Ultimately, however, the renowned open-endedness of the *Stunde Null*—the "zero hour" across Europe when the slate seemed blank and everything appeared possible—has to be reconciled with the realities of transwar continuity. If "Christian democracy" was the unanticipated harvest of the fields of contentious ideological and practical experience across an era of conflict, then it is legitimate to stress that in the end it became the victorious embodiment of new concepts such as dignity, personalism, and rights.

A similar point applies to the study of legacies that the last chapter of this book provides: it is selective and illustrative but not comprehensive or even representative. Study of the full intersection of Christianity and human rights after 1945 remains to be undertaken, both in Protestant ecumenical activism and through the worldwide ramifications of later Pope John XXIII's pivotal encyclical *Pacem in Terris* (1963).[25] Unlike John, Pius XII never referred to the Universal Declaration.[26] But *Pacem in Terris* not only remedied this omission, in what became by far the most trendsetting Catholic endorsement of rights for a global audience; it also reopened the debate about whether commitment to human dignity ratified conservative democracy or pointed far beyond its terms.[27] Without experimental forms of Christianity, further, Amnesty International—the founder of which, Peter Benenson, came out of the Catholic nongovernmental organization Pax Christi, just as many of its early members had close links to ecumenical Protestant networks—might never have been formed, and the shape of contemporary human rights advocacy could look very different. Across the ocean, in an early sign of evangelical Protestantism's conquest of mainline strongholds in the United States and its impending rise to political importance, Jimmy Carter, president of the country in the later 1970s, could give human rights policies unprecedented salience in American liberalism and testify that he did so on religious grounds.[28]

Absorbing and even uplifting as these other stories are, they presuppose rather than negate the importance of the prior victory of Christian human rights as a conservative achievement on which this book focuses. Also omitted in what follows—since I have devoted a prior book to the topic—is how, after a midcentury interlude, the secular left achieved predominant ownership over human rights. The same was not to be entirely true in America, of course, where in spite of a significant community of secular defenders of human rights, many more legacies of their Christian incubation remained strong far longer. While evangelical Christianity helped American liberals discover human rights, thanks to Carter and others, it soon provided a massive boost to the conservative turn that defined the late twentieth century, and "religious freedom" could become a privileged weapon of the religious right in national politics. The modest goal of the last chapter of this book is to provide an indication of how, in Europe, elements of Christian human rights could survive the transwar age of their inception, in spite of the passing of Christian politics and even Christianity itself on its old continent. That this persistence could occur is lamentable, this book contends, precisely because postwar European history generally extricated human rights from their proprietary Christian and especially from their conservative rendition.

The reorientation of conservatives through the 1930s and 1940s—which was often at stake even when actors did not call themselves conservatives—matters because of its lasting effects. Before this period, "human rights" had always been identified with the French Revolution and its promise of secular emancipation. In the face of a Soviet enemy that claimed for itself the mantle of secularism and revolution, a Cold War liberalism arose that featured a tremendously fateful new opening to Christian (sometimes newly called "Judeo-Christian") values and interests, with prior decades of culture war forgotten.[29] This consequential reshuffling haunts politics to this day, as the deepest aspirations of democracy changed, prizing moderation against extremes over liberation of human capacity and restoring order to its regrettable if time-honored status as the centerpiece of justice.

For anyone who wants to revive rather than criticize the promise of secular emancipation, for all its riskiness, the invention of Christian human rights in the era of World War II and after thus provides a window into how the present took on some of its characteristic features—a present in which, after the suppression of the far right, a guarded centrism uniting liberals and conservatives frequently prevails and core values asserted against putative irresponsibility matter more than bids for secular progress.[30]

In the 1940s, as much as in and through some of its contemporary legacies, Christian human rights have been not so much about the inclusion of the other as about policing the borders and boundaries on which threatening enemies loom. And so the story of Christian human rights shows how our premier principles have a complex itinerary. Like all inheritances, it is worth tough criticism rather than unreflective admiration.

The Secret History of Human Dignity

> In the Name of the Most Holy Trinity, from Whom all authority
> and to Whom,
> as our final end, all actions both of men and States must be
> referred,
>
> We, the people of Éire,
> Humbly acknowledging all our obligations to our Divine Lord,
> Jesus Christ,
> Who sustained our fathers through centuries of trial,
>
> Gratefully remembering their heroic and unremitting struggle
> to regain the rightful independence of our Nation,
>
> And seeking to promote the common good,
> with due observance of Prudence, Justice and Charity,
> so that the dignity and freedom of the individual may be assured,
> true social order attained, the unity of our country restored,
> and concord established with other nations,
>
> Do hereby adopt, enact, and give to ourselves this Constitution.
> —Preamble, Irish Constitution (1937)

Chapter 1

"Dignity" is suddenly everywhere in law and philosophy, even though it has long been in decline in general usage. In a popular view, this prominence is essentially due to World War II's aftermath, when in the shadow of genocide the light of human dignity shone forth. More specifically, it is a new emphasis on dignity—channeling Immanuel Kant's pioneering Enlightenment insistence on inherent human worth into the United Nations Charter (1945); the Universal Declaration of Human Rights (1948); and the West German Grundgesetz (1949), or Basic Law, all three of which begin with the dignity of the human person as basic principle—that refounded public law for our time. In this conventional wisdom, Germans after the Holocaust went furthest to rethink constitutionalism and provide an example of how to defend human dignity later taken up in South Africa and beyond.[1] Though it took some time, dignity has since proceeded in the last few decades, in tandem with the larger fortunes of international human rights law, to become a crucial watchword, going global in various constitutions and international treaties and offering judicial guidance for the protection of basic values.[2] Certainly it is true that interest in dignity swarms in legal cases and philosophical discussions today in ways that demand explanation; and the current dispute among judges and commentators about how to interpret dignity provisions is not uninteresting. But is the conventional wisdom about where dignity came from correct in the first place?

The notion of dignity had not been required at any point for the constitutionalization of rights, either in 1776 in Virginia or in 1789 in France—or again in 1946 in France, when the country not only relit its constitutional torch but drew on the flame of constitutional rights guarded by Central and Eastern Europeans in the 1920s.[3] Conversely, West Germans writing the Basic Law were not yet concerned by the Jewish tragedy. And while it is certainly true that Kant occasionally referenced dignity, none of his political disciples have made anything of this fact—and his current philosophical disciples only in the last few years. For that matter, there were no Kantians in Germany of note after World War II (including in the rooms where the Basic Law was prepared and debated), nor really anywhere else. And actually, contrary to familiar beliefs, it was not West Germany that first constitutionalized dignity as leading principle anyway.

Individual human dignity entered global constitutional history in an unexpected place and at a surprising time: Ireland in 1937. It risked—and often still risks—transforming the tradition of rights. After all, 1789 and the liberal secular values for which that date stood in European and world history were not popular in the 1930s or even 1940s and may not have survived the coming of dignity unscathed. More specifically, it was what I shall call "religious constitutionalism" that first canonized dignity: a new form of constitutionalism navigating between the vehement rejection of the secular liberal state long associated with the French Revolution and the widespread demand for an integrally religious social order. To the extent Europeans did not vote with their feet for fascist regimes in an era when most concluded that secular liberalism had failed, it was religious politics that beckoned, indeed almost everywhere at a time of profound intersection of Christian faith and nationalist sentiment. And while outside the Iberian peninsula the new Christian states of the time did not survive the political ecology either of the 1930s when fascism triumphed or of the 1940s when fascism died, Christian Democracy, when it arose after World War II to decades-long dominance in Western Europe, conserved a surprising amount of what came before—notably the central place of religious teachings in public life, including constitutional law.

History matters to the current enthusiasm over human dignity, because while all political and legal concepts are elastic, none ever proves to be exactly as malleable as any other. All bear the marks of their special historical trajectories, so long as partisans of some continuity in their meaning remain to fight on its behalf. This is certainly true of dignity, which emerged as part of an attempt to find a new form of democracy—one that in Europe today, and now many other places too, attracts considerable support. Most important, however, it reveals some of the true ambiance for the crystallization of human rights as a public ideology between the 1930s and the 1940s: a Christian and conservative ambiance. Ireland's early move to Christian Democracy portended the framework that several other Western European countries would take up, which were uncoincidentally the only ones in which dignity had a constitutional presence for a long time.

Traditions of Constitutionalism: Old, New, and Religious

Boris Mirkine-Guetzévitch was the obvious person—the right man in the right place at the right time—to have the most developed insight available into the trajectory of constitutionally declared rights and their fledgling post–World War II internationalization. But he did not mention human dignity, let alone celebrate it.

A Russian-Jewish émigré in Paris and later New York, Mirkine-Guetzévitch (1892–1955) was a founder of the now prestigious discipline of comparative constitutional law. Born in Kiev, from a highly Russified family, he was a liberal who sympathized with Alexander Kerensky until the Bolsheviks took power. After holding on for two years trying to foment opposition, he fled to Paris, ascending to some prominence as a law professor. Compelled to leave France in 1940, he survived World War II in the United States, where he helped found the famous École libre des hautes études. Thereafter he split his time between the two cities that sheltered him.[4] In the 1920s, Mirkine-Guetzévitch had been the premier analyst and proponent of "the new constitutionalism"—as he influentially dubbed it. In his view, the vogue of the rights of man in constitutions had primarily come about as a result of World War I, notably in the constitutions of the eastern European states that arose on the ruins of fallen empires. When he published his analytical study of postwar European constitutions in the early 1950s, he registered the restoration of European democracy after World War II but also the return of the progressive tendency to enthrone the rights of man as the first principles of political order. For Mirkine-Guetzévitch, the victory of Allied arms in World War II allowed not for the invention but for the revival of the new constitutionalism he had first identified and justified.[5]

The old constitutionalism, even when it involved a written constitution, did not typically proceed from the rights of man. Let us recall that the French tradition from 1789, which had taken the Virginian example of 1776 to the national level where the Americans that same year had decided not to proceed (the framers had merely appended a bill of privileges to their federal constitution under pressure), was spurned when it came time to found the French Third Republic in 1870–77. Through modern times, and indeed long after World War II, the British were proud of disdaining written constitutionalism, to say nothing of the constitutionalization of rights. Notwithstanding some Latin American ventures, the end of World War I, therefore, was the true inflection point for the global ascendancy of constitutionally announced rights; and for Mirkine-Guetzévitch, it always seemed as if constitutionalism based on *les droits de l'homme* succeeded by easternizing. The best, albeit short-lived, example remained the Weimar Constitution (1919), but in fact all the postimperial states from the Rhine to the Urals had enshrined rights in a similar manner.[6] After the retrieval of this tradition by the Resistance, the post–World War II consensus about human rights, signaled by the United Nations Charter and made concrete in the Universal Declaration of Human Rights of 1948, finally swept the European continent. It took to a new stage the truly pioneering interwar breakthrough. Given the precedent of the Weimar Constitution, Mirkine-Guetzévitch hoped West Germany's Basic Law was part of this trajectory.[7]

Though it has much to recommend it, no one follows Mirkine-Guetzévitch's presentation of the progress of rights-based constitutionalism today.[8] Present at the creation of constitutionalism founded on human dignity, Mirkine-Guetzévitch may simply have been blind to the era's true breakthrough. Perhaps he did not—or, more generously, could not—understand in real time what has proven to be a considerable step forward in retrospect. It may be, however, that Mirkine-Guetzévitch is a better guide to what mattered just after war and genocide.

After all, for a long time, including in the 1940s, dignity was most strongly correlated with religious constitutions in general—of which the West German Basic Law was merely one among others—and Christian Democratic constitutions in particular. Those constitutions as much broke with 1789 and safeguarded it, let alone rehabilitated it after disaster. The Irish were the true pioneers both in the development of religious constitutionalism and in symbolizing its project through appeals to human dignity. In their 1937 constitution, they gave it foundational placement, as a religiously inspired root concept connected (as in the later West German case) to the subordination of the otherwise sovereign democratic polity to God—and, for many, to the moral constraints of His natural law. This chapter takes up this neglected but revealing fact. It is critical, I contend in what follows, that dignity came to the world as part of the establishment of an alternative constitutionalism—call it "the newer constitutionalism" of Christian Democracy. So far as I know, there is no general historical study of its emergence; and though Ran Hirschl has contributed a valuable overview of what he provocatively calls "constitutional theocracy" today, there is so far no recognition that religious constitutionalism is the framework in which human dignity first became canonized.[9] This newer constitutionalism crystallized precisely in the 1930s when it seemed to so many as if secular liberalism had no future. It was initially part of a replacement package for that secular liberalism; and it remained largely so in West Germany in 1949. The conventional wisdom about the inception of constitutional dignity, in other words, is by and large false.

It then makes more sense that Mirkine-Guetzévitch found nothing of value in dignity; indeed it was as the 1930s passed, when dignity made its constitutional entry, that his liberal trend based on the rights of man was so heartbreakingly cut off by different modes of dictatorial rule, pagan and religious. Every tragedy needs a chorus: "The Spanish Constitution of 1931 was the last act of the new constitutional law of Europe," he recalled grimly twenty years later. "And well before 1939, one after another, the countries of central and Eastern Europe abandoned their democratic constitutions to become totalitarian."[10] It is therefore both crucial and mysterious that, thanks to the Irish, constitutionalism founded on human dignity also came about in this very period. If it is a bequest from history that we have learned to use for our own ends, it is interesting all the same—and perhaps disturbing—that it came from a different place and time than we thought.

To understand the original meaning of constitutional dignity, this chapter proposes, it is necessary to plunge into the confusing years just before war and genocide, for dignity was a response to different circumstances. The most decisive and illuminating context for the move to constitutional dignity, it turns out, is not in the shocked conscience "after Auschwitz" but in political Catholicism before it, which remained its dominant framework for decades thereafter, when the Holocaust still did not seriously figure in global moral consciousness.[11] More specifically, it was in in March 1937 that human dignity made its spectacular entry into world politics—including, thanks to the Irish, into constitutional politics.

Around March 1937: Catholic Dignity between Corporatism and Civil Society

That dignity long ago originated as one status word among others in a universe of aristocratic and hierarchical values is now undoubted. It originated as the literal notion of "rank"—above all, high rank *above other humans*. James Q. Whitman has argued, following Alexis de Tocqueville, that high status was "democratized" over time, but for all its plausibility, this thesis about long-term social relations does nothing to explain the specifics of dignity's ideological trajectory in the 1930s and 1940s—let alone since.[12] As late as the 1930s, in tune with its millennial prior trajectory, dignity was attached to a huge range of objects—humanity rare and individual humanity extremely rare among them. There was thus little prior basis for the novelty of Ireland's constitutional preamble, whatever the circulation of the word in world affairs, including one or two constitutional articles, before then.[13] Then events in international Catholicism intervened, with the Irish constitutionalization of individual dignity as a leading concept as one of their consequences.

In fact, in March 1937, dignity already had an important place in Catholic politics, but it was radically different than the one it has had since then, thanks to the epoch-making reassignment from *groups* to *individuals* the concept underwent. At the beginning of the month, thanks to Pope Pius XI's encyclicals *Casti connubi* (1930) and

Quadragesimo anno (1931), dignity was still attached primarily to collective entities such as workers and religious sacraments such as marriage. Though not utterly without precedent, it was in March 1937 that dignity attaching to individuals (more precisely, persons) crystallized as a visible ideological option. In the 1930s, no one could have guessed what would become of this option, in large part because the Irish constitution's version of dignity reflected such a minority political choice in the landscape of political Catholicism. The years during which it was framed were the period in which Catholic states were rising, typically based on corporatist rather than supplementary individualist notions.

In these states, it was family or labor that was dignified, not persons (and thus not persons with rights).[14] António Salazar's corporatist Portuguese constitution of 1933 was followed a year later in Austria by the purest move to a constitution integrating Catholic social teaching, and "Austro-fascist" leader Engelbert Dollfuss consciously announced it as enacting *Quadragesimo anno*'s economic and social principles. Mirkine-Guetzévitch, a fan of the French Revolution, denounced these as perverse revivals of the Old Regime in constitutionalist disguise; but it surely mattered that these were not only pseudoconstitutional regimes but also ones sometimes echoing the pervasive corporatist assignment of "dignity" to groups.[15] Not long after, Spain—with its secular and indeed anticlerical constitution of 1931—fell prey to war and dictatorship, and Francisco Franco introduced dignity to the quasi-constitutional documents of his regime in allegiance to reigning corporatist orthodoxy.[16] In the international Catholic context, the Irish constitution's framing occurred in the shadow of this trendsetting wave of fully corporatist dignity claims.

Yet it also took place at a time of novel and at first brief and modest availability of an alternative within political Catholicism based in part on the dignity of persons—an alternative it happened to encode. The central source of the conceptual work that made the Irish Constitution's assignment of "dignity" to the individual possible was in a raucous Catholic dispute of the mid-1930s, where survivors of an earlier flirtation with far-right politics squared off against persisting reactionaries about the correct sequel to secular liberalism (which both sides agreed had failed). Historian James Chappel has dubbed this conflict one between corporatist and "civil society" Catholics, and the emergence of the latter helps account for the prominence individual dignity was now accorded.[17]

The intellectual debate and political controversy between these two groups assumed its classic form as a response to the Popular Front, for the dispute raging in 1934–36 was about how to match the frightening alliance of communists and socialists of the era. These two groups of Catholics concurred in rejecting the modern, liberal secular republic in the name of the dispersal of authority to the "natural" social hierarchy established by God and descending through and including religious institutions, local communities, and patriarchal families. Their agreement was perfectly obvious to contemporary witnesses, such as celebrated political theorist Michael Oakeshott, who in this era offered readers a conspectus of European political thought in which "Catholicism" was a possible option alongside "representative democracy," "communism," "fascism," and "National Socialism." Catholic social theory, rooted in God's natural law, opposed liberalism and its historical associations with individualism, secularism, and relativism.[18] But where the civil society Catholics distinguished themselves was in their assignment of importance to what they called "the human person" as an alternative to the dissolute individualism they joined with other Catholics in stigmatizing.

The human person, a central icon of civil society Catholicism after 1934, would become the increasingly popular bearer of "dignity." Corporatists themselves, Chappel shows, referred to the human person too; just as some of their civil society foes ended up supporting the Vichy regime. But it seems clear that "the dignity of the human person" mainly became one slogan for civil society Catholics attempting to stave off both secular liberalism with its destitute atomism and corporatist reaction with its demand for clerical forms of authoritarianism—or flirtation with Nazi Germany and other fascist regimes that were viewed as fit for support in spite of their "paganism."

In spite of the emergence of the civil society option, corporatist ideology offered the dominant version of political Catholicism until the outcome of World War II made the religious authoritarianism in Spain and Portugal or even National Socialism in Germany seem not like the wave of an exciting future but a relic of past mistakes. Seriously outnumbered in spite of sharing many premises with their corporatist foes, civil society Catholics opened another path in the 1930s, which few took until later; individual dignity emerged, essentially, as a marker on that path. Consider as an example of civil society dissidence Joseph Vialatoux's speech to a Catholic summit in Lyon, just at the time of the finalization of the Irish

Constitution. Its title was "Dignity of the Group? Or of the Human Person?"[19]

"It may not be excessive," Vialatoux commented, "to say that this very question defines the historical moment in which we live." He inveighed against specifically biological and generally naturalistic approaches that tended to view the human group as the locus of significance, arguing instead that Christianity brought the metaphysics of spirituality—which made the human person the site of dignity. Yet Vialatoux's preference for individual dignity, it bears noting, did not at all connote the corollary of "human rights." That revolutionary concept, in spite of its ostensible priority of persons, remained in what Vialatoux called a "bastard union" with "naturalist philosophy." For this reason, it had elicited the equally erroneous sequels: the secular temptation of revolutionary nationalism swept Europe in the nineteenth century, and now counterrevolutionary racism in the form of National Socialism was extending it into the twentieth. The "dignity of the human person" was to be a response to all these mistakes. It was now critical to assert dignity against the "depersonalized individual" of the secular liberalism associated with the French Revolution and the equally secular racist extremism that now sought to overturn it. Dignity would save the "person" buried in secular and later revolutionary politics from its own misguided proponents and make it the foundation stone of a spiritual community rather than the materialist totalitarianism of communism and fascism alike.[20]

Vialatoux had posed his question of whether to give individual or group dignity priority in early 1937 but, far from crying in the wilderness against totalitarianism, by summertime when he gave his lecture, it must have seemed as if the individualist option had garnered the highest possible support: from the pontiff himself. It was for this reason above all—and not because of the Irish constitution—that March 1937 was a great month for civil society Catholics. That month, stung by the failure of earlier overtures toward and negotiations with Nazi Germany, Pope Pius XI condemned German incursion on church rights in *Mit brennender Sorge*, and a week later issued his stirring encyclical letter *Divini redemptoris* "on atheistic communism." The dignity of the individual surged in world public discourse essentially due to *Divini redemptoris*. Interestingly, however, "dignity" was basic only in the second, anticommunist encyclical letter.

In fact, the failure to respect the dignity of the human person was repeatedly identified—and starting in March 1937 was to be for decades—as communism's central error. Communism, the text reads, "strips man of his liberty, robs human personality of all its dignity, and removes all the moral restraints that check the eruptions of blind impulse." Simultaneously too authoritarian and too liberatory, communism reduced man to matter and thus also interfered with the source of moral agency. That it "denies the rights, dignity and liberty of human personality" thus mainly made it an affront to moral norms. Put differently, dignity offered an individualism that, far from atomizing humanity, offered the true first principle of community and society, for "each individual man in the dignity of his human personality . . . is supplied with all that is necessary for the exercise of his social functions."[21] It was thus not strange that in Irish hands, individual dignity connected with the common good and the theological virtues (likewise constitutionalized), since it shared in the premise that the day of destitute secular individualism was done.

For "human dignity," *Divini redemptoris* was epoch-making, for it gave the concept as an incident of individuals or persons by far its highest profile entry in world politics to that date. Without at all deciding papal policy toward political form (only World War II would do so), the letter also gave a lift to the civil society Catholics' insistence that dignity did not exclusively attach to groups. And the crucial revisions of the Irish Constitution that led to the appearance of individual dignity in its preamble also occurred in this period—very precisely, in the immediate aftermath of the encyclical. This accidental coincidence forms the basis of my case about what dignity meant when it became an Irish touchstone, anticipating many later developments.

Ireland and the Coming of Religious Constitutionalism

The many historians of Ireland's Constitution, notably the accomplished Dermot Keogh, have simply missed the relevance of its invocation of dignity. Unaware of Ireland's comparative priority when it comes to dignity, they have therefore failed to place the document in international context to explain this priority.[22] The Irish Constitution, of course, needs to be read in a number of contexts, of which the one I will emphasize—international Catholic thought and politics—is merely one. But it is this context that matters inasmuch as the Irish Constitution registered an international development that would later mark the

United Nations Charter and the Basic Law—and thus make possible everything that followed based on their language.

Éamon de Valera, Fianna Fáil party leader and, from 1932, new Irish prime minister, wrote the Irish Constitution, after brief and informal consultation with a tiny group of advisers, before unveiling his handiwork in April 1937 for approval. Though the wave of the Catholic future may well have seemed to be corporatist constitutionalism on the European continent at this moment, the Irish constitution clearly could not go there—in spite of the hopes of some Irish Catholic integralists consulted during the process. De Valera was not an enemy of democracy (and in any case, it is doubtful Great Britain would have allowed him to take Ireland down the Spanish and Portuguese road), but he did help bring about a new kind. An evanescent movement of Irish fascists trumpeting Catholic principle known as the Blueshirts rose and fell in the mid-1930s; and around the same time as the Constitution was in preparation, Paddy Belton's fearsomely reactionary militant group, the Irish Christian Front, emerged.[23] But de Valera had no truck with these groups, nor with any other version of undemocratic corporatism.

Indeed, the primary impulse for engineering a new constitutional process was a negative one. De Valera had long since committed himself to scuttling the Constitution of the Irish Free State of 1922 in the name of a new order. That the Anglo-Irish treaty of 1921 had not allowed Ireland full sovereignty, and that the first constitution imposed a galling loyalty oath to the British crown (which de Valera deleted immediately in 1933), gave both so repulsive a stigma as to make them unsalvageable.[24] For the history of dignity, however, the happenstance that the drafting of de Valera's long-sought replacement of the unacceptable text with a new one occurred in the winter and spring of 1936–37 proved consequential. The process replaced a document of the "new constitutionalism" (and the earlier era of progress Mirkine-Guetzévitch celebrated) with a very different constitutional affair.

The Irish Constitution was not just a "negative" success after all. The country's move beyond its prior dominion constitution to assert its "rightful independence" reflected Catholic social thought in its positive outlook in a series of ways, and not surprisingly given the centrality of Catholicism to Irish nationalism in the 1930s and long after. As Perry Anderson puts it, Ireland led the way in the "distinct sub-group" in "the history of 20th-century nationalism"—along with India and Israel later—in which

> religion played a central organising role from the start, providing so to speak the genetic code. . . . The success of [leaders such as de Valera who emphasized the faith commitments of the national projects] was due not just to the faltering of the first wave of office-holders, but to their ability to articulate openly what had always been latent in the national movement, but neither candidly acknowledged nor consistently repudiated. They could claim, with a certain justice, to be legitimate heirs of the original cause. . . . [T]hey operated constitutionally, if in each case with certain prewar sympathies for European fascism.[25]

More to the point, 1937 presented de Valera with a moment of specifically Christian opportunity—though within a constitutional framework—to advance a controversial social morality.

If he was a devoted Catholic passionately committed to the greater presence of the country's dominant religion in the constitution, however, de Valera was above all a politician. He deftly maneuvered to take account of the views of the episcopacy and various Catholic authorities while also assuming final control of the details of drafting. In particular, de Valera saw the preamble as the place to achieve symbolic Christianization of the document, while specific articles—notably on church and state, family, and property—would offer a considerable incorporation of Catholic social thought into (though not a total lock on) Irish politics. In this approach, de Valera may have been more canny than most comparative scholars of constitutions, who regularly slight preambles, though they are the most meaningful and memorable parts of founding texts to citizens.

In the preamble and in general, de Valera never wanted to go, nor could go, as far as reactionary or even doctrinally conservative Catholics desired. "De Valera had little or nothing in common with the authoritarian Catholic leaders of the 1930s," Keogh remarks, a bit apologetically. "He did not make a fetish out of religion like the 'monkish' [António] Salazar of Portugal. He was repelled by the extremism of General Francisco Franco's *cruzada*. De Valera exhibited none of the demagoguery practised by the Central European Catholic dictators of the 1930s. . . . [He was] both patriotic and loyally Roman Catholic, but in a very independent way."[26] But he had even less in common with socialists and communists who offered the main alternative to religious authoritarianism in many countries—until they were brutally suppressed.

The constitutionalization of the freedom and dignity of the individual, in short, can be taken above all as a symbol of de Valera's larger balancing act of crafting a Christian Democratic synthesis throughout the document. In an era of the victory of Catholic corporatism or outright fascism, Ireland proved a peripheral laboratory of civil society Catholicism or even post–World War II Christian Democracy. Dignity now meant more than the anticommunist politics of *Divini redemptoris*, for de Valera's registration of the individualist rather than simply the corporatist strand of dignity talk within political Catholicism of the moment encapsulates this broader stance toward the place of religion in politics and the availability of a third-way religious constitutionalism. Negotiating between forsaken secular liberalism and ascendant Catholic reaction, this novel constitutionalism offered religiously inflected conservative democracy. As such, this project powerfully marked the emergence of constitutional dignity. Illustratively, when Oakeshott concluded his compilation of sources on "Catholicism" as a free-standing option in the political thought of Europe in 1939, he reprinted the Irish Constitution's preamble and most revealing articles.[27]

Comparison of de Valera's constitution with the 1922 predecessor he patriotically scuttled makes this graphically clear. The earlier document had very much been in the spirit of the liberal "new constitutionalism" of the immediate moment after World War I in its attitudes to church and state, religious pluralism, and gender; its 1937 replacement was a Christianizing document of a "newer" constitutionalism of religious democracy.[28] Its approach to property, for example, drew substantially on *Quadragesimo anno*, while the provision on religion acknowledged the Catholic Church's "special position." The article on family and gender perhaps went furthest in qualifying the secular liberalism of the prior constitutional exercise.

Irish feminists, agitating for the group most obviously affected by such changes, responded to its consequences immediately and with outrage. The new draft constitution deleted the existing constitution's promise of equal rights without distinction to sex, which feminists feared might even strip women of the hard-won vote. (They succeeded in restoring the clause during ratification debates.) And as ratified, the constitution's controversial Article 41 enshrined a traditionalist vision of the family. On a symbolic level, the article made clear that whatever the dignity of persons meant, it was inseparable from the natural priority and social centrality of families, which in turn depended on women's "life within the home." More substantively, the provision constitutionally prohibited divorce, a ban lifted only six decades later in the constitution's fifteenth amendment.[29]

Religious Constitutionalism between Drafting and Ratification

Thanks to recent publications, it is relatively easy to chart the formation of the constitution's preambular allusion to "the dignity and freedom of the individual."[30] De Valera clearly saw the preamble doing essentially symbolic work, unlike the body of articles potentially justiciable in courts (including in constitutional review).[31] The comparatively uncontroversial preamble nonetheless underwent its own evolution.

A Jesuit committee set up in late 1936 with de Valera's permission, led intellectually by Father Edward Cahill and basing its text in large part on the 1921 Polish Constitution, offered large parts of the surviving preamble.[32] The Polish source that provided a template for the Jesuits, however, did not mention dignity. Cahill, founder of the modest Irish branch of Catholic Action (An Ríoghacht) that elsewhere became strongly linked to civil society Catholicism, had definite views about the dominant role Catholicism should play in the drafting process and threw himself into his task. For him and his yet more conservative colleague Dennis Fahey, the Catholic prophylaxis against modern evils—from liberalism to communism, spread by Protestants, Jews, and freemasons—needed to provide the packaging and the details of the new document. In his own social thought, Cahill promoted *Quadragesimo anno* and adopted a version of corporatism known as vocationalism.[33] However, even as late as the close of 1936, his main contribution occurred too early for him to inject individual dignity into the proceedings, and in his many communications with de Valera, he did not mention it.

As the process went on in spring, the draft constitutions de Valera circulated to various circles from March 16, 1937 did not yet include the preamble—with which de Valera and his staff appear, on the basis of the original Jesuit suggestions, to have tinkered on their own throughout the period. Three days after the first rough draft, *Divini redemptoris* was issued to wide global reception, including in Ireland and especially in *The Irish Press*, the newspaper de Valera had helped found.[34] There is no better evidence than this matter of timing that the encyclical inspired the insertion of dignity. At this point, de Valera may have made the crucial revisions on his own or with the advice of John Charles McQuaid, then president of Blackrock College (later Dublin's archbishop) and de Valera's close contact in this decisive period.[35] In any event, when de Valera met on April 3, 1937 with the pope's ambassador, or nuncio, he showed him a draft of a preamble invoking "the dignity and freedom of the citizens."[36] By April 11, in new documents sent to the papal nuncio, the preambular phrase had assumed its final form—an important revision since to restrict dignity to "citizens" might seem to ignore its natural foundations and thus its role in constraining the state.[37]

These changes were uncontroversial and no evidence suggests any dispute about them—an unsurprising fact given that the dignity clause is much more important in retrospect than it was at the time. (Often what later seems like an extraordinary departure occurs without fanfare.) But the documentation is rich enough to provide a clear sense of the timing of the constitutionalization of dignity, in the immediate aftermath of *Divini redemptoris*, and thus provides a clue about what it meant. Its linkage with constitutionalism, however, could not help but associate individual dignity with a new sort of political enterprise. Religious change in recent decades has left de Valera open to constant and severe criticism for how far Catholic social thought surrounding the role and rights of families, education, property, and the Church itself impacted his constitutional vision. At the time, however, de Valera worried most—and rightly so—about disappointing his most fervent Catholic advisers.

In particular, even as feminist complaints were marginalized, a huge dispute swirled throughout this period (and indeed long after) around the wording of Article 44, a provision that Cahill and others wanted to name the Catholic Church as the true Christian Church. But in spite of his own apparent sympathies, de Valera ultimately understood he could not do so, setting out to balance Catholicism's preeminence with acknowledgment of minority faiths and religious freedom.[38] It was, after all, a country with a Protestant population of 25 percent (if one included the contested north, which the constitution claimed as part of the nation). Article 44 illustrated, once again, that the larger constitutional effort balanced between competing extremes of secular liberalism and religious authoritarianism.

This article also caused no little difficulty for de Valera in his search for ecclesiastical imprimatur. In mid-April, two weeks before unveiling his handiwork to the public, he sent his emissary Joseph Walshe to Rome for endorsement. But Eugenio Pacelli, then Vatican Secretary of State communicating for the already sick pontiff whom he would succeed two years later, refused to comply. Pacelli reminded Walshe that failure to acknowledge the Catholic Church as the one true church was technically heretical, though Pacelli said he grasped that de Valera felt his situation forced him into theological error. "*Ni approvo ni non disapprovo; taceremo*" (I do not approve, but I also do not disapprove; I will remain silent), Pacelli told Walshe in the pope's name—which was nonetheless a crushing result for de Valera, who had striven to explain to Rome that he was constrained by the fact of his Protestant minority from the more full-blown Catholic ideal he personally desired for the document. "It did not shake him when I contrasted the expressly Christian character of our new Constitution with the liberalism (continental sense) of the old," Walshe reported back glumly.[39]

De Valera thus did not go as far as some of his Catholic advisers and ecclesiastical authorities desired. But he did intend the Irish Constitution to mark the appearance of a new sort of Christian state, and the preamble in which dignity now appeared had a special role here. In the pained negotiations with the Vatican, dignity—which did not come up—was not enough to convince Pius XI (or the future Pius XII, speaking in his name) to sign off. Nonetheless, when in the ratification process some months later de Valera faced unexpected opposition to the constitution for its excessive secularism (rather than its excessive confessionalism), the Christian credentials of dignity proved helpful. In spite of the pope's earlier reluctance, the Vatican newspaper, *L'Osservatore Romano*, providentially seemed to endorse the constitution. "It differs from other constitutions," it noted, in an affirmation reported by the *Irish Press* that had a large impact in satisfying the religious vote, "because it is inspired by respect for the faith of the people, the dignity of the person, the sanctity of the family, of private property, and of social democracy. These principles are applied in a unique religious spirit, which animates the whole constitution."[40] It seems that Ireland's pioneering venture in a newer constitutionalism, in which individual dignity came to the fore, was generally understood in these terms by its friends as well as by its critics. Certainly the document went far enough as to allow disputes to swirl for many decades around the degree to which Ireland had made the natural law of God's morality a profound constraint on democratic choices as well as judicial interpretation.[41]

From the Irish Constitution to the Basic Law

That some Catholics sought an alternative to authoritarian and fascist solutions by appealing to individual human dignity in these years, of course, does not mean that the faltering republics of Europe were generally defended on their terms. It simply means that some Catholics hewed out a conceptual possibility that was to have an unlikely fate in later years (up to and including our era). Liberals such as Mirkine-Guetzévitch did not frame their republicanism in terms of human dignity, either before or after World War II. Most revealingly, when Vichy authorities proposed their own constitutional plans in 1944, to regularize their emergency rule, their proposed constitution began with dignity. Where the Irish constitution had registered human dignity in passing in its preamble, the Vichy constitution made it the leading first article—for the first time in history.

According to Vice Admiral Jean Fernet, Philippe Pétain's adviser who left the most detailed published memoirs on the subject, the marshal was never sure his fealty to the French nation was compatible with the whole exercise of written constitutions.[42] In 1941, the goal was to break thoroughly with the Declaration of the Rights of Man and Citizen in the name of different principles—nation, family, religion, along with duties to community far more than rights for individuals—in a restorative act after republican dissolution.[43] Yet already when an initial draft was entertained in summer 1941, strong emphasis on the authoritarian nature of the state remained compatible with a section on "the human person" with his "duties and rights." The reason was a vision of far-right rule that leaned more toward Christianity, and its unique version of counteracting liberalism, than the Nazi regime countenanced. In this vision, according to the constitution, the moral law was above sovereignty and even the authoritarian leader was subordinate to it. Often inspired by the corporatism and familialism of Salazar's 1933 constitution, but also by an explicit desire for Christian personalism to replace liberal individualism, the 1941 draft—unlike the Portuguese document—even mentioned "dignity" in a subsidiary article that explained: "The state recognizes and guarantees the rights of the human person, liberties that are essential to its dignity and the realization of its higher ends."[44]

As the war wore on, the first constitutional try began to look premature, and the winds shifted against a more purist "National Revolution" that the initial draft had reflected. Yet in two more stages, the revision process made Christian personalism even more important to the text, as the document was "republicanized" in order to seek an adjusted path.[45] Grudgingly, Pétain—pressured and to some degree displaced by head of government Pierre Laval on this matter, especially as the German defeat seemed ever more likely—was prepared to allow more continuity with the "habits" of overthrown democracy, rather than constitutionalize formal autocracy, even though it meant disappointing hard-core reactionaries. (According to Fernet, some trusted confidants whom Pétain consulted were "shocked by the liberal character of the project," especially "given the Marshal's justified critiques of the shortcomings of demagogic parliamentarism.")[46] Finalized in late 1943, the constitutional proposal now placed human dignity at the very top, within a larger scheme of reference to communitarian social principle. Indeed, the result was a first article disturbingly similar to more famous postwar ones: "The liberty and dignity of the human person are supreme values and intangible goods." It added: "To guarantee them demands order and justice of the state, and discipline from the citizens."[47] But German proconsul Otto Abetz would not allow the plan to be enacted because of its "clerico-bourgeois-reactionary" character.[48] After the war, former Vichy official Xavier Vallat, who organized Jewish deportation for the regime, claimed that Pétain had asked him to revise the now excessively republican constitution further into the summer of 1944, but it now seems doubtful that this is true—and in any case, Vallat's text left the leading article on dignity undisturbed.[49] Human dignity left many Christian political options open long into the war.

Then Allied guns decided the conflict. Through the war, just a few Catholics believed that allegiance to "human dignity" entailed allegiance to "human rights," which most Catholics following modern popes still considered the baleful child of the French Revolution and secularist evil and which Catholics under authoritarian regimes were commanded to spurn. Indeed, as the next chapter documents, Catholic thinker Jacques Maritain, chief theoretician of civil society Catholicism and later premier interpreter of the Universal Declaration, did not connect dignity to "human rights" until 1942 at the earliest, even if an intermittent papal usage intensifying from 1937 on opened a path to travel.[50]

But between 1942 and 1945, as the Allied war effort after Stalingrad looked forward to its ultimate triumph, more and more Catholics in general linked "the dignity of the human person" hewed out in the prior decade to "human rights." Pius XI had not ceased the rhetoric of dignity before his death. "Christian teaching alone gives full meaning to the demands of human rights and liberty because it alone gives worth and dignity to human personality," the *New York Times* reported him saying in late 1938—a nearly exact anticipation of the Universal Declaration's formula ten years later.[51] Even while remaining publicly silent on de Valera's constitution, Pius XII said similar things, in tune with *Divini redemptoris*, both before and after his election as pope.[52] But in wartime, his public claims about human dignity accelerated to a striking degree. In his high-profile Christmas message to the world for 1942, Pius XII offered five principles to inform a future peace, of which "the dignity of the human person" was the very first. Such wartime invocations provided a bridge between what might otherwise have been a passing peculiarity of a few dissident theorists, along with the Irish constitution, and the postwar trajectory of the concept.

It was thanks to Pius XII, as the meaning of such rhetoric became clear even to him as reactionary politics failed, that individual dignity became incredibly common stuff across the Atlantic during the later phases of World War II, though much more work remains to be done to excavate wartime percolation. Far less ambivalently than in Pétain's constitutional discourse, the few who joined French Resistance on Catholic principle to criticize the Vichy regime's popular claim to restore religious morality and civilization found in human dignity the authority for human rights.[53] To take another of sundry examples, Edmund A. Walsh, American Jesuit (and founder of the Georgetown University School of Foreign Service that still bears his name), wrote in 1942: "The conflict is between the rights of individual men, endowed with the dignity of the human personality and elevated to the adopted sonship of God, on the one side, and the dehumanized, totalitarian state of Fichte, Hegel, Treitschke, Nietzsche, Hitler and the Tanaka Memorial of Japan on the other. This means not a world campaign of conventional belligerents [but] a World Revolution seeking to capture the soul of humanity."[54] Abetted by Catholic and Lutheran clerics who participated, when the German conservative elites around the Kreisau circle led by Helmuth Graf von Moltke turned to organize resistance midwar and drafted their own constitutional statements, the same pattern applied. "The government of the German Reich sees in Christianity the foundation for the moral and religious renewal of our nation," the group's document on basic principles read. "Breaking the totalitarian coercion of conscience and recognition of the inviolable dignity of the human person [form] the basis of the aimed-for order of law and peace."[55] How many people understood the global conflict as a crusade for dignity is unclear, but conservative Christians arrayed against "totalitarianism" were the most frequent.

As in interwar debates, dignity in such usages carried with it a communitarian and religious streak intended to distinguish it from the secularism of nineteenth-century liberalism. Writing in *Fortune* magazine shortly after discovering the contiguity of dignity and rights, Maritain castigated modern man for "claim[ing] human rights and dignity—without God, for his ideology grounded human rights and human dignity in a godlike, infinite autonomy of human will." But he now referred to the apparently alternative "concept of, and devotion to, the rights of the human person" as "the most significant political improvement of modern times."[56] By the time of Pius XII's exceptionally influential Christmas message to the world of 1944, human dignity in a similarly invidious conception teemed to a degree completely unprepared even by prior papal exhortation.

The goal for and therefore also check on democracy, and a commitment that would save it from leveling equality and secularizing materialism, the dignity of the human person became one of Pius XII's key slogans for good. By late wartime, with authoritarian corporatism (or outright fascism) both outmoded, dignity, for Pius XII, implied conservative democracy to keep communist or even liberal politics at bay and to make Christian moral norms central. "The holy story of Christmas proclaims this inviolable dignity of man with a vigor and authority that cannot be gainsaid—an authority and vigor that infinitely transcends that which all possible declarations of the rights of man could achieve," the pope observed. True Christian democracy would protect human dignity, he warned. False democracy, by contrast, would sacrifice it on the profane altar of secularism, materialism, and relativism, subordinating the natural law and common good to the whims of the masses, exaggerating defensible liberty into appetitive license, and accelerating acceptable equality into colorless uniformity—all travesties of human dignity rather than its enthronement.[57] Continental Western

Europe followed this advice after World War II, with restabilization occurring under the auspices of conservative
democracy, supervised by a new sort of Christian political
party, with Catholics in the lead.[58] For a long time, dignity summarized these developments in a single term. The
Irish Constitution was thus in spite of its initially accidental and local ramifications a premonitory document of the
direction political Catholicism would eventually take after
guns decided the larger direction of history.[59]

It was papal usage that proved most relevant to postwar affairs—the bridge from the late 1930s to the late
1940s. Arguably, even the United Nations Charter registered it, for there is no other obvious source. As political
theorist Charles Beitz has lately discovered, it was Barnard
College dean Virginia Gildersleeve, in her cosmetic work
on South African politician Jan Smuts's draft of the United
Nations Charter's preamble in San Francisco in 1945, who
edited the document so that it would "reaffirm faith in
fundamental human rights, in the dignity and worth of
the human person." But it is self-evident that the prominence of dignity in wartime—explaining its eligibility for
Gildersleeve's fix—was due to the Pope more than all others, even all others combined, including in its connection
to rights. (No American sources, in particular, conjoin
human dignity and human rights earlier than or outside
the framework of the Christian sources mentioned earlier
and in the Pope's widely circulating language above all.)[60]

In response to the powerful findings of papal and
more generally Christian usage during the war, Beitz has
plausibly responded that the specific associations that
conservatives attached to dignity need not have accom-
panied its promotion into the United Nations Charter and

later documents such as the Universal Declaration. "While this confluence of factors may explain why references to human dignity began to appear in discourse about human rights during the war," Beitz writes, "they supply no reason to believe that there was any substantial common idea." Looking more closely at the United Nations Charter, he adds, "The employment of the term 'human dignity' is evidence that this term had a positive valence in the vernacular of the moment, but the offhandedness of the decision to place it early in the preamble and the absence of any consideration of its significance argue against inferring any shared, articulate purpose."[61] As persuasive as this is, however, the argument does not do well in explaining the near exclusive use of human dignity in Western European constitutions in the moment just after World War II, coinciding and overlapping rather precisely with the time and place that conservative Christian Democracy ascended to rule. More broadly, Christians celebrated a victory in the language. "We discern in the Charter's avowal of . . . the dignity of the human person," Carlos Romulo, Philippines delegate to the United Nations and crucial American ally, observed in 1949, "the Christian belief in a brotherhood of men equally precious in the eyes of God, each deserving of His Justice and worthy of His love." It was by restoring the basis of natural law to the national and international future, with all the moral implications that went along with it, that dignity found its stride.[62]

Not surprisingly, when conservative democracy came to postwar West Germany and elsewhere, dignity could now have a crucial role, in constitutions that—like Ireland's before them—were grounded on the Christian God and human dignity together, as the first principle of a new sort of constitutional regime. This gesture occurred in Germany in the form of the several subfederal *Länder* constitutions before it was repeated in the Basic Law of the new federal republic. Unlike Austria, which restored the post–World War I liberal constitution Hans Kelsen had drafted, West Germany and Western Europe generally were allowed by the Allies (and especially the Americans) to go another way. First, both in time and significance, was the absolutely critical Bavarian Constitution of 1946, whose preamble, written personally by Christian Democrat Alois Hundhammer, began as follows: "Before the field of rubble, to which a state and social order without God and without knowledge and respect of human dignity have led the survivors of World War II. . . ."[63] The horrendous regime and conflict they had experienced was clearly the immediate background in the mind of the framers of the West German documents—even if the Holocaust of European Jewry was clearly not. (Hundhammer, for example, had spent a month in newly opened Dachau in 1933, then sold shoes until his conscripted service in the Wehrmacht for the entire war.) But constitutions are always also prospective blueprints for rule, in which God, dignity, and morality were intended to play a special role, much like in Ireland before.

As much or more influenced by Christian Democratic thinking, the Italian Constitution (1947) similarly includes both dignity and "the human person" before the Grundgesetz (and the Universal Declaration), though not in its preamble or as its first article. It also constitutionally preserved the fascist-era Lateran Treaty with the Holy See, whose provisions concerning religion and public life continue to be at stake in current controversy.[64] Of course, to emphasize general correlation is not to insist on absolute identity of dignity with conservative outlooks. In particular, Germans could draw on a deep well of usage of "human dignity" in their classical period of letters and philosophy, and simultaneously with the Bavarian Constitution, the Hessian constitution forged under more socialist authority made room for the notion—albeit not at the top but in a later article, and then at the end of a list of other values.[65] But the evidence clearly shows that in regions where socialists exerted more control, they were far less likely to invoke dignity in constitution making; and while socialists participated fully in the origins of the federal constitution, though they would not rule for decades, their own early suggestions did not make reference to the principle. Given this general picture, it seems fair to say that Germany's federal constitution in 1949 was part of a trend, localized wherever Christian Democracy was strong (and exclusively there for a long time), that founded new republics on—and limited them through—the morality of dignity.[66]

Mirkine-Guetzévitch did not note it, but the strong presence of Christian Democrats in the French constituent assembly allowed the preamble of both the abortive April and final November 1946 constitutions of the new Fourth Republic to begin with the human person—though it did not allude to God or dignity.[67] (It begins: "In the aftermath of the victory won by the free peoples over the regimes that strove to subjugate and degrade the human person . . .") Perhaps it was out of awareness of Vichy discourse, and the strength of socialism, that in spite of its postwar promotion, French law skirted "dignity" until as late as the 1990s. In any case, the country's Christian Democrats, through their Mouvement républicain populaire party, did not take power, as in the rest of continental Western Europe.[68]

All things considered, the framework that human dignity provided human rights and liberal constitutionalism in and through the war is hard to greet as an uncomplicated breakthrough—if it was not a retrograde concession. Human dignity mainly helped wrest both rights and constitutionalism from the heritage of the French Revolution specifically and from political secularism generally, with which they had hitherto been associated in European history. Now the latter were represented in transatlantic public culture as easy stepping stones to totalitarianism. Just as World War II had seen strange bedfellows in a popular front to defeat fascism, after that alliance fractured, the Cold War united onetime enemies against a new threat, with fateful consequences for all concerned. Dignity's main role for a long time remained public and private Cold War rhetoric, not constitutionalism, as Westerners generally adopted Catholicism's understanding of the central failing of communism. A founding document of the American Cold War, NSC-68, says the point of the struggle is the defense of human dignity, and President Harry S Truman agreed that "[b]oth religion and democracy are founded on one basic principle, the worth and dignity of the individual man and woman."[69]

Conclusion: Did the Irish Save Civilization?

This chapter does not claim that the Irish Constitution is important in itself. Indeed, when Boris Mirkine-Guetzévitch put out the forlorn 1938 revision of his handbook of European constitutions, he took the corporatist Austrian and Portuguese constitutions to be much more significant, since they broke fundamentally (rather than, as in the Irish compromise, partially) with secular and liberal democracy.[70] The Irish Constitution matters not intrinsically but instrumentally: in the current enthusiasm over human dignity, it decisively establishes both the right chronology and the "original meaning" of its constitutionalization in the circumstances of religious democracy. It is, as it were, like a tape recorder that, because it was on at the right time, captures the moment in which an accident happened that still determines our moral speech.

Needless to say, for the Catholic world and European politics generally, the Irish assignment of dignity to the individual human being in 1937—like the other tentative proposals of Christian Democracy at the time—certainly did not settle matters. That took a war, in which illiberal corporatism was taken off the table as an option for political Catholicism, with much blood spilled in the process, though the survival of "clerico-fascist" Spain and Portugal for many decades allowed some diehards to cherish the flame of reactionary dignity. Dermot Keogh long ago proposed seeing de Valera as a pioneering "Christian Democrat."[71] The trouble with this otherwise illuminating interpretation is that there was no Christian Democratic hegemony in Europe until after World War II—whose violence was required to open the possibility for its decades-long reign. But after it, de Valera's originally eccentric and peripheral synthesis of Catholicism and democracy suddenly became modish, and individualist dignity became a more prevalent foundation stone, in the

West German Basic Law not least. Constitutional dignity entered history as part of what became the unanticipated post–World War II supremacy of Christian Democracy— and more broadly as an aspect of the earliest version of religious constitutionalism since gone global.

The crucible for human dignity that religious constitutionalism provided thus establishes a potentially troubling starting point. Of course, more than a half-century on, dignity's functions today are no longer fully controlled by its original deployments. It was unexpected secularization that ultimately occurred in Ireland (and Germany), which also had the tributary effect of making human dignity open to new understandings. Those living under the regimes of the "newer constitutionalism" of Christian Democracy surely could depart from original meanings, and unquestionably did so as the post–World War II era wore on. In fact, in both Ireland and Germany, the huge influence of Catholicism on constitutional theory and practice has waned so substantially over the intervening decades that its founding centrality risks being forgotten or suppressed.[72] In any event, it is fair to say that human dignity is no longer tightly, let alone exclusively, tethered to the framework of religious constitutionalism.

In the end, therefore, my emphasis on religious constitutionalism not only acknowledges but even insists that some rather recent account is required for the salience today of a very different version of human dignity.[73] In law, no doubt the wave of recent constitutions invoking human dignity, and the South African probably above all, is the main factor in the current preeminence of the concept. Famously, dignity in West Germany was initially a *nicht interpretierte These*, or strictly symbolic provision, but German judges departed from this original understanding long ago, and the Irish story is roughly similar.[74] Dignity's role in judicial interpretation of old and new constitutional law in turn excites considerable attention today. Connected with the sudden relevance of and commentary on international human rights law, dignity is much more free-floating and contested than at the start. Its almost required status in constitutions in the last two decades means that dignity opens up specific fora for interpretation around the world, even if this process is potentially (though not necessarily) kept in boundaries by its concurrent interpretation in international human rights law.

In the academy, the belated and surprising return of Kantianism to prestige contributed a great deal, to be sure, with the proviso that contemporary secular liberals claiming Kant's mantle did not turn to the touchstone of dignity until very late in their revivalism. Kant accorded individual dignity importance in his moral philosophy, but few of his followers have until recently. For most of the period since the 1940s, dignity was something like a proprietary Catholic concept, generally restricted to natural law circles.[75] Kantians before the recent present, both in their late nineteenth-century guise with Hermann Cohen or late twentieth-century guise with John Rawls, have not focused on it. Of the preeminent philosophers who have published a book, chapter, or article on dignity in the last few years, none featured or in most cases even mentioned it before; the common assertion of dignity's immemorial theoretical presence simply does not fit with its strikingly meteoric rise.[76] In international law, for a long time it was exclusively conservative naturalists in the guild, such as Myres McDougal and especially Alfred Verdross (by far its most prominent promoter in Cold War international law anywhere), who organized their thought around human dignity. (Verdross, a Viennese pupil of Kelsen's who turned to Catholic natural law, had been a loyal admirer of Dollfuss and an ardent supporter of his regime before becoming postwar Austria's greatest international lawyer.)[77] In great numbers, since then, liberal constitutional and international lawyers have now turned to dignity, generally concurring in the same move that philosophers have made toward Kantian thought as their basic framework.[78]

The priority that Kantianism has today in sometimes overlapping academic and legal circles occasionally prompts a wishful assumption about the constitutional presence of dignity. But if constitutional dignity originally posed a bar, it was much more to democracy in the name of a posited anterior morality, to stave off the risk of the secular incursion or "totalitarian" expansion of the state. It is true that in Catholic social thought, a utilitarian basis for policy calling for hedonic calculation was also anathema, but not because it preferred the autonomy of Kantian persons. It insisted on *constraint* on autonomy, individual as well as collective. Dignity thus did not originally portend now current debates concerning individual prerogatives versus collective goods—the distinction between which the notion of the "human person" was supposed to overcome.

The constitutional beginnings of individual human dignity were rather distinctive compared to the present time. They affected human rights, hitherto a liberal conception, profoundly and for novel conservative uses. At a very different historical moment than ours, human dignity originally entered world and constitutional politics as some Catholic actors struggled to establish it as a valuable tool; and it spread at a moment when Christian Democracy was cementing the rule it was to enjoy across Western Europe for decades—conservative rule.

The Human Person and the
Reformulation of Conservatism

In summer 1947, the Institute for International Law
reconvened after a ten-year hiatus. For decades the self-
appointed tribune of European "civilization" and the legal
conscience of humanity, the Institute now hoped to retake
its former role. Given its prominence in the rhetoric of
Allied new order during World War II, human rights—
though international lawyers had never even flirted with
the concept before—had become the first item on their
agenda.[1] The atmosphere was one of bitter disappoint-
ment: whatever the idealism of wartime dreams, the sad
but obvious fact was that when it came time to enact a
peaceful order, the allies had proved grim realists. Already
in the Dumbarton Oaks documents, the pivotal first drafts
from 1944 of international arrangements in which human
rights did not figure, it had been clear that a theory of
sovereign power politics would rule. The same basic ver-
dict applied to the United Nations Charter, which great
powers adorned with the concept of human rights without providing the notion either a clear definition or any
means of defense.[2] The international lawyers of Europe

were, the Institute believed, perhaps the last best hope for making good on what now seemed like broken promises.

"Neither the Charter not diplomatic wrangling is reassuring," noted Charles de Visscher, Belgian international lawyer and judge (1946–52) on the International Court of Justice, who prepared the Institute's report and proposal on human rights, in his opening remarks at its reunion meeting. "International organization," he ruefully complained, "looks like a mere bureaucracy with neither direction nor soul, unable to open to humanity the horizons of a true international community." A new international law, based on human rights and theorized and implemented by the caste of jurists, might, however, provide the "morally-inspired salvation" that the world clearly needed. Now comes a very curious statement: "Since the end of the second world war, a powerful current of ideas has arisen against the nameless abuses that we have witnessed: it is the personalist conception of society and power. The intellectual elites of all of the countries with liberal and democratic traditions are rallying to this conception." According to de Visscher, this "personalist conception" alone could provide the basis of an authentic turn to human rights and guide the response of law to Machiavellian power.[3]

Given the current discussion of the origins of human rights, one would be hard pressed to understand what this leading international lawyer was talking about. In fact, however, personalism was a principal feature of the human rights moment of the 1940s, especially, though not exclusively, on the European continent. But what was personalism? How was it possible to view it as the key to the turn to human rights—saving them from their entombment by the very United Nations organization that announced them? And how thoroughgoing a resonance did personalism really have in the postwar moment? Forgotten now, the spiritual and often explicitly religious philosophy of the human person was the conceptual means through which continental Europe initially incorporated human rights—and, indeed, became the homeland of the notion for several decades.

In fact, recovering the centrality of personalism through the 1930s and 1940s should deeply unsettle prevailing opinion about what the concept of human rights really meant in its founding moment. This chapter surveys a few of the sources of personalism, looks at the breadth of its percolation (not least in legal thought), and evaluates the significance of the vehicle it provided for human rights in the 1940s. If this episode is missing from the emerging understanding of now core precepts, it should also drive home a larger lesson about the teleology, tunnel vision, and triumphalism that has so deeply affected current historiography. Universalistic and formalistic languages always have a historically specific and ideologically particular meaning, which it is the mission of historians to seek out. In early postwar Europe, human rights were—contrary to current expectations and desires—best associated neither with a revolutionary nor a republican heritage. For almost nobody were they the essence of post-Holocaust wisdom, not least since the worst crimes of Nazi evildoers were not yet understood to be ones specifically directed against the Jewish people. Instead, human rights were most closely associated with an epoch-making reinvention of conservatism. This defining event of postwar Western European history is familiar from the more general historiography of the period in the form of Christian Democratic hegemony but is absent so far from human rights history—even though this same Western Europe became the earliest homeland of the concept. In sum, human rights came to the world not just as part of a wartime internationalization of the American New Deal but also, and just as crucially, as one element of a European reinvention of its humanism as it tried to put self-imposed disaster behind it. The first surprise, perhaps, is that the concept of "the person" not only preexisted the mid-1940s but had originally served different forces.

The Origins of an Obsession

"We are neither individualists nor collectivists, we are personalists!" So proclaimed perhaps the earliest personalist political manifesto, put out by the rightist club "New Order" (*Ordre Nouveau*) in 1931.[4] In its 1930s popularization, the person was an antiliberal conception, and the chief task of following its eligibility for its postwar role is to trace the reversal that led it to imply rather than forbid formalistic conceptions such as rights—or even a reinvention of international law based on it.

The sources of "the person"—besides the Thomistic rendition of Jacques Maritain, who would become the premier postwar philosopher of human rights—were varied. Personalism had sprung up in motley and mostly disconnected and unrelated versions in several branches of modern thought in the nineteenth century.[5] In the twentieth century, one important reference was the émigré Russian Orthodox philosopher Nicholas Berdyaev, who brought to the West an old Russian tradition of religious personalism.[6] Most decisive, according to the historian John Hellman, may have been the influence of the originally Russian-Jewish convert Alexandre Marc, who founded *Ordre Nouveau* together with the shadowy guru Arnaud Dandieu, an atheist follower of Friedrich Nietzsche whom many considered the secret genius of personalism (though he was a mere librarian by day). In Germany, the most prominent personalist was Max Scheler, who also exerted influence elsewhere.[7] Not just the cacophony of voices starting in the early 1930s but the essential indeterminacy of the concept itself made personalism highly ambiguous: it was after all the common but deeply contentious cause of Christian and para-Christian intellectuals from the far right to the communitarian "left." The thinker who forged the most durable version of personalism, Jacques Maritain, could generously acknowledge as much: "There are at least a dozen personalist doctrines, which, at times, have nothing more in common than the term 'person.'"[8]

Yet the ambiguity of personalism was, in a sense, its genius; it signaled the identity of the opposition clearly, while leaving flexibility about what the alternative program was. (Its ambiguity was also a minimum condition for its eventual extrication from its generally reactionary and always illiberal origins.) Personalism—linked quickly to spiritualism and humanism and not infrequently to European identity—meant a repudiation of the rival materialisms of liberalism and communism. In the first place, then, personalism was different than individualism, for it championed a figure who was supposed to overcome the destitute atomism in the politics and economics of the nineteenth century. If, however, the person provided a connection to community that individualism ruled out, it also provided the key source of value omitted in, and a political bulwark against, communism. Most boldly, personalists claimed that capitalism and communism, apparently foes, deserved each other, and canceled each other out, in their common materialism.

The spectrum of opinion championing personalism in the inaugural years of the early 1930s ranged from the far right to the farrago of publicists now known as "nonconformists." The so-called Young Right (*Jeune Droite*), an up-and-coming cohort of young reactionaries, self-proclaimed "defenders of the West," were originally part of Maritain's reactionary circle in his days as a charter member of the Action Française. But they remained within the fold of the conservative revolution *à la française* even as Maritain himself departed the far right. As we will see, their source for claims about the person was that very mentor who, many years later, would offer up the concept as the foundation for human rights. "Before the tragic failure of materialist prosperity," one of these figures, Thierry Maulnier, wrote in 1932, "political humanism—the just reckoning of the person, and its possibilities and rights—would seem the sole formula . . . to furnish the acceptable elements of a reconstruction."[9] A group such as *Ordre Nouveau* was representative of nonconformism, a set of movements "neither right nor left" or rather both, since many thought what was true in Marxism and communism—their opposition to bourgeois decadence and their hankering for the death of individualism—had to be saved in order to redirect justified revolution against the bourgeoisie onto a spiritualist and often explicitly Christian new path.[10] These were the early themes of personalism, then. But if the essential meaninglessness of the person was a minimum condition for the fact that it could eventually be extricated from its reactionary and nonconformist origins, one must at least also note that, for a time after 1934, communism also tried to claim it. Nicolai Bukharin transformed the appeal of communism in the West when he claimed in that year that the Soviet Union would make the realization of "the personality" for "the first time . . . a mass phenomenon and not just . . . part of the slave-owning upper class in its various historical variants." This startling assertion came to profoundly affect the way ordinary Soviet citizens imagined and constructed their identities. But the ramifications were also legal, as the Stalin Constitution (in whose drafting Bukharin played an instrumental role) shows.[11]

Without question the man who made the intellectual fortune of personalism, however, was Emmanuel Mounier, due to the terrific impact of his nonconformist journal *Esprit* from the early 1930s. Drastically expanding the purchase of the theme of the person in his early essays, Mounier proposed going back to where modernity started out in the Renaissance, which had merely led to "established disorder," and trying again with a genuine humanism that freed Europe of the secular and liberal mistake of individualism. For Mounier, the challenge was to use the person to insist on respect for self-realization that "collectivism" ruled out, while pressing it to imply a community that brought atomized individuals back together. This common idea was one that Mounier developed at length, including in his famous *Manifeste au service du personnalisme*. Far from implying rights, this central personalism of the 1930s sought new forms of postliberal politics as well as a personalist economy to go with them. "On the altar of this sad world," Mounier wrote in an illustrative passage, "there is but one god, smiling and hideous: the Bourgeois." Mounier explained:

> He has lost the true sense of being, he moves only among things, and things that are practical and that have been denuded of their mystery. He is a man without love, a Christian without conscience, an unbeliever without passion. He has deflected the universe of virtues from its supposedly senseless course towards the infinite and made it center about a petty system of social and psychological tranquillity. For him there is only prosperity, health, common sense, balance, sweetness of life, comfort. . . . Next in line among bourgeois values are human respect and protection of rights. . . . Law is for him not an institution for justice, but the defence of the injustices he inflicts. Thence comes his harsh legalism.[12]

Repudiating France's then minuscule Christian Democratic party—in a notorious fracas with Paul Archambault, who considered him dangerous in the extreme—Mounier declared that "the ideology that we are combatting, and which still poisons all democrats, even Christian democrats, is the ideology of 89," whose principles such as individual rights had to be "evaluated in the light of our conception of man [and] of the Community that completes him."[13]

The puzzle is how the person, in spite of all these associations, would be readied for its intellectual—and harsh legalistic!—role later; and much of the solution to that puzzle depends on Jacques Maritain, who would, not coincidentally, become the most prominent thinker of any kind across the world to champion rights in the postwar moment. Personalism survived its original connotations, as the communitarian third way that it promised between individualism and communism survived its reactionary (and occasional leftist) connotations to be linked tightly to Cold War conservatism.

Maritain from Authoritarianism to Human Rights

Maritain actually had a plausible claim to have introduced "the person" first, in his popular Action Française–era book *Three Reformers* (1925). He argued that the catastrophe of modernity, due to the sensualist heresiarch Martin Luther, the solipsist metaphysician René Descartes, and the bourgeois reformer Jean-Jacques Rousseau, left behind St. Thomas's "person" for the new individual. Thus not just generally, but in Maritain's own case, the basic claim of the sociopolitical relevance of "the person" antedated any break with the far right of his day, rather than driving it. "Are you well-informed about the ideological adventure that two pages of *Three Reformers* [those that originally introduced the person/individual distinction] have allowed?," Maritain's disciple Yves Simon could ask him in a letter as late as 1941, when the person still remained chiefly a reactionary conception, in spite of Maritain's extraordinary labors by then to make it mean something different.[14]

For Maritain had left the personalist revolution to others for a decade, while he continued his main interests in metaphysics and aesthetics. In the mid-1930s, this changed. As much as the negative example of the far right, it was Mounier's para-Catholic and this-worldly combat for a personalist rupture that pushed Maritain to elaborate his own politics. (Intellectually and organizationally, Maritain had been instrumental in Mounier's path to *Esprit*, but the obverse of the relationship has not been sufficiently stressed. Maritain opposed Mounier's drifts into apparent proximity to fascism but would never have become a political thinker without Mounier's example.[15]) It is also clear that, though by then an anticommunist of quite long standing, Maritain was angered by the huge propaganda successes of communism in the West in the mid-1930s in the cultural preparation of Popular Front antifacism, as figures such as André Gide and André Malraux responded to Bukharin's new propaganda by insisting that the Soviets might have the true recipe for the achievement of the dignity of the human personality.[16] Yet even in his *Integral Humanism* (1936), in which he spelled out his politics of personalism in their most classic form, Maritain endorsed the person without endorsing rights, a clear sign of his proximity to nonconformist and illiberal currents in European thought.

We cannot understand Maritain's conversion to rights—and that of the whole continent—without looking to the larger Catholic Church's conversion to personalism. How this happened was unexpected and dramatic, and due above all to events in the mid-1930s that prompted Pius XI to commit the Church to antitotalitarianism.[17] The move toward the later twentieth-century embrace of rights talk as the essence of Christian social thought occurred neither at a slow and steady pace nor all at once in a single transformative moment. It is not impossible to find allusions to the person and even to rights (though always in relation to family or labor) before this moment. These usages, however, were "neither comprehensive nor tightly systematic."[18] The crucial leap occurred when Pius XI began to use the terms in a more serious and organizing way toward the end of his papacy.

This remarkable turn against "statolatry" by no means compelled any embrace of rights as an organizing doctrine; but it did involve the assertion of religious sovereignty over personal conscience. And most frequently, this sovereignty attached to the previously peripheral figure of the person. Interestingly, it was most frequently antiliberal premises that led to what may seem a liberalizing outcome in the pope's denunciation of the era's dictators (Benito Mussolini usually exempted), with the modern and "secularist" separation of state from church often presented as having allowed the menacing totalitarian hypertrophy of the state to occur.[19] In any event, it was at this moment that Pius—who knew Maritain well and esteemed his work—turned emphatically to personalism as the foundation of Church's spiritual alternative to totalitarianism in 1937–38. "Man, as a person," Pius declared, "possesses rights that he holds from God and which must remain, with regard to the collectivity, beyond the reach of anything that would tend to deny them, to abolish them, or to neglect them."[20] This phraseology, from the anti-Nazi encyclical of March 1937, *Mit brennender Sorge*, was matched by the anticommunist encyclical of the same month, *Divini redemptoris*, the latter placing greater emphasis on the right of property in the context of a more general picture of the rights of the person against the totalitarian collective.[21]

It was thus in a moment of discovering two extreme political ideologies that, in its view, left no room for

Christianity that the Church discovered its sovereignty over the "human," over which in turn no merely temporal politics can claim full authority. In summer 1937, Eugenio Pacelli, soon to be Pope Pius XII, rendered the centrality of this new figure against the backdrop of "a vast and dangerous conspiracy" threatening unlike any prior occasion "the inviolability of the human person that, in his sovereign wisdom and infinite goodness, the Creator has honored with an incomparable dignity." Further, Pacelli cited the critical line from *Mit brennender Sorge* to make clear that this inviolable dignity gave rise to some set of rights. Of course, personalism implied community, not atomism. All the same, "if a society adopted the pretense that it could diminish the dignity of the human person in refusing it all or some of the rights that come to it from God, it would miss its goal."[22]

What such changes in papal political theory meant on the ground, in the context of other doctrines and the inherited weight of tradition, varied widely—especially after Pius XII's election a year later to face the final crisis of the 1930s and the difficult choices of the war.[23] With respect to the language of rights as well as in other ways, Pius XII, like any good strategist, left his options open, encouraging some possible lines of future development and tolerating others.[24] In summer 1941, on the fiftieth anniversary of his predecessor Leo XIII's great social encyclical *Rerum Novarum*, Pius was forthright about the precedence of the common good of the community to the rights of the human person, even as he was clear that the state could not suppress the latter in the name of the former. "To safeguard the inviolable sphere of the rights of the human person and to facilitate the fulfillment of his duties should be the essential office of every public authority," Pius observed.

> Does not this flow from that genuine concept of the common good which the State is called upon to promote? Hence it follows that the care of such a common good does not imply a power so extensive over the members of the community that in virtue of it the public authority can interfere with the evolution of . . . individual activity . . . in opposition to the personal duties or rights of man, and to this end abolish or deprive of efficacy his natural rights . . . To deduce such extension of power from the care of the common good would be equivalent to overthrowing the very meaning of the word common good, and falling into the error that the proper scope of man on earth is society, that society is an end in itself, that man has no other life which awaits his beyond that which ends here below.[25]

Perhaps most important, in different national contexts, rights talk had different fates: the new language of the rights of the human person was not just passively received but creatively interpreted from place to place and moment to moment. As historian Paul Hanebrink has shown in the case of Hungarian debates, for example, what was at stake for some churchmen and Christian politicians was only "the rights of (Christian) man," chiefly the defense of the right of conversion against racist essentialism, still in the name of a exclusionary vision of a Christianized nation. Similarly, Piotr Kosicki offers a disturbing story about a Polish "rights talk" fully compatible with anti-Semitism in the era.[26]

But in America—before Maritain ever turned to rights—a small band of liberal Catholics chose a different direction. In tune with his final thought, Pius XI had written barely two months before his death that "Christian teaching alone gives full meaning to the demands of human rights and liberty because it alone gives worth and dignity to human personality." In this usage, "human rights" meant threading the needle between the twin totalitarian obstacles, without falling back into liberal secularism and materialism: "The Catholic," he explained,

> is necessarily the champion of true human rights and the defender of true human liberties; it is in the name of God Himself that he cries out against any civic philosophy which would degrade man to the position of a soulless pawn in a sordid game of power and prestige, or would seek to banish him from membership in the human family; it is in the same holy name that he opposes any social philosophy which would regard man as a mere chattel in commercial competition for profit, or would set him at the throat of his fellow in a blind brutish class struggle for existence.[27]

In a pastoral letter in response to this statement in honor of the golden jubilee of Catholic University, American bishops took the argument a (textually unwarranted) step further: "His Holiness calls us to the defense of our democratic government in a constitution that safeguards the inalienable rights of man."[28] American Catholic liberals opposing Father Charles Coughlin's Jew-baiting founded the publication *The Voice for Human Rights* in 1939.[29] Historians who have examined the crucial early war years to trace the rise of the hitherto largely unused phrase (in English) of "human rights" have discovered only minor percolations until something happened to bring the term into its immediate postwar moment of increased use. Completely neglected among these percolations so far highlighted, however, is the comparatively early Catholic articulation of the human rights idea.[30]

As the war continued, papal pronouncement remained open textured enough for Catholics to infer widely different messages from it. But one of the Catholic bishops who formed a committee to promote the papal peace points in the United States, Aloyisius Muench of Fargo, North Dakota, entertained the belief—at least according to his later testimony—that Franklin D. Roosevelt's later language of new order and four freedoms merely amplified the pope's call for a postwar political settlement based on universal moral principles. This was especially so thanks to the 1942 letter Roosevelt wrote to American bishops after the country's entrance in the war that the United Nations (as the alliance was called before it became a prospective organization) would seek "the establishment of an international order in which the spirit of Christ shall rule the hearts of men and nations." "We were assured by the late President Roosevelt," Muench recalled just after the conflict, when he had become papal nuncio to a defeated Germany, "that the war would not be one of vengeance but to establish a new order in the spirit of Christ [and] a crusade for the preservation of the rights of men."[31] American Catholics were in advance of others, and even their president, in deploying the phrase "human rights," but by 1941–42, Catholics in Germany and France would also be using the language too. The nuance and specificity of wartime human rights discourse remains to be studied; the defense of the human rarely meant any special concern with the Holocaust and frequently went along with fierce Christian anticommunism in which enthusiastic support for Adolf Hitler's anti-Bolshevik crusade could coexist with dissent from his depredations against life.[32] Nevertheless, the language is there, as a possible new basis of Christianity's political identity, for those who had stopped dreaming the dream of "holy empire." German bishops, in a common pastoral letter of Easter 1942, rose in protest of their regime's trampling not just of the church's rights (in disregard of the earlier concordat) but also of human rights—"the general rights divinely guaranteed to men." The extraordinary clandestine resistance group of French Catholics, *Témoignage chrétien*, republished this letter and amplified the call in its summer booklet "Human and Christian Rights."[33]

Maritain intersected this earlier but episodic, unsystematic, and selective Catholic tradition of rights and made it his most enduring contribution to the twentieth-century church and world. Maritain had already, by the late 1930s, begun a geographical and intellectual voyage to the American scene—one that would be fateful for the future of Catholicism as a whole. He originally went to North America in 1933, when he accepted fellow Thomist Étienne Gilson's invitation to lecture annually at the new Institute for Medieval Studies in Toronto; he first set foot in the United States in 1938.[34] But it was only the war that led his Christian humanism in the direction of rights. This is not to say that the Catholic rights turn described earlier did not have an immediate effect: in speaking on the Jewish question in 1937–38, Maritain rose in defense of "a pluralism founded on the dignity of the human person, and established on the basis of complete equality of civic rights, and effective respect for the liberties of the person in his individual life." Even as it was "thoroughly opposed to the ignominious medievalist Hitlerian parody," the defense, however, also had to be immediately couched in absolutely clear rejection of "the old Liberalism." Rights, Maritain emphasized, were only going to be retrievable "in a general new régime of civilization, freedom from the ills of capitalistic materialism as well as from the even greater ills of Fascism, Racism, and Communism."[35] But far from becoming the self-evident entailments of the dignity of the human person they would shortly become (let alone the key watchwords of politics), rights remained highly uncertain in the place they initially found in Maritain's thought: in a Chicago speech from the same period, Maritain still claimed to his American audience, in perfect fidelity to integral humanism, that "democracy can no longer afford the luxury of drifting. Individualism in the sense of individual rights and comforts must cease to be its chief objective."[36] Fortunately, he continued, there were emerging signs that America planned to rediscover the religious imperatives of its civilization. In his Théâtre Marigny speech, just after the Munich agreements and a year before German tanks rolled into Paris, Maritain lavished praise upon Roosevelt's remarkable State of the Union address for 1939 in which he endorsed religion as the foundation of democracy. In the same address, Maritain likewise cited Walter Lippmann marveling that "the President, who is the most influential democratic leader in the world, should recognize religion as the *source* of democracy . . . [which] is a fundamental reorientation in the liberal democratic outlook upon life."[37] It was time to revisit the familiar rejection of liberal democracy as a threat to Christianity, as both converged after saving themselves from their inherent extremes.

On an American sojourn when France fell, but transmitting his ideas back to the continent throughout, Maritain made himself the premier interpreter of human rights amongst Catholics, and indeed almost single-handedly reinvented them as a Christian tradition. By itself, personalism could have led Maritain, like so many others, into the arms of the Vichy government, whose leader, indeed, himself proclaimed that "individualism has nothing in common with respect for the human person" (a respect he promised his regime would restore, along with religious civilization as a whole). Maritain's formulae of the "primacy of the spiritual" and "integral humanism" were even used as sloganeering buzzwords by Vichyite intellectuals and youth.[38] But Maritain, in exile, opposed Vichy uncompromisingly and soon became an inspiration for the Resistance, even if he was ambivalent about Charles de Gaulle as the Free French leader, on the grounds that the latter would not concur with his vision of personalistic democracy.[39] It was most clearly in early 1942 that Maritain transformed into the philosopher of human rights that he had never been before. In *Natural Law and Human Rights*, Maritain took what would be a fateful step for postwar intellectual history as a whole, making the claim that a revival of natural law implies a broad set of prepolitical human rights.[40] "The dignity of the human person?," Maritain asked. "The expression means nothing if it does not signify that, by virtue of the natural law, the human person has the right to be respected, is the subject of rights, possesses rights."[41]

What would have been—and still is—curious about this claim, of course, is that whatever their opinions of the origins of modern rights talk, nearly all histories of the political language concur that the rise of rights in political theory occurred after and because of the destruction of the Thomistic natural law tradition.[42] In either a stroke of a master, or a sleight of hand, or both, Maritain—as if the Thomistic movement had not long and unanimously rejected modern rights—claimed that the one implied the other and indeed that only the one plausibly and palatably justified the other. Thanks to Maritain above all, the older view that Christianity's political and social doctrine could not be reformulated in terms of rights was dropped in exchange for the claim that only the Christian vision placing the personal entitlements in the framework of the common good afforded a persuasive theory of rights.[43] Some Catholics wondered then and since if Maritain conceded too much to modernity ("dressing up poor Thomas Aquinas in the rags of a laicist apostle of democracy," in Aurel Kolnai's hilariously grim assessment); yet Maritain's view of continuity between natural law and natural rights has generally won the day.[44] By his Christmas message of 1942, Pius too was laying out his postwar vision in terms of the dignity of the person and human rights.[45]

A communitarian framework had emerged for the new rights talk that both updated the former and domesticated the latter. "Why have philosophers devoted so much attention in recent years to the distinction between person and individual?," asked one Catholic philosopher at this moment, concluding that the Thomistic terms in which

Maritain often defended the distinction were baseless. "In this matter, they are motivated chiefly by the desire to provide a philosophical answer to the claims of totalitarianism," the observer concluded.[46] By 1942, British Catholic and later Harvard University professor Christopher Dawson—who had imported Maritain in his reactionary phase to Britain along with Carl Schmitt in his Catholic phase for English-language readers—was sounding similar themes. "We are standing against an order in which all human rights and the human person itself are immolated on the altar of power to the glory of the New Leviathan," he wrote. Alluding to Roosevelt, Dawson now explained, in spite of his formerly reactionary politics, "The liberties which we demand and which humanity demands are not the right of the strong to oppress the weak or the right of the ambitious to enrich themselves at other men's expense: but the elementary right which are to the human spirit what air and light are to the body:—freedom to worship God, freedom of speech, freedom from want and freedom from fear." All the same, he clarified that if Christianity now implied some sort of democracy, it could not be a liberal kind:

> It must be a social order directed to spiritual ends. . . . From this point of view the use of the term "Democracy" as the definition of our cause is not completely satisfactory. For Democracy has a restricted political significance which by no means covers the whole field of values that has to be defended, and the confusion of Democracy as a general term for our tradition of social freedom, and its more limited but more accurate political meaning, is apt to produce misunderstanding

84

and disagreement. For the cause that we are defending is far more fundamental than any form of government or any political creed. It is bound up with the whole tradition of Western and Christian culture. . . . No doubt Democracy as an ideal does stand for these things and is the outcome of this tradition. But in practice modern democratic culture often represents only a debased and secularized version of this ideal and in many respects, as de Tocqueville saw more than a century ago, it prepares the way for the coming of the new mass order which achieves political form in the totalitarian State. What we are defending, in short, is not democracy but humanity.[47]

Dawson's argument made sense in light of prewar conceptions of democracy, which prioritized its formalistic associations as a "bourgeois" electoral and economic phenomenon that both far-left and Christian politics were agreed in rejecting. As the war continued, however, one of Maritain's main purposes was to lay out a new, Christian conception of democracy that transcended these narrow limits, and soon the Pope would agree. Democracy and humanity could coincide.

In the flow of Maritain's political theory in these years, in fact, the Catholic position of the nonindividualist person in the nontotalitarian community remained stable, as the overall governing framework into which rights were introduced. In other words, the superimposition of rights on personalism meant as much continuity as change. In an atmosphere in which many Catholics understood the defense of the West to mean all-out war against Bolshevism even at the price of an alliance with unholy forces on the secular right, Maritain's message was primarily directed at the Christian preference for fascism as the lesser evil. "An obscure process of leniency toward totalitarian forms that lying propaganda tries to picture as the upholders of order," Maritain regretted at the University of Pennsylvania bicentennial in 1940, "has thus invaded parts of the believing groups in many countries."[48] "The error of those Catholics who follow Pétain in France or Franco in Spain," Maritain wrote Charles de Gaulle in 1941, "is to convert Catholic thought, through lack of social and political education, in the direction of old paternalistic conceptions of history rejected in the meantime by the popes and condemned by history."[49]

In the process, Maritain's often harsh view of the catastrophe of modernity became more irenic (though it never reversed). His relative move toward an affirmation of a specific kind of state framework within which alone a "new Christian order" could come about forced Maritain to quietly but decisively drop his old associations of formal liberties and formal democracy with liberal individualism on its deathbed. He broke more fully with visions such as Marxism or Mounier's personalism that treated formal rights and democracy as elements of a hypocritical sham. Formal or "bourgeois" liberties, formerly condemned, now had to be resurrected as providing the legal carapace of the Christian state and interstate order. Arguably, however, these innovations were in the service of keeping personalist communitarianism the same in new circumstances.

It is true, though, that this substantive vision now prompted a less critical attitude toward formal guarantees and political structures or, indeed, even invested them with considerable significance. One could say something similar of Pius XII who, having adopted the rhetoric of the rights of the person, was by his 1944 Christmas message following Maritain by endorsing democracy on condition of differentiating between its Christian communitarian and reprobate secularist version. By 1944, the rights of the human person, as galvanized by Maritain's enthusiastic promotion and as the ground of his reappropriation of democracy, were understood by activist Catholics to be the main bulwark against Hitlerian racism.[50] And such Catholics also claimed that the concept provided the key slogan for the postwar settlement, which would have to be based on principle not power. The answer would be a vision of human rights that split the difference, or rather found the proper reconciliation, between self and collective. As Pius expressed things: "In a people worthy of the name, the citizen feels within him the consciousness of his personality, of his duties and rights, of his own freedom joined to respect for the freedom and dignity of others. . . . [But] if men, using their personal liberty, were to deny all dependence on a superior Authority possessing coercive power, they could by this very fact cut the ground from under their own dignity and liberty—by violating, that is, the absolute order of beings and purposes."[51] This was subjective rights for the sake of submission to objective morality, not of exercise of personal autonomy or maximization of individual utility.

But the availability of rights had been achieved. Appealing to Pius XII's Christmas message of 1942, Richard Pattee explained on the radio in 1945, "The genius of Catholicism is perhaps no better illustrated than in the subtle and profound harmony that is established between the dignity of the human being as a singular person, and the obligations and duties of that person as a member of society."[52] "Defend These Human Rights!" British Catholic John Eppstein wrote in a 1948 pamphlet, explaining that this meant *la défense de la personne humaine* first discovered by Catholics in the later 1930s. ("This was somewhat different from the familiar enumeration of 'the Rights of Man and the Citizen,'" he explained, "since by 'the human person' the Christian opponents of State absolutism meant particularly man as a *spiritual* being.")[53] Even in America, in a 1950 essay, the major postwar Catholic thinker, Jesuit, and follower of Maritain John Courtney Murray, argued that the human rights turn showed that the modern world had finally imbibed Catholicism's message rather than vice versa: "The growing conviction of the old attempts to solve the problem of human liberty and social order in purely secularistic, positivist terms had created a new openness to the world of metaphysical and religious values. [The Christian human rights idea provides] such a basis because it is metaphysical in its foundations, because it is asserted within a religious framework, and because it is realist (not nominalist), societal (not individualist), and integrally human (not rationalist) in its outlook on man and society."[54]

The work of saving the person from its antidemocratic votaries arguably depended on the deeper commitment to a moral and communitarian ethos. And it allowed leaving reactionary versions of the person behind, almost as if they had never been. "To avoid all misunderstanding, I must add," de Visscher put it rather charmingly in 1947, "that the personalist conception must be defended against some of those who claim it and who have sometimes compromised it in the very process of advocating for it."[55]

After the War

Even Mounier, who remained in France, embraced rights after a fashion—albeit very briefly. After having flirted with identifying the National Revolution as a personalist one—he criticized Maritain for his treasonous defense of American democracy before being shut down by the regime—Mounier penned a declaration of "the rights of persons and communities."[56] This made an important difference to his followers, many of whom essentially made Maritain's move to reconcile personalism with formal democracy while Mounier notoriously moved from nonconformism to the far left in the postwar era. Mounier had, it is clear, a far more serious impact on Belgium and France, while Maritain's message found its most significant hearing in Italy and Latin America.[57]

Followers of Mounier in the briefly if meteorically successful postwar Mouvement républicain populaire were able to be more faithful than Mounier was to his brief rights-based revision of personalism. A good example of a Mounier disciple who played a major role in the postwar European human rights moment—besides Charles de Visscher—was François de Menthon, who headed the French prosecution team at Nuremberg. In his spectacular opening address, now understandably attacked for developing the juristic novelty of "crimes against humanity" while failing to mention which part of humanity actually suffered the crimes, Menthon identified the German acts as "crimes against the spirit," a clear reference to interwar and wartime antimaterialism that contemporaries, unlike Nuremberg's many historians since, would have readily identified as such. "National Socialism," he thundered, "ends in the absorption of the personality of the citizen into that of the state and in the denial of any intrinsic value to the human person." Even his glancing reference, at the end of his address, to "citizens of the occupied countries categorized as Jews" singled out the damage done to "their personal rights and to their human dignity."[58] The personalist framing of crimes against humanity was far more central than the much later heirs of Nuremberg—who have made the Holocaust more ethically central to their activities than the trial's own sponsors—might like to admit. It shows the ethics of the trial were often more concerned with a particular vision of moral order rather than with today's intuitions about social justice.

As for Maritain, he continued to defend a personalistic conception of human rights wherever he went. It should be said that, unlike most other proponents of Christian human rights in the age, Maritain—though a conventional anti-Semite in his Action Française days—both knew and cared about the vicious Jew hatred of the 1930s and 1940s in general, and the Holocaust in particular (his wife Raïssa having been born a Jew under the Russian empire). Nevertheless, there is no evidence for thinking that Maritain championed human rights because of this exceptional awareness or in response to the Jewish plight.[59] Instead, human rights became his talisman as one of the hallmarks of a new Christianity, including in his work for the United Nations Educational, Scientific and Cultural Organization (UNESCO) on the philosophical grounding of human rights and as

French Ambassador to the Holy See (where he decisively influenced later popes who would finally overcome institutional resistance within the Church to a full move to human rights language two decades later).[60] And though Maritain was certainly the most prominent thinker on the postwar scene to defend the concept of human rights, it was political shifts that made its fortune in the Western European polities that would become its early homeland. Still, because Christianity aspired to be and to some extent was even then a global phenomenon, there should be no surprise in discovering that personalism went far and wide. Though not yet seriously researched, personalism's radiance among emerging postcolonial elites was clearly enormous, and its third-way promise played a similar role among those who repudiated communism and claimed to save the West from its materialist and imperialist mistakes. For example, in South Vietnam, the authoritarian Ngô Đình Diệm and his brother both frequently trafficked in claims to realize the human person, to the outrage of their opponents (and the confusion of their allies).[61] More specifically, the personalistic framing of the global human rights blip of the era affected the language not simply inside continental Europe but far beyond it. This included, most obviously, the move to human rights at the level of international organization, essentially rhetorical though it was (as European international lawyers were not wrong to note).

Indeed, the human person became a key figure of thought at the United Nations, thanks to Christians who were impressed by papal language and who injected it into founding documents. In a multiculturalist age, it is tempting to look back at storied figures in the origins of human rights at the United Nations and claim them for the third world and alternative values, when in fact they themselves insisted—before the right audiences at least—that they were making a Christian contribution.[62] Charles Malik, a Lebanese Christian who is responsible for the personalistic language of the Universal Declaration proper, is a case in point. "In Christianity, the individual human person possesses an absolute value," Malik explained in 1951. "The ultimate ground of all our freedom is the Christian doctrine of the absolute inviolability of the human person."[63] Carlos Romulo, Philippines delegate to the United Nations and a crucial figure in the General Assembly debates on the Universal Declaration, provides another illuminating example, as his lectures on the natural law foundation of international law developments make clear. "Of all the acts of the United Nations," he argued, "the Universal Declaration of Human Rights has demonstrated most clearly the tendency . . . to work out a system of international law conforming as closely as possible to natural law. . . . We may yet find ourselves confronted by the seeming paradox of Christianity emerging as the only practical program for lasting peace and equitable order in our troubled world."[64]

There was, however, very little true international human rights law for decades, and the real story of human rights in the early postwar period, with due allowance for the importance of symbolism, is of its nationalization and regionalization. It would go too far to claim that the vogue of declarations of rights in the postwar moment reflected a personalistic consensus.[65] Early steps in European unification and the—also initially quite unimpressive— European human rights regime, however, certainly did. As Wolfram Kaiser has shown, Christian Democracy, hegemonic as the continent restabilized, made a politics of personalism and dignity central to its work nationally as well as to its construction of Europe regionally.[66] "In the inter-war period catholicism had been closely linked to nationalism and the League of Nations had been presented as being a dangerous centre of masonic power," Richard Vinen observes, in a similar vein. "After 1945, this changed. Catholic organizations were enthusiastic proponents of international harmony, within the western bloc at least, and Christian Democrat parties in all European countries were so intimately linked to European integration that some began to feel that Europe was being built under the aegis of the 'catholic international.'"[67]

It is true that personalism, in both Maritain's and Mounier's renditions, could have had left-wing implications, and to some extent did, prompting an evanescent "left Catholicism" that quickly sputtered.[68] This was not, however, because of any dispute about the role of the state in the economy: though continental Europeans needed Americans in the 1940s, it was not to learn commitment to an economic new deal. As de Visscher argued, no one believed that personalism implied a return to "the economic liberalism of the eighteenth or nineteenth centuries."[69] Rather, left and right Christians agreed that some management of the economy was necessary and diverged from there. Very quickly, however, left versions of personalism were extinguished, and the ideology underwrote a reinvention of conservatism in power.

This "re-recasting of bourgeois Europe," as one may call it, occurred under the political hegemony of Christian Democracy, even if one wants to see it as redounding t⁄ the benefit of liberal economics in the long run. As Ma⸱ Conway observes, "perhaps the most durable cha⸱

European political life brought about by the war was in fact conservative in nature. . . . . Catholicism in the later 1940s and 1950s . . . , while presiding politically over the postwar reconstruction of Western Europe, retained within it the intellectual components of a profound critique of liberalist and individualist values which underpinned that same process of reconstruction."[70] It should not be surprising, therefore, that many of the chief founders of the European project, both in politics generally and in the tradition of European human rights specifically, were avowed personalists (for instance, Robert Schuman, Paul-Henri Spaak, and Pierre-Henri Teitgen).[71]

Of course, human rights law gained only slightly more traction in its Europeanized form: the case of the European Convention (1950) involved—in the early decades when there was no right of petition and little serious activity, not least because of its inapplicability during colonial emergency—much more ideological signaling about the values on which Western European identity depended than it did legally enforceable guarantees. Common Christian identity mattered a lot here, only now it meant the centrality of the human person. The Convention itself, given signal British participation in its origins, is not an exception to this statement but illustrates how powerfully the revolt against materialism as the essence of Europe resonated in these years. As the Convention's historian Brian Simpson has emphasized, the Convention emerged thanks to Britain's commitment to the "spiritual union" of Western Europeans against communism, in Ernest Bevin's phrase. "In the event Bevin's idea of a spiritual union came to be secularized," Simpson drily comments, "but this was not perhaps how it began."[72]

That the incipient Cold War would soon come to be widely understood in terms of the defense of religion and "the West" that the Church's struggle against communism had already been for three decades was no doubt crucial in the larger postwar spiritualist consensus among Western European liberal-conservatives.[73] In this sense, it was not only that British commitment to "spiritual" values in international affairs, which had also antedated the war, that allowed for new collaborations with Catholic politics in the postwar years, of which the Convention is only one example.[74] More generally, there had been important Protestant defenders of third-way personalism all along (perhaps most importantly, Swiss writer Denis de Rougemont, who had been a nonconformist close to both Marc and Mounier before becoming a Europeanist).[75] The larger phenomenon, without which the picture would remain incomplete, is the cross-denominational ratification of human dignity as part of a reinvention of Christianity of both Catholic and Protestant varieties. A few notes on the German case—a crucial link in the Catholic international but with meaningful Protestant participation—are useful in this regard.

Of course, there is no reason to hypothesize the direct impact of thinkers in the Francophone orbit on German developments, though the full ramifications of dissident networks across the Rhine in the interwar period are still only beginning to be reconstructed.[76] Certainly, the spiritualistic antimaterialism and emphasis on "the dignity of the human person"—including sometimes human rights—prevalent in the early years after World War II suggest that German Christians developed their own versions of the doctrines canvassed so far, based easily available papal pronouncement as well as Protestant sources. Even if it is true that they had no homegrown Maritain, a cognate spiritualist credo came close to providing the central ideological fulcrum of Christian Democracy in Germany.[77] As the last chapter suggested, it is best to read the Federal Republic Basic Law's opening affirmation of human dignity not just retrospectively as a response to the Nazi past (and certainly not reflecting horror in response to the Holocaust specifically) but prospectively as an allusion to the kind of moral future that would best overcome that past. It is a mistake, in other words, to think about the "recivilization" of West Germany without appreciating the religious consensus that provided its justification and explained the specific, nonsecular, moralized form it was supposed to take.[78]

The transformation of Christianity works far better than the background of fascism to explain the centrality of dignity and rights not just in postwar politics but also in postwar law—most famously, of course, postwar German constitutional law.[79] Catholic jurists such as Willi Geiger and Josef Wintrich, although at times quite compromised during the Nazi regime, could in the postwar period draw directly on new papal traditions, to give a strongly communitarian view of the Basic Law's implications. As a judge on the new German constitutional court, Geiger, for instance, championed the centrality of dignity and rights in public and private law in the early Federal Republic, which he saw as totally different in basis now that they had been reassigned from being Weimar-era products of the sovereign will to being rooted in the preconstitutional nature of persons.[80]

But others found relatively independent routes to similar conceptions. The transatlantic "ecumenical movement" of Protestants—which will be taken up in more detail in the next two chapters—had developed its own version of personalism across the same approximate period.[81] Protestant Gerhard Leibholz, an émigré in Britain during the war (and Dietrich Bonhoeffer's brother-in-law), early established contact with the crucial intermediary figure between British and resisting German Protestants George Bell, bishop of Chichester. Bell's postwar writing shows that Anglicans too signed, if slightly less frontally, onto antitotalitarian Christian personalism. As he put it, "Chief among [the idolatries of the day] are the worship of power, the totalitarian State, nationalism, racialism, the craving for riches. . . . Put against them the great Christian ideas of the sovereignty and fatherhood of God, the solidarity of the human race with all its varieties, the sacredness of the human personality . . . [T]he rights of men derive directly from their condition as children of God and not of the State."[82] Developing Protestant versions of antitotalitarianism emphasizing spiritual freedom, both Bell and Leibholz worked together with Anglican Alec Vidler and continental Catholic refugees to argue for a return of natural law based on the person. "Must not theonomic thinking demand that the State ought to abandon the idea of being a self-contained sovereign entity with only rights of its own, and acknowledge that it is a member of a community of nations each and all of which are bound to serve the rights of the human person?," Leibholz asked in 1946. In the postwar era, and his return to West Germany, where he served as a judge on the nation's highest court, he tirelessly promoted the centrality of the human personality (*Persönlichkeit*) as the foundation stone of democratic order.[83]

The intellectual and cultural sources here were not individualist in general or Kantian in particular, certainly not in the early going. In a first moment, in fact, the dominant view was to connect the human dignity affirmed at the outset of the Basic Law with naturalistic premises, and indeed "the dominant Catholic natural law teaching possessed in the first postwar years such a powerful radiance amongst constitutional experts that Protestants themselves could not withdraw from it."[84] In a second moment, Günter Dürig, Catholic personalist and author of the leading commentary on the Basic Law, moved away from natural law to a theory of human dignity, and rights generally, as "objective values" (here, Scheler's critique of Kant's putatively subjectivist proceduralism in the name of material values provided the main source).[85] In both moments, personalist conceptions of dignity purporting to leave behind the choice between the individual and the collective provided the dominant framework and affected many aspects of what human rights meant within the postwar constitutional framework.[86]

Conclusion

It may be true, then, that (as Mark Mazower has argued) there was a conceptual shift from group to individual in diplomatic and legal circles that set the stage for the post–World War II human rights moment. But there was also a shift afoot from the individual to the person, and in terms of its *cultural meaning* at the time, and the embedding of its ideas in postwar European politics, the Universal Declaration is a profoundly communitarian document—precisely a moral repudiation of dangerous individualism, albeit one equally intended to steer far clear of communism.[87] Indeed, in my view this is the key to placing the document—along with the human rights idea in general—more securely in the ambiance of the war's aftermath, as part of the moral reconstruction of Europe perceived to be necessary to stave off future world crises and conflicts.

One significant irony of this history is that the availability of a now far more familiar paradigm of the moral value of the person—one with roots in Roman law and embedded in Immanuel Kant's political thought—may easily elide the primacy of a very different human person in the years when the Universal Declaration was framed and the concept was embedded in early postwar European law. Kantians were few and far between in the 1940s. In a later era, communitarianism could come to seem a major challenge to rights talk, but few in this more recent debate have grasped that rights talk in immediate postwar Europe did not exclude communitarianism but instead presupposed it.[88]

In short, the original context of the European beliefs about human dignity and the rights of the human person—surprisingly short-lived in this form—was in Christianity's last golden age on the continent, which endured for two decades before the shocking reversal for the fortunes of religion after the mid-1960s. The "death of Christian Europe," as one might call it, forced—along with many other developments—a complete reinvention of the meaning of the human rights embedded in European identity both as a matter of formal treaties and substantive values since the war.[89] The only serious thread of persistence was, ironically, in Eastern Europe, and especially in Poland, not coincidentally the main exception to Christian decline. There, Maritain, Mounier, and Scheler enjoyed huge discipleships, not least in the personalism of Karol Wojtyła, eventually Pope John Paul II.[90] But by the time of the explosion of human rights in the later 1970s, when the concept gained a currency out of all proportion to any other moment in history, Christian personalism, while not absent, was decidedly peripheral. Human rights had become a secular doctrine of the left; how that happened is another story.

The First Historian of Human Rights

In November 1948, the German scholar Gerhard Ritter traveled to Basel, Switzerland, to lecture on the history of human rights. They were then the subject of intensive discussion in the United Nations and were to be canonized by its General Assembly in the Universal Declaration a month later. Ritter's lecture, "The Origin and Nature of Human Rights," appeared in print the following year in the *Historische Zeitschrift*, in the first new volume of the storied journal since the war had interrupted its publication.[1]

It is fair to say that it was the first history of human rights ever written: the first intentional attempt to find a lineage for their new postwar role.[2] This precedence would not matter if many professional historians entered the field immediately or eventually. But strikingly, Ritter's venture was not matched, either at the time or for decades, by anyone in the Anglo-American sphere, where the history of human rights is a genre that has appeared and exploded only in the last few years. (No article with the phrase "human rights" in the title ever appeared, for example, in the *American Historical Review* before the late 1990s, even though within an astonishingly short time, contributions to the genre proliferated, and it became possible to proclaim that every historian in effect works in the field.)[3]

If Ritter's intervention is worth remembering, it is not simply because it was a crucial statement by a scholar who—though generally forgotten since—once epitomized the discipline of history as one of its handful of internationally leading figures. Both its similarities to and differences from more contemporary approaches to the subject matter make it a startling precedent to record. And not least because of the surprise that Ritter, of all people, was responsible for it: for Ritter was a conservative Christian and German nationalist whose turn to human rights is best seen as part of his larger struggle—together with that of many European conservatives—to make sense of the world in bewildering defeat.[4]

Naturally, given his onetime standing, Ritter has received much attention over the years, from Anglo-American commentators worried about his resumption of old nationalist habits and (more recently) in a large wave of German scholarship more critical than ever before of the historical discipline's postwar founders.[5] But though it provides indispensable context for understanding Ritter's interest in human rights, the accumulated literature has neglected this episode in his career. After all, in general and in his writings, this topic might have seemed marginal had the historiography of human rights not emerged so spectacularly today.

Almost unanimously, contemporary historians have adopted a celebratory attitude toward the emergence and progress of human rights, providing recent enthusiasms with uplifting backstories and differing primarily about whether to locate the true breakthrough with the Greeks

or the Jews, medieval Christians or early modern philosophers, democratic revolutionaries or abolitionist heroes,
American internationalists or antiracist visionaries. They
have been less ready to concede that human rights have
been only one morality among others. At the point of origin for postwar human rights, however, Ritter knew that
these truths were not self-evident: that they had emerged
out of and against other moral schemes and continued
to face stiff and plausible competition. And while Ritter's
history is selective, appropriative, and manipulative, the
very flaws in his approach provide a bracing reminder of
how easy it was—as it clearly still is—to construct a field
with the goal of crafting a usable past for new imperatives.

Given his onetime fame, Ritter provides an excellent
example of Christian human rights that it might otherwise seem convenient to forget. Recently it has become
popular to revisit the 1940s as a kind of dry run for our
time, but Ritter's case documents that, in doing so, it is
easy to proceed selectively. Omitting the conservative
and religious enthusiasm for human rights at the time is
not possible when it comes to Ritter, for it would mean
leaving him out entirely. His case thus forces us to take
another look at what human rights may have meant when
Ritter was their historian, before later and different gen-
erations became their inheritors. For example, Ritter's history clearly demonstrates that whatever the teleological
bent of current constructions of the immediate postwar
moment, the concept of human rights in its founding era
need not—frequently could not—imply the planting of a
seed of activist reformist idealism that would bloom only
decades later. Similarly, human rights were not a response
to the Holocaust, not for Ritter but also for next to no one

in the era. Instead, they most often involved above all a kind of cultural signaling about the need for the defense of inherited identity at a moment of unprecedented crisis and threat. And Christianity was central to that identity.

If his vivid case forces a reckoning with what human rights could mean before many later departures made them eligible for new kinds of support—and before they attracted new chroniclers—then Ritter's value is emphatically not in his lasting contributions. Rather, he is worth remembering for the emphasis he placed on the difficulty the new morality of human rights would face, like all moralities that matter, in its encounter with the violence of politics. Just as he joined the transnational Christian defense of human rights, Ritter affiliated with "Christian realism," which was never a uniquely American position, in spite of its prominent defenders in this country from theologian Reinhold Niebuhr, to presidents Jimmy Carter and Barack Obama, and beyond.

Christian realism—which approaches international order with tolerance for violence and doubts about whether morality alone can best the forces of sin and evil in the world—was and remains dubious. Yet in this first historian's hands, it teaches a useful historiographical lesson. Just as they have moved to create a Whig interpretation of the history of human rights, contemporary scholars rarely show interest in how the intentions of morality are in fact swept into the violence of politics that it is their goal to reshape. In their narratives, the idea of human rights is obviously a good one, and the task of its historians is to show its emergence in the past in order to encourage its fortunes now. If human rights evolve slowly, it is because of evil opposition, not because they can themselves be caught up in evil. But Ritter, though his project is otherwise dead, remains at the forefront in his awareness that in actually lived history, the moralization of politics, however laudable, does not necessarily work out for the best.

A Brief Life

Born in 1888, Ritter affiliated with the standard narrative of Germany's modern trajectory as a search by the nation for the state, pioneered in the nineteenth century by Leopold von Ranke and followed by a nearly unanimous consensus thereafter.[6] After events had led to a Prussian solution, and a rapid Prussification of German history in the later nineteenth century, Ritter's dissertation dealt with how the project of national unification had had to overcome the initial skepticism of Prussian conservatives, before they became—such as Ranke himself—swift converts to Otto von Bismarck's empire as the salvific agent and embodied realization of historical progress. From an early date, however, Ritter also was attentive to how state politics and religious morals fit together in history, and it was this problem that may have concerned him most, though in interestingly different ways from regime to regime.

A devout Lutheran, Ritter won initial renown for a general study of the origins of Protestantism and its bequest to the modern world, and the German state in particular. Yet although he always emphasized Martin Luther's contribution to morality in these works, notably in a synthetic biographical study that first appeared in 1925, Ritter praised the founder of Protestantism as a "national hero." As the 1930s continued, Ritter moved from uncertainty through moments of enthusiasm for Nazism to opposition, penning perhaps his most widely read book, on Frederick the Great, identifying with the antiracist Confessing Church, and joining resistance circles in Freiburg, where he taught for decades. Ritter was especially loyal to Carl Goerdeler, a conservative opponent of Adolf Hitler whose biography he would later write. After the failed plot to kill Hitler in July 1944, and the roundup of many thousands in conspiratorial networks, Ritter's membership in the resistance became known, and he spent months in Ravensbrück concentration camp and the Lehrter Strasse prison in Berlin's Moabit district. Nicolas Berg has emphasized that in his postwar memory, Ritter downplayed the penetration of Nazi ideology in his own university and town. The victimization of Jews was not, Berg shows, a major theme of his work, either in the Nazi years or after the war, when he favored the German resistance of which he had been a part with his scholarly attention.[7]

Ritter had not written about human rights before his release and did so in the later 1940s only in the context of his return to his Freiburg professorship where, with extraordinary vigor, he revised several of his books for reissue and played a major role in the reconstruction and reorientation of West German historical scholarship. In old age, Ritter turned to a multivolume study of German militarism whose later volumes became, after Fritz Fischer famously laid blame for World War I on Germany's doorstep, an acrimonious public diatribe against his enemy. If memory preserves anything of Gerhard Ritter, indeed, it is the image of a German nationalist who lost the attempt to salvage any sort of uplifting history of his country and defend it against totalizing opprobrium for its twentieth-century crimes. "It is more than doubtful whether the 'dean of German historians' accomplished what he perceived to be his last great mission," V. R. Berghahn commented soon after, summing up a broad consensus.[8] By a few decades into the postwar era, with its original spirit under heavy assault, Ritter left the stage of history with his whole project in ruins; it soon was to be unintelligible. But in 1948, he was doing something now considered to be at the cutting edge: to place human rights, surging in public discussion in his time as they have once again today, in the vast historical framework that only a specialist's learning could provide.

Ritter's History

There was, Ritter began, "hardly another theme of political history that touches the burning problems of life of our present so directly."[9] His German ancestors of the prior half century knew that their own predecessors of 1789 and 1848 had taken rights seriously, but "the alacrity with which these forefathers had allowed themselves to lose their heads over so abstract and unreal an object" had until recently been simply amusing. Times change. "For we have in the meantime," Ritter wrote, "experienced a reality without human rights. . . . Now we know: on the belief that the premises of human rights are valid, on the fact that they are a reality and not a mere program, depends nothing less than the continued existence of Occidental culture; or, even more plainly stated, on human rights depend in the end whether life on this old European continent will remain worth living or not."[10] Thus Ritter signaled right at the start that the new human rights were about conservative defense of old verities, not progressive betterment of the world. Their content was neither commitment to the humanization of world politics through international law, nor affiliation with any movement of well-meaning transnational advocates acting in the name of human rights (not surprisingly, since there was as yet no such thing). Instead, they prompted a recognition of moral limitations to and on politics.

Yet Ritter also insisted that the new acceptance of the crucial role of human rights as "the essential hallmark of Occidental civilization in contrast to 'totalitarian' state slavery" meant a transformation of recent political attitudes and called for a reformulation of conservatism.[11] It would be wrong not to admit, he explained, that human rights were of a narrow bourgeois origin, at least in their "one-sided" typical expressions that had properly led Germans to be critical of them.[12] Fortunately, the better history he would now provide showed that they did not necessarily have to be about the "self-protection of a bourgeoisie seeking political comfort, but [were] the expression of a highly idealistic activity, from both political and economic points of view."[13] If so, the original confusion of German nationalists who had understandably vilified human rights as the accoutrements of Anglo-Saxon or—worse—French shopkeeping could be dispelled, and their new centrality to politics after World War II seemed less a rude injection or wholesale import than a sober embrace of common Christian and "Occidental" identity. They could save conservatism from its immediately prior mistakes.

To do so, Ritter had to locate their origins properly and carefully. "Historical observation shows," he suggested, "that they are a relatively recent project of this Occidental civilization."[14] True, the Stoics of antiquity had understood the common brotherhood of all men in their insistence on universal reason. But the Stoic cosmopolis drew its votaries away from society, not into it for the sake of institutionalizing morality. The Greeks and Romans more generally, as modern liberals saw, recognized no limits to politics—where modern human rights were to insist precisely on such limits. The Stoics had advocated an "unpolitical, invisible spiritual community, in which one took refuge from the tumult of political struggle."[15] For this reason, "there would need to be many intellectual bridges, to proceed from reason ruling the world to the concrete state and its political and juristic formation."[16] The same insistence on discontinuity applied to early Christians, whose kingdom was also—as Jesus always insisted—not of this world.

The most one could say for the Stoic-Christian contribution—lionized by Ernst Troeltsch, the great church historian, in an earlier number of the prestigious *Historische Zeitschrift* in which Ritter's article appeared—is that it made possible Scholastic natural law, which embraced the project of moralizing politics.[17] St. Thomas Aquinas and others, Ritter wrote, propounded "the idea of an eternal order of right which stands over the state, the idea of a justice and a peace that all earthly powers must serve."[18] In a sense, this guaranteed the purposes human rights were later to serve, without the sociopolitical transformations that were to provide the forum for their annunciation. "So long as Christian belief remains still really living in society, there can be no totalistic claim by the state; for not the highest worldly power, but the Christian God, compared to whose majesty each earthly glory must fade, is the object of the highest love and greatest fear. This double-poled Christian existence relieves the true believer of all fear of men, and makes him in his innermost ethical-religious core independent of all state command and gives him already a sphere of life that is free of the state."[19] In other words, religious civilization provided functionally—through the alternative authority of God's morality—limitations on the hypertrophic state that human rights would, later, try to afford some other way. At the same time, the crucial value content of human rights had been achieved by the Scholastic terrestrialization into the social order of the otherworldly universalism of Stoicism and Christianity alike into the social order.

It was because it preserved the inward, moral sphere that religious freedom emerged as the first of all human rights. Impressively, Ritter generously acknowledged not the Lutheran Reformation but the Dutch and English dissenting traditions, which eventually were to find their ways to American shores, for the truly pioneering theoretical breakthrough in this regard. Theirs was not a scheme to protect and promote bourgeois comforts, as Germans once charged, but a high-minded and spiritual origin for rights that Germans could now recall. True, propounding freedom of conscience had not been the most common result of Protestantism's advent. On the one hand, even in England, the Reformation could easily smash, rather than reinforce, the old double-poled distinction between spiritual and temporal authority, promoting bloody confessionalization. On the other, the principles of religious freedom the dissenters introduced were not a simple source for the more full-blown rights of the American Revolution, which instead introduced a permanent dilemma to anyone who thought to champion these principles.

At the turn of the twentieth century, German political scientist George Jellinek had claimed the direct Protestant origins of modern rights.[20] Yet as Ritter observed, in colonial America "the general paradigm is English privileges from the king and freedoms of Englishmen handed down from time immemorial; and in any case the Christian character of colonial society was assumed and went without saying." In contrast, by 1776, "emancipation from the Anglican Church played no further role. An article on freedom of religious conscience was inserted late in the in the Virginia Bill of Rights, and not without opposition from the state church, which itself hoped to be established." Something new drove the colonists: "not religious, but essentially material complaints." Unlike the right of religious freedom expressing "spiritual ardor," American secession reflected "purely worldly and politically irrepressible desire for recognition, an authentic nationalism of the young colonial people."[21] Thus the limitation of the state that had been unnecessary to proclaim in the Middle Ages was only one modern implication of the invention of human rights, which indeed had another face. In modernity, human rights could also take a form less spiritual and more material, as well as less morally constraining and more politically licentious. If Americans leaped from the long-developing list of English privileges against the king to the annunciation of general principle—"the general phrases of natural right, that applies to all humanity," as Ritter put it—it was because they had moved from religion to revolution.[22] Which lesson did the rise of rights teach, then? Not simply the translation of the state's limitation that religious forces had once introduced but also successor and competing developments that pointed toward very different results.

It mattered utterly, Ritter continued, that the ambiguous transformation had occurred in a wholly atypical place, in a "colonial hinterland."[23] "Only on the virginal soil of colonial America," Ritter put it, "was there, after the yoke of English dominion had been shaken off, a society so completely without tradition, one which achieved this without its revolutionary subversion." The same, however, was not to be true for the next destination of human rights: France. What made sense in America, with its wide-open spaces and untraditional equality, could not directly apply to Europe, especially continental Europe where it was the *resistance* of the old Stoic and Christian legacy to transformations in the direction of American individualism and especially economic freedom that mattered. For the Declaration of Independence "had in reality nothing more to do with Christian natural law."[24] It went so far as to base social ethics on the natural desire of men to pursue happiness, a telltale—and somewhat disturbing—concession to eighteenth-century materialistic utilitarianism. "For Christian social ethics," by the starkest of contrasts to modern self-involved hedonism, "men have the same worth as God's children, but only and above all on condition of like responsibility before the eternal judge." From Christian thought followed "the recognition of each man as a person, that is, as bearer of an eternal distinction, in an ethical order."[25] It was precisely the difference between these earlier conceptions and the potentially anarchistic implications of "human rights" from 1776 and since that explained why the more democratic states became, the less they resembled moral communities, courting totalitarian abuse of rights rather than their protection. History, Ritter insisted, had shown as much. What was safe in Philadelphia was explosive and dangerous in the extreme in Paris and elsewhere.

Thus the distant roots of human rights in the Christian Occident needed to be remembered but only in light of the perversions of democracy with which rights had since, alas, become bound up. This history, which Ritter covered in his discussions of the trajectory of Jean-Jacques Rousseau's principle of popular sovereignty and of its apotheosis of the French revolutionary Declaration of the Rights of Man and Citizen, had to be recalled now too—not least because it led, long down the road, to Hitler's triumph. On the continent, democracy was "wholly foreign to history," and applied there it "was profoundly destructive, compromising the very freedom of the personality that it was alleged to secure."[26] He continued, "If it was the point of human rights to restrict the sovereignty of the state in the name of an individual sphere of freedom, this problem could not really be solved with a radically interpreted sovereignty of the people that led directly to the submission to the masses."[27] No wonder that the nineteenth-century consensus—even in the Frankfurt revolutionary parliament in 1848, where heartfelt appeals to rights cast them as German inheritances rather than natural or hedonistic entitlements—retreated from American and French radicalism.[28] True, the Germans debating rights in the Frankfurt Paulskirche had played a dangerous game and deserved condemnation for their excesses, as their "National Liberal" followers saw; but even their early emphasis on the importance of German rights within a German state achieved a useful embedding of rights without yet risking the democratic wildfire that America had invented but contained and which France unleashed on the world, leaving nothing but terror and destruction. For its assertion of rights *against* democracy, "we look back on the liberal nineteenth century with so much wistful longing."[29] Twentieth-century history was not to be so kind to German lands, as the destitute form of rights as mass emancipation and totalitarian slavery won out.

Ritter dealt with the disaster in a final page. In his lifetime, the "unholy" story had been one of "the shattering of traditions." The drive to spiritual uniformity of both World Wars with their "total" absorption of all facets of life in the state had provided a climax to earlier trends, with their moral corruption and idolization of the political nation; and the technologization of life with its "corrosion of the concept of the person" had only abetted the profane results. And "behind it all, stood the advancing secularization of the Occidental world." On a political level, the baleful Rousseau had the last laugh, in the form of "the doctrine of the national general will, which realizes itself without restriction of eternal law." The "inner logic" of *volonté générale* was the *Volksgemeinschaft* of the National Socialist movement.[30]

If there was no going back to a Christian era before the ambiguity at the heart of human rights had to be confronted and mastered in the first place, then the key now was to isolate and prioritize their good version. Freedom of the person, not vulgar equality, mattered; and especially, high-minded spiritualism, not low-minded materialism, had to govern the meaning of human rights, so that the memory of the social ethics that Christianity had once provided without human rights could be defended against the hedonistic and democratic guise the latter could easily assume. Against the Soviets, especially, the rationalistic interpretation of human rights could afford no defense, since the promise of collective material happiness had now passed over to communism, in spite of its American origins.[31]

The move to economic and social rights, whether in the Weimar Constitution, the Atlantic Charter, or emerging United Nations language (including its draft universal declaration), was in this sense treacherous, as the Stalin Constitution of 1936, which included similar promises, showed their real meaning was terror. Not that they were unimportant, and they might be crucial, given the collapse of liberal capitalism that had caused so much misery in living memory.[32] But everything depended on whether the new "human rights," both political and social, were an attempt to restore and revive by other means the wisdom of Christian social ethics or simply a prelude to democratic and materialistic totalitarianism. "On human rights depend in the end whether life on this old European continent will remain worth living or not" thus meant most of all whether the right interpretation of them would prevail.

The Narrative in Conservative Context

The basic topics of Ritter's history of human rights, from the Stoics to the present, largely track most later exercises in the genre. Yet its idiosyncrasies are obviously reflections

115

of the time in which it was written—suggesting that contemporary forays into this charged field, too, might say much more about very recent experiences than about the deeper past that they ostensibly narrate. To encounter Ritter is, therefore, first of all to worry about what sorts of short-term concerns might affect how the human rights that historians want to cherish are placed in a grand narrative. And placed in context, the main revealing feature of Ritter's argument is about the contemporary reorganization of the politics of religion with which his whole interpretation was bound up.

Among the key elements in Ritter's cultural signaling is the recasting of the relationship between Christianity and "the Occident" of the postwar era, a topic of overwhelming importance that has barely begun to be analyzed. It is a transformation to which Ritter provides an interesting guide, because it was the fate of the Christian Occident that Ritter understood to be most at stake in the efflorescence of human rights. Indeed, in 1949, in a commentary on the new Grundgesetz (Basic Law) of the Bonn Republic, which refracted human rights into West German domestic constitutionalism, Ritter insisted again that Christian social ethics, though now unavailable as a potentially direct foundation of collective European life, must assume the task of informing human rights to avoid their secular or revolutionary perversion, or all would be lost.[33] Though Ritter never gave up his sense of the superiority of the German Lutheran tradition, what mattered to him, as to many others in the postwar period, was transcending an older politics of sectarian dispute leading to ecumenical compromise and unity in the face of unprecedented fear and catastrophe. Ritter made a striking place for Catholic principles. And while Axel Schildt and others have shown that there was a real tendency in postwar West German conservatism to exclude America from "the Occident," Ritter found Atlantic Protestantism crucial.[34] Both moves affected his history of human rights fundamentally.

As far back as 1942 (in a piece published only after the war), Ritter had bemoaned the terrible price for "the Occidental idea" that Hitler's state had exacted and signaled that only the unification of Christians could save it now.[35] According to his student Klaus Schwabe, Ritter's participation in the Freiburg Circle resistance group in his mostly Catholic university town had softened his revulsion toward the Roman Church and sensitized him to the riches of Scholastic natural law traditions; Ritter, in turn, testified that his experiences with Catholics while in prison opened his eyes to the fact that what Christians shared mattered far more than what separated them. But after the war, the escalating threat of secularism counted just as much as a rationale for closing ranks.[36]

The lessons about the crucial legacy of the Catholic background even for German Lutherans were drawn in a dramatic talk, delivered on the four hundredth anniversary of Luther's death in 1947, that Ritter updated to give in English in Washington, DC, in December 1952 to fellow Reformation scholars.[37] It was now, he insisted, crucial to acknowledge the medieval Catholic attempt to join God's revelation and worldly affairs, whatever its flaws, rather than taking Lutheranism's escape route to individual faith alone as the one thing needful. After all, Luther, while spiritually uncompromising, had assumed "the risk of breaking up the whole universal Christian order of Western civilization," while Catholicism, however defective, had striven mightily to provide "the spiritual basis for the domination of the whole of life by the church [and above all] that application of the Christian spirit in the practical sphere, by which was determined the political, economic, and social order of the world." It was Catholicism, therefore, that had provided "a cultural unity in the Christian Western lands," one "which possesses in it a strong power of rebirth and recovery after disaster."[38]

No feature of Ritter's history of human rights is more surprising than its assignment of a sort of acme to Catholic natural law for concretizing religion in social norms in a way Lutheranism never succeeded in achieving, whatever the deep validity of its critique of Catholic intermediation between God and man. To be sure, the Lutheran correctly suspected that the attempt to embed morality in the world— even a morality of rights—also brought with it a terrible risk. "Was there ever a mob-rising of chaos against order, of the masses against their overlords, was there ever a revolution or a grave breach of the law that was not embellished by a proclamation of the innate natural rights of man?," Ritter asked. "Indeed the worst memories of mankind come to mind when we hear talk of such 'natural rights,' and we never understand more clearly what the Bible means by 'original sin' that when we witness the inextricable confusion of true and false pathos, idealism and acquisitiveness, noble intention and utter mendacity, in which mankind fights its way onward."[39] All the same, the worry that had understandably led Lutherans to avoid politics before was at most a cautionary proviso in the present emergency.

In the immediate postwar era, in fact, it was Anglo-American Protestantism that stood the best chance of saving the dire situation, and Ritter opened himself to it in remarkable ways both in theory and practice. He joined the "ecumenical movement" among Protestants, which after many false starts experienced a wave of success, due not least to vigorous American wartime work for Christianity to contribute to the future peace. Two months before his lecture on the history of human rights, Ritter attended the epoch-making Amsterdam conference of the World Council of Churches (WCC) in 1948, where the ecumenical movement finally coalesced.[40] He eagerly reported that Christians, unlike many secular Americans and Englishmen, treated Germans as brothers but had understood far before their German fellows the need for Christianity to infuse the political world. In his most important article, Ritter reviewed the history of the ecumenical stirrings in wartime, with special attention to Republican Party internationalist and Presbyterian John Foster Dulles and the "six pillars of peace" that his Commission to Study the Bases of a Just and Durable Peace formulated on behalf of the American Federal Council of the Churches of Christ. In this phase, Dulles and his colleagues hoped to push Americans toward a peace based on godly morality, rather than power considerations alone, while also rejecting the pacifistic temptations of their religious brethren; and among other things, and like other American private groups, they called for an international bill of rights—in particular, for the sake of ensuring the protection of religious freedom.[41]

Ritter saw in this—and in light of Dulles's postwar path, in which the assertion of rights against totalitarianism that already featured in the earlier documents was amplified further amidst new anxieties—a precious resource. Ritter explained to German readers that Dulles embodied in person the spirit of American Protestantism today, because he announced the need for Christians to mobilize to secure "world order" against potential chaos now. Already in a 1947 letter, Ritter had said he had found such idealism moving once he discovered it in Dulles's wartime career and affirmed that such ideas would prove to be Germany's sole defense against totalitarianism. These assumptions were likely ratified when he heard Dulles urge fellow ecumenical Christians in Amsterdam the next year to incline to an American rather than Soviet model. In any case, Ritter praised the defense by Dulles, the WCC, and American statesmen of human rights for early recognition that their articulation had to be understood as a Christian moral mission. "Geopolitically," Ritter concluded, "there can be no doubt that the future of everything that we customarily regard as the heritage of Christian-Occidental culture depends on the almost religious zeal with which today's America defends the principle of general human rights against the totalitarian state system."[42] No wonder, then, that Ritter had tracked the history of human rights, this newly pivotal concept, to an American epicenter, first in the colonial defense of religious freedom and then, albeit more ambiguously, in 1776. As Americans had shown, the Christian "must demonstrate what being a Christian means in the world itself, not in a spiritual void."[43]

Like Catholicism, Anglo-American Protestantism showed the world could not be left to itself. The wartime and especially postwar editions of Ritter's Luther biography, which had once influentially celebrated his hero as the "eternal German," were revised accordingly.[44] Ritter dropped that moniker and altered his old statement that it remained open to question whether Lutherans should "join the 'modern' world and want to join it, if by this one means the spirit of Anglo-Saxon and Roman culture." Now the same line concluded: "if by the modern world one means the spirit of an un-Christian world," implying that Germans had to make peace with old enemies to oppose the greater foe of un-Christian secularism.[45] The justification for these new alliances was, self-consciously, the need for Christian unity and worldly engagement against the Soviet Union, the common enemy of common values. "How uncannily near to our own doors," Ritter worried, "stands the culture-destroying power of the East, and how darkly is German life already overshadowed by the night of barbarism!" The order of the day was to "re-erect with brain and brawn a sort of emergency structure of human culture out of the old rubble and ruins" and embrace "the cause of reconstruction and the consolidation from within of the old Christian culture of the western world." (In this era, as the next chapter will also show, Orientalism most frequently targeted secularism, while human rights often stood for the West's religion.)[46]

To illuminate the significance of the moves Ritter was making, his trajectory deserves comparison with that of Jacques Maritain, a Catholic and French counterpart with whom he converged in important ways in the postwar moment. If Ritter was the most prominent historian of human rights of the era, Maritain was by any measure the leading philosopher enthusing about the concept and promoting it widely.

Early in his career, Maritain had once been a leader of a reactionary French Catholic circle reviving St. Thomas as a bulwark against Rousseau's founding of democratic idolatry (in this era, Maritain saw Luther not as a moral alternative to the disease of liberalism but as the cause of the virus). As the last chapter showed, Maritain's complex evolution occurred much more slowly in the direction of human rights than did Ritter's, after the pope's 1926 ban of his favored political group Action Française drove him into a decade of experimentation. By the early 1940s, a few years before any German equivalents, Maritain had come to argue—contrary to the overwhelming weight of his own tradition—that Catholic natural law teachings were the best framework for modern human rights. Indeed, Maritain did most to link the idea of the "human person" so central to Ritter's essay with the idea of human rights. Along with the powerful revival of natural law in Germany, the activism of a figure such as Maritain to make old Catholic theories seem like the only viable framework for the new human rights cannot but have influenced Ritter's historical narrative and contemporary attitudes.

True, Ritter acknowledged more honestly than Maritain that the old natural law metaphysics of the "human person" did not flow directly into the new human rights; instead, for Ritter, human rights were at best a proxy for the primacy of that person that Christianity had once protected without modern compromises. Yet just as with Ritter's ambivalent championship of human rights in the postwar moment, Maritain's depended on a distinction between their good, communal, and religious form that centered on the person and their evil, soul-destroying, and Jacobin perversion that unleashed both the individual and the totalitarian state that claimed to meet the individual's hedonistic preferences. Writing in *Fortune* magazine as early as 1942, Maritain praised the "concept of, and devotion to, the rights of the human person" as "the most significant political improvement of modern times" but—as chapter 1 of this book mentioned—also warned darkly of the perilous temptation to "claim human rights and dignity—without God," for an "ideology" grounded in "a godlike, infinite autonomy of human will" led only to catastrophe.[47] In a similar vein, Ritter remarked to an ecumenical correspondent, "As Christians we possess the standard with whose help we can distinguish mere assertion and glorification of man from true, ethical understanding of society's obligations to the individual; the so often haphazard and arbitrarily strung together catalogue of 'human rights' has to be checked against our standard."[48]

Ritter also fits with a general fear of democracy and the role of rights in keeping it at bay. The perception of "Cold War liberals" that Rousseau paved the way for totalitarianism originated as a commonplace of Christian intellectuals in their interwar reactionary days—and they did not change their minds when circumstances drove them to invent a new kind of conservatism after the war. For Ritter, as for later Cold War liberals, revolutionary-era rights were revolutionary—and violent. Conservative historian of international law Wilhelm Grewe agreed in 1948, for instance, that Rousseau could not be invoked as a founder of the new human rights when his own doctrine of the *volonté générale* had historically been so prejudicial to them.[49] Jacob Talmon, to take a different example, shared the suspicion of appeals to abstract rights, promises of material happiness, moves to social entitlements, and voluntarist, revolutionary means for realizing them. "Carried away by the idea of the rights of man, and the

Revolutionary hope of salvation, and exasperated by famine and shortage," Talmon wrote, "the masses confusedly and passionately clamoured that the Revolution should carry out its promises, that is to say, should make them happy."[50] To such figures, indeed, claims for French Revolution as direct origin of more recent human rights would have seemed not simply mistaken but an extraordinary and dangerous perversity. In other words, it is hard to avoid the impression that when human rights were invented and accepted in the 1940s, it was often on the grounds of an energetic critique, explicitly Christian or generally spiritualistic in basis, of the French Revolution, an event emotionally rejected by figures now conscripted under the banner of Western spiritual unity. Their attempts to separate rights from revolution, in the radically different atmosphere of conservative restabilization of the post–World War II moment when human rights were canonized, were a central feature of the concept's birth.

In any case, many other examples show the invention of human rights as a signal for the need to unify Christians to be far from Ritter's idiosyncrasy. Like Maritain, most religious figures—especially the Catholics who were to be so significant after the war—had once rejected the idea of rights as secularist and solipsistic. The Catholic Church's long-term vilification of the political language is a classic fact, though the institution reshaped itself later. Commenting in 1940, to take another example, George Bell, the highly influential Anglican bishop of Chichester, commented, "Of course you can dress up the ideas of 1789 and adapt them to the conditions of 1940. But the present situation is the result of secularism. To add a further dose of secularism to what the patient has already absorbed is to add poison to poison. . . . No amount of secular Declarations, no number of claims for human rights, without spiritual sanctions, will save us from destruction."[51] Yet by the postwar period, in part thanks to Maritain's agitation and in part due to independently successful attempts to capture the language, many prominent Christian intellectuals were championing the rhetoric of human rights—on condition that it reflected a Christian moral community. These years saw Bell insisting that "the rights of men derive directly from their condition as children of God and not of the State," given "the sacredness of the human personality."[52] When leading Swiss Protestant theologian and ecumenical icon Emil Brunner addressed the topic in 1947, he insisted, similarly, that "[h]uman rights live wholly from their ground in faith. Either they are *jus divinum* or—a phantom."[53]

For such spokesmen, as for Ritter, the priority of religious freedom mattered most, and its pivotal role in his history reflected a consensual priority. Charles Malik, a Lebanese Christian and principal drafter of the Universal Declaration, later recalled his fear that "if we should lose th[e] Article on freedom of conscience and religion, namely, if man's absolute freedom were to be derogated from in any way, even by the subtlest indirection, my interest in the remainder of the Declaration would considerably flag."[54] (According to his cousin by marriage Edward Said, who sat at his feet during these years, Malik's devotion to rights as a proxy for Christianity flowed unacceptably into doctrines of "the clash of civilizations, the war between East and West, communism and freedom, Christianity and all the other, lesser religions.")[55] By contrast, few serious non-Christian intellectuals were theorists or partisans of the new idea of human rights—or even rights generally—until several decades later.[56]

Such intellectuals were likewise representative of the immediate postwar trajectory of human rights in politics, when the idea survived nowhere in the cacophony of world ideology, except in what became their Western European homeland, in an era of Christian hegemony based on a reformulated conservatism.[57] The internment of Hungarian Cardinal Jószef Mindszenty rapidly became a cause célèbre in transatlantic Christian circles and also defined very quickly what international human rights politics might look like, not least since the United Nations General Assembly—within a few months of passing the Universal Declaration—issued resolutions condemning communist interference with religious liberty.[58] The fact that there were socialist and indeed Soviet invocations of the idea in the 1940s did not succeed in establishing some powerful alternative human rights discourse; apparently, they mainly succeeded in convincing Westerners such as Ritter that human rights had to be saved from their totalitarian abuse, which he worried would occur in their name, if these rights came to imply the pursuit of happiness rather than the fear of the Lord.

However threatening, human rights were defended by Ritter in the immediate postwar years as a last genealogical connection Europeans had to a Christian past in which the limitation of the state went without saying because of primary religious loyalties. Ritter's deep history of human rights, though, actually reflected the extremely recent, if quite pervasive, transformation of a politics of religion that had only shortly before veered in the direction of confessionalism and nationalism. Now it offered a continental and transatlantic spiritual cultural unity that was crucial in the face of the baleful materialism of the Soviet east. "The whole over-concentration on 'the West' is only religious nationalism extended in cultural scope," political theorist Judith N. Shklar put it incisively in 1957, criticizing the common tendency by Christian conservatives of the era to broaden geographically and modernize politically a religious and anticommunist politics that had previously fastened more narrowly on defense of sect and homeland.[59] Most of all, therefore, Ritter's history provides a potentially uncomfortable reminder that, whatever their secular and progressive later uses, human rights were so often a religious and conservative enterprise in their founding era. They were, in other words, Christian human rights.

Christian Realism

As his sympathy for Dulles's critique of pacifism makes clear, Ritter's appeal to human rights remained compatible with the exercise of power. Even as he distanced himself from the cult of power for its own sake in the postwar period, Ritter also insisted that the attempt to moralize politics must face forbidding challenges. True, as his many critics have insisted, Ritter's goal of redeeming German history from its supposed Nazi deviation defined his project, fully as much as his suprastate embrace of Christian and "Occidental" identity did. But it may be that, in his trajectory to a morality of human rights that did not forsake their dependence on power, a redeeming feature of Ritter's otherwise local and time-bound embrace of

human rights is to be found. For interestingly, and perhaps uniquely, Ritter embraced human rights as part of
the transnational invention of "Christian realism," a connection that few other founders of that political theology
made, even though it was exploding throughout the West
at just the same time.

Why Basel? The venue of Ritter's lecture on the
invention of human rights—the Basler Historisch-
Antiquarische Gesellschaft—may have been pregnant
with significance. The national myth of the German
people then being under forced revision, it was to Swiss
Basel—where Jacob Burckhardt had provided the skeptical nineteenth-century counterpoint to the historiography of the triumphant Prussian state—that many were
making a pilgrimage, though not always so literally. Most
famously, and remarkably, in that same year of 1948, Ritter's older contemporary, the likewise conservative Friedrich Meinecke, delivered his absorbing meditation on the
contrast of Berlin and Basel and of Ranke and Burckhardt.
Meinecke's career had once involved histories of Germany's break with Enlightenment cosmopolitanism and the
rise of nationalism in its stead. Now at the ripe old age
of 86, he conceded rather disarmingly that Burckhardt,
the skeptic toward power, might have been right all along.
Meinecke's once instinctive preference for the narrative of
the apotheosis of the triumphant Prussian state had now
been shaken, he explained, with the benefit redounding
very largely to Burckhardt's pessimism; it might even lead
to a rejection of the state not simply as a subject of history but also as an object of identification. Hugh Trevor-
Roper and, more recently, Lionel Gossman have made
Meinecke's lecture central to their penetrating treatments

of the postwar relevance of Burckhardt's thought at a moment that the principles of German *Machtpolitik* had to be rethought.[60]

Ritter could not go so far. In his self-labeled "war book" of 1940, *Machtstaat und Utopie*, Ritter had already turned to Niccolò Machiavelli and Thomas More and their contending modern legacies, as well as the fraught relation they symbolized between power and morality. It was to be reissued after the war, with major revisions, as *Die Dämonie der Macht* and appeared in English then as *The Corrupting Influence of Power*.[61] In response to Burckhardt's curt apothegm that "power is evil," Ritter drew back in his own reflections. "Power is not simply evil, as Burckhardt thought," Ritter affirmed right at the start of *Machtstaat und Utopie*. It was an estimate he did not change, and even amplified, after the war. "Power as such, even combative power, is not altogether evil, as Jacob Burckhardt thought," he added, for good measure.[62]

Ritter had first turned to his meditation on power in the aftermath of his teacher Hermann Oncken, who had long before inducted him into critical reflection about the liberatory transcendence of power that utopian schemes promised. As far back as 1922, in fact, Ritter had published a translation of More's *Utopia*, to which Oncken added an introduction that detected below the surface of the progressive humanitarianism of the book a rationale for future British imperialism.[63] In his own reflections, in a very new context, Ritter turned to explore why his own nation inclined to the Machiavellian pursuit of power for its own sake and to investigate what the alternative to it really was. His basic conclusion in 1940, and indeed in all editions of his book, was that geographical circumstances determined the necessary German embrace of Machia-vellianism, in which More's *Utopia* ought to be read, in content and context, as a reflection of "insular" humani-tarianism that only safe isolation from the interne-cine struggles of neighbors allowed and that in any case masked its own selfishness.[64] It was, Ritter insisted there-after, a veiled criticism of Hitler, but it was also possible to read as a defense of the German struggle. For even in his somewhat revised version, Ritter praised national power at the expense of humanitarian morality, at least in a mod-ern, German situation.

One source of this view, and certainly the most prom-inent, was Ritter's continuing affiliation with Machiavel-lian realism, even as Meinecke himself was now leaving it behind. Ritter stuck to the position that Machiavelli set the terms for continental politics, which could not be ashamed about its affronts to morality when necessary. "He ought to be praised for illuminating the daemonic aspect of power and for revealing its very nature in so ruthless a fashion," Ritter insisted. Yet whatever his per-sisting Machiavellianism, Ritter now did add that some conceptual alternative needed to be found: "And still, everything in us refuses to accept meekly what he said, or even to talk of it in Machiavelli's elegant, not to say joyous, manner. In spite of all that we have seen, we cannot and have not resigned ourselves but are making the attempt to construct an order of things which is based on healthy, reasonable, and moral considerations. We still believe that there must be—somewhere—a moral basis for all social life."[65] If Ritter was to remain a realist, it would have to be on the basis on Christian morality, not Machiavellian power alone.

Yet Anglo-American utopianism—long since rejected by Meinecke and Ritter—still did not fit the bill. Machiavelli's great contemporary More had indulged in the fiction of island separation to dream the dream of humanitarian morality by itself. True, More himself insisted on the state's power to defend itself and, as a Christian, knew that human sin meant the bankruptcy of excessive optimism about earthly affairs. Yet *Utopia* ultimately stood for the "program of peace and humanitarian welfare which was to replace the power politics of war and conquest"—and indeed the need for a propertyless, "communist" state to advance that program.[66] Ritter admitted that such a humanitarian utopia might, as More hoped, start out on its course by taking advantage of its natural borders and distance, fortifying its ports but not waging endless war. More nevertheless knew, Ritter observed, that economic relations and population growth would still embed his polity in the continental syndrome from which it only claimed to be free. To be sure, More proposed that planting colonies on virgin soil abroad, steering clear of continental conflicts, comported with eternal justice and allowed the humanitarian utopia to avoid the cult of power as an end in itself. But then, Ritter responded, this "humanitarianism" was simply an imperialism caught up in its own high-minded propaganda. And utopia's claims to humanity in warfare, which the islanders most certainly conducted in More's scheme, grated when from the continental point of view it looked like selfishness dressed in the rhetoric of universal ideals. Humanitarian utopianism, far from offering a real alternative, simply hid power beneath justice's mask, which was "doubly in the wrong since [the utopians] now appeared—in the eyes of the Machiavellian!—as deceitful and pharisaic, in fact like wolves in sheep's clothing."[67] As a result, if Ritter wanted human rights to infiltrate politics after the war, it would have to be in full awareness of political theorist Carl Schmitt's celebrated interwar dictum, a piece of Machiavellian wisdom that survived the ruin of the German cause: "Whoever invokes humanity wants to cheat."[68]

This critique of morality as the propagandist's delusion competed, however, with a very different argument in Ritter's arsenal that became more and more prominent now: morality needed power and would have to reckon with its frightful implications. "Without some assistance from real power," Ritter insisted, "no ideal has ever been able to survive for long in the field of power politics." And if so, "the moral code fails to remain self-contained and absolute."[69] The Machiavellian could try to dispense with the utopian, but the reverse was not the case, and this lesson still applied in the postwar scene—applied with more force, since the order of the day was to moralize politics. Ritter never got very far in resolving this dilemma. Though in the later versions of his book on Machiavelli and More, Ritter extended the story from World War I to World War II and transformed his postscript into a chapter revealing what he insisted he could not say under dictatorship. Yet the revelation of how to resolve the controversy between the claims of morality and the demands of politics remained sketchy and inadequate.[70] Self-evidently, in his various versions of the defense of power, Ritter hoped to isolate and defend the main line of modern German nationalism from its alleged deviation in the Nazi movement and its wars—which he blamed in any event on Western and especially French democratic incursion.[71] He pursued this quixotic agenda most directly in his book-length postwar response to attempts to draw a line from Teuton forests, through Lutheranism, Prussianism, and Bismarck, to twentieth-century aggression.[72]

It was a stance that, perhaps by chance, caused what was almost certainly the first dispute over the history of human rights, in the pages of the *Times Literary Supplement*. In March 1950, an anonymous notice on the new volume of the *Historische Zeitschrift* singled out Ritter's piece on human rights as its "most important article" and gave a respectable summary of it.[73] In April, Geoffrey Barraclough, whose then recent studies sought a medieval explanation of Germany's modern errors, inveighed against this complacency. Barraclough worried about "subtly reactionary and nationalist trends" in the new journal and charged that Ritter wanted to "prove (put with a brutality which he would certainly deplore) that the ideas of Human Rights that developed historically in England and France, and the liberal parliamentary democracy that went with them, are the historical source of 'totalitarianism.'"[74] Was this more than a bit unfair? Clearly wounded, Ritter (who had met Barraclough in his home when he visited England in October 1949) wrote first to his critic privately, then in a letter to the editor, decrying this "total misapprehension" of his views. "As I explained on the first page," Ritter noted coldly, "I wanted to oppose the traditional skepticism in German history of the practical meaning of so-called human rights." Why it mattered most of all to save human rights from their secularist perversions Ritter made clear in his conclusion: "I also wanted," he added, "to participate as a historian in clarifying the inner tension between the principle of freedom and that of equality in the catalogue of natural-law

Human rights [a phrase he left in English in his German letter] of 1776. This tension has grown only clearer in the course of the last century and a half. If equality is understood not as equality of opportunity but as equality of life entitlements, then the danger of a communist revolution, and the destruction of a liberal social order, lie very near."[75]

Conclusion

That a long train of critics such as Barraclough have indicted Ritter for continuing the nationalist traditions of German historiography is understandable. The evidence for that conclusion is there to see. Much more interesting to note, however, is that if Ritter struggled to fit the need for a morality now formulated as human rights together with the role of "power," it was not simply out of nationalist apologia. His vision harmonized with the transnational crystallization of Christian realism that, in America and England no less than in Germany, insisted on the realities of power as a framework for moralism. Just as he esteemed Dulles, Ritter heaped praise on Reinhold Niebuhr and his fellow Christian "theologians of a new world order." (Niebuhr, like Ritter, attended the WCC Amsterdam congress, but it is not clear whether they met.) Similarly, Ritter floridly welcomed the spectacular emergence of Cambridge don Herbert Butterfield as a prominent Christian theorist of international affairs whose emphasis, like Niebuhr's, fell on the permanence of sin and the need to grant's power inevitable role and not simply deplore it moralistically.[76]

Recent affiliates with Christian realism typically take the emphasis on a fallen humanity as warrant for belligerence in an evil world, rarely seeing its relevance—as Niebuhr certainly did—for their own potential conduct. Accepting his Nobel Peace Prize in 2009, American president Barack Obama appealed to Christian realism to explain why he must still fight wars, making the hard choices in a world of enemies that the "human rights lobby" in his country and especially Western Europe finds abhorrent.[77] Yet it is worth noting that few of the early Christian realists cared much for the percolation of human rights; Niebuhr, most notably, disdained them.

Almost uniquely for his time and since, and perhaps precisely because he knew his own country had indeed gone so wrong, Ritter strove to make Christian realism compatible with devotion to the new human rights. Instead of rejecting them as hollow optimism, Ritter simply insisted that like all idealistic moral aspirations, human rights were ambiguous in their implications because they depend on politics to be embedded in national life and world affairs. Besides constraining states, Ritter knew that appeals to such norms can consecrate dangerous "crusades for idealistic ends," including ones specific states are empowered to conduct.[78] Ritter's history claimed human rights but without treating them as a refuge of moral safety that could ever remain free of the impurity of power.

In this sense, if in no other, Ritter's priority as the first historian of human rights is deserved, no matter the suspect origins of his argument and the very ambiguous legacy of Christian realism. After all, so far historians of human rights as an emerging group have most frequently identified closely and empathetically with the moralization of world politics, offering the validation that deep roots seem to provide and favoring uplifting tales in which struggles are followed by success. Less examined, let alone explored, has been the relationship of the embrace of this set of norms to concrete results—including their multiple pathways and blatant failures. Ritter, however, had a pronounced sense of how norms can justify and embellish state action as much as they channel and limit it. He understood how such norms are often annexed to the extension of power in incomplete, exclusionary, and even violent ways as much as they force power to do their bidding. And he therefore knew that they needed to be treated dispassionately rather than celebrated blindly. When Ritter made himself into the first historian of human rights, it was not least out of an increasingly familiar confusion, a half century before Americans constructed the field anew and entered it in droves, about how to make sense of the inescapable but perilous connection between morality's aspirations and power's realities. We may have different reasons to approach his problem, but it is—or ought to be—ours all the same.

Chapter 4

From Communist to Muslim
Religious Freedom and Christian Legacies

In January 1999, Belgin Dogru, an eleven-year-old Muslim girl living in Flers, a small French town in lower Normandy, began wearing a headscarf to school. Her teacher ordered her to remove it for gym class, and the school expelled her because she refused to obey. Dogru invoked her right to manifest her religion but found no relief from administrators or courts. She remained in Flers, finishing high school by correspondence as her case made its way through the French national judiciary to the European Court of Human Rights, which agreed in a 2008 ruling that no violation of her religious freedom had occurred.[1]

Christian human rights did not die entirely with the extraordinary decline of Western European Christianity that began in the 1960s. A series of decisions by the European Court of Human Rights in the era of the contemporary pan-European headscarf controversies has thrown open an important debate on the trajectory of the principle of religious freedom—the most prestigious norm for Christian proponents of human rights, and which this chapter therefore revisits and singles out for special focus. The court, most recently in the spectacular case of *Lautsi v. Italy* permitting crucifixes in Italian public schools, adopts a forgiving attitude toward Christian symbols and practices permeating the public sphere but does not offer comparable protection to Muslim symbols and practices suppressed by state legislation and administrative decisions.[2] Together, these interlocking attitudes suggest that the renowned European devotion to a neutral state above contending religions is more image than reality. (*Lautsi* approved the accommodating attitude toward Christian symbols made possible by Benito Mussolini's Lateran accords with the Holy See of 1929, which were subsequently incorporated in Italy's post–World War II constitution.)[3]

Dogru's case was not an isolated one.[4] Do these cases merely reflect a Christian Islamophobia in the principled garb of secularism? Friendly commentators see nothing wrong with the court or the European Convention of Human Rights norm of religious freedom. At worst, there is simply a mistake in the way the court applies the norm. In a rare dissent in one of the cases, for example, Judge Françoise Tulkens viewed the result merely as a misapplication of the notion of religious freedom, without inquiring into why the court would view the wearing of a headscarf as a threat to democracy in the first place.[5] So it is worth attending to the more thoroughgoing criticism that insists that the judicial decisions follow from a deeper and longer syndrome, in part because more uncompromising critics are right to resist ascribing the results to accident alone. One case can be an honest mistake, but an almost unbroken trend demands some other interpretation. For both defenders and critics of the court's mission to sustain a supranational human rights regime—indeed to be in the vanguard of such regimes and thus a model for the world to emulate—much is at stake in deciding how to interpret the history of religious freedom. Is it possible that the norm is poisoned at the root?

In several of the cases, the European Court itself works with a historical narrative of the rise of secularism close to that which John Rawls offered in his late "political liberalism." In this story, the secular political space is the outcome of a bloody era of early modern religious warfare: what began with the nervous truce of a *modus vivendi* evolved into an overlapping consensus featuring not only peace but justice too.[6] In this narrative, religious freedom is a long-term companion of the creation of a secular political space, in which a transcendent state rises above the attempt by sects to infuse public matters with their private faith. Faith is protected in private on condition of staying there.

Ironically, those skeptical of European secularism see the same tight relationship between religious freedom and secular politics. They agree that the former became early allied to and swept up in the rise of the latter. But since secularism amounts to little more than what Edward Said once denounced as "orientalism" in particularly effective disguise, for these critics the bias against Muslims in the European Court cases is entirely unsurprising. On this view, precisely because of religious freedom's long-term links to the creation of a secular political space, it has proven discriminatory in practice.[7] A pretextual neutrality in the service of discriminatory results is precisely the syndrome that the thoroughgoing criticism of "secularism" so influential today has diagnosed as a glaring form of orientalism. In her essay on the politics of the veil, to take one example, Joan Wallach Scott worries that the secularism of public authorities is simply "a mask for the domination of 'others,' a form of ethnocentrism or crypto-Christianity.... Its claim to universalism (a false universalism in the eyes of its critics) has justified the exclusion or marginalization of those from non-European cultures (often immigrants from former colonies) whose systems of belief do not separate public and private in the same way."[8]

In spite of the plausibility of this account, however, large and perhaps principal aspects of the history of religious freedom point in a very different direction. The deepest background of the principle of religious freedom indicates as much, since from the early modern period on, religious freedom was most often an instrument of intra-Christian pacification for the sake of Christianity, not "secularism." Forsaking that distant background, this chapter offers instead close analysis of the era when religious freedom was internationalized through the Universal Declaration of Human Rights and Europeanized in the form of the European Convention itself. As in its earliest origins, so in its mid-twentieth-century iteration, religious freedom was not part of a secularist enterprise, whether one defines it as the project of privatizing religious affiliation, creating a naked public square, or—with the critics of secularism—concealing the Christian faith behind the mask of neutrality. On the contrary, religious freedom was historically a principle that was most often intended, and often quite explicitly, to marginalize secularism.

In Christian human rights, indeed, religious freedom was always the leading entitlement that alone would ensure the postponement of secularism rather than its victory. Gerhard Ritter's enthusiasm for religious freedom as the keystone principle that would guarantee the Christian vocation and the moral importance of the entire enterprise of human rights, surveyed in the previous chapter, was in this sense hardly unusual. Similarly, it was as part of a broad campaign to keep secularism at bay that the European Convention in general and its Article 9 on religious freedom first appeared little more than a half century ago. The paradox is then that Christian human rights live on in the Muslim headscarf cases from beyond the grave of the transatlantic Christianity that originally birthed them.

The Court and the Cases

Article 9 of the European Convention for the Protection of Human Rights and Fundamental Freedoms (1950) has two clauses. Announcing the principle of religious freedom, it begins by closely following the Universal Declaration of Human Rights: "Everyone has the right to freedom of thought, conscience and religion; this right includes freedom to change his religion or belief and freedom, either alone or in community with others and in public or private, to manifest his religion or belief, in worship, teaching, practice and observance" (Art 9(1)).[9] But the European Convention also assumes that, unlike the inviolable right to the sanctity of the *forum internum* of conscience, the right to manifest internal beliefs could be overridden: "Freedom to manifest one's religion or beliefs shall be subject only to such limitations as are prescribed by law and are necessary in a democratic society in the interests of public safety, for the protection of public order, health or morals, or the protection of the rights and freedoms of others" (Art. 9(2)).

Already before 9/11 the European Court—which had not really taken up Article 9's promise of religious freedom until the 1990s—had shown itself willing to interpret that last provision in ways that treated Islam as a second-class religion not entitled to the same sort of consideration as the Christian faith. Notably, the European Commission (the since dissolved former parent body of the European Court) sided against a Muslim applicant from Great Britain claiming that Salman Rushdie's *Satanic Verses* violated the then extant common law ban on blasphemy—though the commission, like the court later, was willing to uphold blasphemy prosecutions in cases of offense to Christian sensibilities.[10] Since then, it has issued a series of decisions that granted European states wide latitude to ban Muslim symbols, such as a Swiss ban on minarets.[11]

In *Dahlab v. Switzerland*, a Christian schoolteacher who had converted to Islam and began to wear a headscarf to work was told by authorities to choose between her headscarf and her job. A Swiss federal court held that public safety and order justified the administrative decision. But if *Dahlab* dealt with a teacher, allowing the court to emphasize the power of a role model in the classroom (though no student or parent had complained), *Leyla Şahin v. Turkey*, like *Dogru* and a series of cases testing France's famous 2004 law banning conspicuous religious symbols, concerned Muslim (and sometime Sikh) students. The most visible and discussed of these cases, *Şahin*, involved a medical student who had worn the headscarf in her training in Vienna but was told she could not do so at her Turkish certification test.

The *Dogru* court, following the *Şahin* ruling, emphasized "the State's role as the neutral and impartial organiser of the exercise of various religions, faiths and beliefs." The state's service as secular arbiter above the fray, a hard-won outcome of Reformation conflict, remained "conducive to public order, religious harmony and tolerance in a democratic society."[12]

The most recent of the court's decisions on these matters extended these troubling trends. In *S.A.S. v. France* (2014), the court sided against a young Muslim girl who claimed that France's 2010 law prohibiting coverage of the face in public by the niqab violated her religious freedom. Concealing her face in public, France contended, offended the core social requirement of "living together" (*vivre-ensemble*), since individuals who do not show their faces will "break the social tie" without which society cannot survive.[13] While contesting other rationales for the law that the government offered, the court agreed with it that

> the face plays an important role in social interaction. It can understand the view that individuals who are present in places open to all may not wish to see practices or attitudes developing there which would fundamentally call into question the possibility of open interpersonal relationships, which, by virtue of an established consensus, forms an indispensable element of community life within the society in question. The Court is therefore able to accept that the barrier raised against others by a veil concealing the face is perceived by the respondent State as breaching the right of others to live in a space of socialisation which makes living together easier.[14]

It was this rationale that survived the scrutiny the court is charged with providing in the name of the human rights it is supposed to protect—in this case, the right to manifest religion.

In all these cases, the court prominently referred to local interpretations and ingrained traditions (in France, Switzerland, and Turkey) of secularist political order. Invoking its well-known judge-made doctrine of "margin of appreciation"—a perennially controversial principle of deference to national policy—it found that these particular European countries might well have the latitude to forge especially stringent interpretations of secular space. But in doing so, the court also developed its own interpretation of what democratic societies require, one that the headscarf or other Muslim religious practices offends. This "democratic minimum" analysis, this chapter contends, proves to be the most valuable clue to the legacy of history in the court's cases. In this connection, the most revealing case is *Refah Partisi v. Turkey* (2003), a decision declining to uphold the claims of Turkish applicants whose Islamist political party had been banned. Though already strongly implied in *Dahlab*, the latter case made it even clearer that, in the court's judgment, Muslim practices can be plausibly viewed as threats to a democratic minimum, justifying state abridgment of rights to manifest; the "minimum" was cited again in *Şahin, Dogru,* and *S.A.S.* for precisely that proposition.[15] This complementary element of the European Court's Article 9 jurisprudence—in which the minimum "necessary in a democratic society" (Art. 9(2)) does not protect the religious practices but allows for their suppression—turns out to be equally important to evaluating the legacy of history as the court's deference to national policy. This doctrinal basis on which the cases ultimately rest had nothing originally to do with religion in general or Islam in particular. Instead, its source lies in Cold War anxiety that secularist communism would topple Christian democracy.

If so, the secularism of the European Court's headscarf jurisprudence is a recent artifact, primarily following from the collapse of European Christianity in living memory. Even more ironically, this chapter contends, the European Court headscarf cases actually owe part of their doctrinal rationale and perhaps their exclusionary implications not to the secularist associations of religious freedom but to the legacy of the religious struggle against communism once feared as secularism incarnate. The Muslim has taken the place of the communist in the contemporary European imagination—and above all in the history of the religious liberty norm.

How Religious Freedom Became an International Human Right

In the depths of Western history, before the Protestant Reformation, crucial steps had already been taken to wrest control of public matters from the church, opening many new possibilities. There had to be a state for anyone to propose the separation of church and state, just as "politics" had to become, in a revival of classical ideas, an imaginable domain for anyone to hope to purge religion from it. The very notion of the "secular" as a nonreligious space, superimposed on the term's original temporal meaning (still preserved in the Virgilian motto on the American

145

dollar bill, *novus ordo seclorum*, or "a new order of the ages"), rose on the basis of medieval distinctions between property that belonged to the church and property open to seizure from it. Yet whatever the preliminaries were to distinguishing state from church institutionally or politics from religion imaginatively, it remained possible long into modernity not simply to have states with established churches but to have religion pervade politics in the most direct and intimate of ways. The central point is that the formal split of authority between what belonged to Caesar and what did not hardly implied the decline of religion as a public force. Put differently, secular possibilities of long date did not translate into secularism.

Perhaps the most important reason, therefore, to doubt that there was an age-old alliance between religious freedom and political secularism is that for a long time, the former made its way as a Christian principle while the latter simply did not exist. Contrary to an older view, it is now obvious that promotion of something called "liberty of conscience" was not an avowed end of the Reformation of Christianity. The progress of this principle has been, over the long term, more a matter of a means becoming an end in itself, since toleration rose originally as a tool in regimes of religiosity and even persecution. In the beginning, freedom of conscience was not at all a secularist ideal (let alone a religious one masquerading as secularist); it was born in an age in which the highest social premium still fell on collective achievement of some one true faith. It was a device to continue the struggle for the true Christianity, not to end that struggle.

An international human right to religious freedom was not a response to the nineteenth-century secularist republicanism in France or the twentieth-century secularism in Turkey. Instead, it was a project, faithful to the early modern origins of religious freedom, of preserving religion, now in the face of a disturbing new form of secularism. The Soviet Union was the first country founded to promote secularism, in a radical version aimed at stamping religion out altogether. Eventually it recognized religious freedom too as a formal principle: the Soviet Union's 1936 "Stalin" Constitution, though propounded in an era of terror, includes the most extensive list of human rights ever recognized in history, including its Article 124 offering religious freedom. But the devotion of the Soviet Union to a thoroughgoing secularism to deprive the masses of their then favorite "opiate" prompted it to establish an unapologetic public tilt against religion, going far beyond the separation of church and state that allowed religion to be a private matter and churches to shepherd believers. The regime's Commissariat of Enlightenment was intended to take public reeducation in hand in the name of a glorious secular future, and a League of the Militant Godless arose among civil society activists to promote scientific atheism.[16]

It was not least in view of the Soviet Union's avowed secularism that, in what remains one of the massive causes of nongovernmental activism of the entire twentieth century, organized religion mobilized around depredations against Russian Orthodoxy and minority faiths (and later Catholics and Protestants in the Soviet Union's satellites). Prior to World War II, however, no one would have said that the attempt to internationalize the ideal of religious freedom seemed a central device in this campaign. The specter of revolution at home in still highly unstable democracies and a shifting international system meant a much more visible and fateful mobilization against liberalism, viewed as a stepping stone to communism. Compared to the threat of communism, fascism and reaction seemed to many believers and churchmen not a "totalitarian" companion of communism but the lesser evil to choose (if not a positive good to embrace).

Then the Allies—the Americans in league with the Soviets—won the war and took political and often clericofascist reaction off the table as an option for postwar Europe, the Iberian peninsula aside. In its wake, not secularism but religious freedom to ward secularism off was promoted. During the war, when the idea of "human rights" began to circulate for the first time in the English language, American mainline Protestants responded to Franklin D. Roosevelt's Four Freedoms promises (the second of which promised freedom of religion everywhere in the world) by making human rights central to international activism for the first time in history. They outstripped any other nongovernmental activists in this regard in the United States—and they made religious freedom the human right that mattered most. These American Protestants put aside their internal disputes about whether Christianity demanded pacifism (and staying out of the European war). After the war's end, they were by any standard most responsible for the original move to the internationalization of religious freedom and, in fact, for the presence of the entire notion of human rights in international affairs.[17]

Their groups, spearheaded by the Federal Council of Churches of Christ (FCC) and its Commission of Churches on International Affairs (CCIA), always placed freedom of religion first among all other causes, as the foundation of all other rights, and offered it up as the most basic premise of their early struggle against the Soviet Union and in defense of far-flung missionary activity.[18] During the war, an FCC group headed by John Foster Dulles, the Commission to Study the Bases of a Just and Durable Peace, issued its widely circulating *Six Pillars of Peace*, early incorporating calls for an international bill of rights, which—it insisted—must prioritize freedom of religion as its essential linchpin.[19] Thanks to the indefatigable functionary Frederick Nolde, the FCC and CCIA were deeply involved in getting human rights into the United Nations Charter in San Francisco, and Nolde's good friend, Lebanese philosopher Charles Malik, Eastern Orthodox but with strong Catholic leanings, considered freedom of religion the keystone of the Universal Declaration of Human Rights, which he helped write. It is true that Malik was not simply motivated by anticommunism in his goal of internationalizing religious freedom; he also held out hope for the conversion of the entire Mediterranean basin to Christianity, just as several of those most deeply connected to the promotion of religious freedom as a new international principle were animated by the desire to safeguard the premises of missionary activities in East Asia and elsewhere. Nonetheless, communism provided the essential glue of the campaign to internationalize religious freedom.

Primarily a federation of Protestants agreeing to put aside their once bitterly divisive differences in the name of common geopolitical interests, the FCC and its European allies were in the van of history in perfecting "freedom of religion" as the main principle with which to oppose communism, before the wartime alliance frayed or the Cold

War even began. The work of the FCC's Joint Commission on Religious Liberty, founded during the war to survey the state of religious freedom and suggest avenues for its promotion after the war, makes this clear.[20] British and continental European ecumenical Christians were full participants in this discourse.[21] Many Anglo-Americans, it is true, eventually found the World Council of Churches (WCC) too soft on communism, as Dulles's tutorial on the subject at the Amsterdam summit suggested, but the transatlantic coalition remained united in taking the individual right of religious freedom as the core one. Ironically, the FCC's rise and promotion of religious freedom internationally paved the way for what David Sehat calls a "liberal moment" in the United States during which, exceptionally in the country's history, religious freedom was not primarily understood as a device of Protestant public hegemony and moral control. Liberal Protestants were indeed some of the most committed to civil rights for African Americans.[22] In international affairs, however, the "liberal moment" remained very much part of a campaign about the fate of Christianity in a world in which the Soviets had defeated Nazism, as well as a struggle for the continuation of the Christian cause in an age in which missionary proselytizing remained a humongous global enterprise.[23]

Meanwhile, at home, mainline American Protestants were involved in an epoch-making renovation of national identity which, for the first time, brooked the admission of Catholics and Jews to the national project in the creation of a "Judeo-Christian" or "tri-faith" America that explained in the eyes of a succession of presidents and their people what the country stood for in its emerging struggle against the Soviet foe. Far more so than ever before, Protestants relaxed confessional disputes and especially their anti-Catholicism, uniting with other Christians and even Jews—who were instrumental in accepting the bargain of inclusion in the "Judeo-Christian West" on condition of stigmatizing secularism.[24] This episode has tended to be forgotten, not least because this move by mainline Protestant elites inadvertently set the stage for the destruction of their long-term American dominance. The decision by the hitherto Protestant university to diversify, for example, ended up driving rather than forestalling secularism, even as the Cold War promoted the boom of an evangelical conservatism away from mainline fortresses. But if America's mainline Protestant elites no longer enjoy their dominance today as a result, the same was not true in the immediate years after World War II ended. One of the most important developments in Cold War historiography of late is to show how, even as the US Supreme Court turned to impose a "wall of separation" between church and state, America's self-avowed Christian statesmen viewed their task as a holy crusade against secularism. It was at this point that Americans pledged allegiance to a nation proclaimed to be united "under God" and therefore indivisible.[25]

With the Western powers dominating the United Nations for a few years, during the period the Universal Declaration of Human Rights was propounded, the immediate postwar trajectory of human rights in international politics shows how central religious freedom was to this antisecularist venture. Of the few causes generally understood as human rights concerns in international politics at the time, the most prominent by any measure involved depredations of religion under communism, as United Nations

General Assembly attention to the once famous internment of Hungarian Cardinal Jószef Mindszenty shows. (Mindszenty's arrest occurred the month of the Universal Declaration's passage and was condemned soon after, during the short time the West controlled the United Nations forum; Czech Cardinal Josef Beran suffered the same fate soon after, and comparable resolutions followed.)[26]

The new individual human rights centering for so many on religious freedom left behind a League of Nations minority rights regime that did better in recognizing collective, practical, and political dimensions of religious affiliation, given the regime's protection of insular group minorities in Eastern Europe often living in relatively closed faith communities. In this regard, Mark Mazower is absolutely correct that this interwar episode shows that few had trouble thinking about religious identity in terms that were collective and practical rather than individual and conscientious alone.[27] Indeed, in a brilliant recent work on the Universal Declaration's Article 18 on religion, Linde Lindqvist suggests that its focus on individual conscientious choice was in many respects novel, depending most for traction on concern about communism but frequently defended by Malik and Nolde in Christian "personalist" terms that emphasized spiritual freedom. Also new and unprecedented at the time was the right to *change* religion, articulated in Article 18 on similar grounds but strongly motivated by perception of threat to historic missionary activity (it ultimately caused several abstentions in the General Assembly vote on the Universal Declaration on the part of Muslim states).

The critique of secularism often traces the individualization of religion—defining it in terms of internal belief and personal choice—to deep Protestant origins, but long ago rather than late and with an eye toward twentieth-century geopolitics.[28] The emphasis on the *forum internum* of the human being beginning in the Universal Declaration's preamble, as determined by Malik's advocacy, actually invoked the medieval Thomist formula of humanity's "reason and conscience" but with one eye toward potential conscientious nonconformists suffering under communism. By contrast, in United Nations debates, the Soviets proposed that instead of giving special protection to conscientious choice of religion, the law should focus instead on carving out a secular space for "freethinkers" who—they insisted—were historically beset by the fanaticism of religion. Their own draft of Article 18 noted that such "freethinkers" had "led them to discard old-fashioned beliefs and religious fanaticism" and were those whom a human right should most of all protect, given that their acts had always been "crucial for the development of the sciences." (Obviously, the Soviet suggestion was rejected.)[29]

Of course, the internationalization of religious freedom in wartime and after did not come out of nowhere. There had been clauses guaranteeing religious freedom in various European treaties after the Reformation settlement—indeed they were the distant source of the contemporary norm of "the responsibility to protect," albeit one forged by Christians for Christians.[30] It should also be acknowledged that in the most fledging steps toward the internationalization of the norm of religious freedom before World War II, the targets were very much Oriental despotisms—especially the Ottoman Empire—where Christians and Jews were imagined as beset by backwards misrule. The early, modest institutionalization of this norm occurred neither because of a Christian nor because of a secularist impulse in foreign affairs. Rather, Jewish notables and eventually Jewish organizations invoked religious freedom strategically on behalf of their foreign coreligionists to encourage the imperial policymaking France and Great Britain to take seriously the rhetoric of superiority of the tolerationist Christian West—in order to commit Christian states to the defense of the Jewish people abroad. In fact, in several treaties and eventually at Versailles, internationalist Jews were able to embed the ideal of religious freedom in fledging ways in the international order against "backwards" sovereigns in Poland, Romania, and elsewhere that were Christian rather than Muslim.[31]

In spite of these extremely modest antecedents, however, the internationalization (and Europeanization) of religious freedom in the 1940s took its historical quantum leap under the auspices of a Christianity positioning itself geopolitically for antisecularist struggle. By the interwar period, a large range of defenders of religious freedom existed, and the norm percolated into traditions of constitution-making across modern times and around the world. But in its midcentury internationalization and Europeanization, the secularist defenders of the principle who now supported it in many domestic circumstances were not the main agents. To complete the picture, but above all to explain how this strategy defined the Western European human rights regime, Catholicism demands the lion's share of attention, since it was its historically surprising, but geopolitically crucial, alliance with transnational Protestantism that deserves most credit for solidifying the international politics of religious freedom in Cold War form.

Catholicism and the Origins of the European Convention of Human Rights

Prior to the Cold War, many Catholics favored explicitly Catholic states in crisis circumstances (in Austria, Portugal, and Spain before World War II and then Croatia, Vichy France, and Slovakia during it) and fascist states when this first best option was not available (in Germany and Italy before World War II and most of Europe during it). Indeed, forsaking state capture still seemed radical in the 1940s, when a powerful Vatican current remained stalwart in its defense of the older view that an endorsement of religious freedom made sense only as a "hypothesis" in those situations in which Catholics were in the minority—as in the United States—rather than a general principle or "thesis." Through the 1950s, and in fact through Vatican II, the Church opposed religious freedom, against a strong set of dissidents such as Jacques Maritain and others. After the war, critical figures such as Cardinal Alfredo Ottaviani (last head of the millennial inquisition) inveighed against religious freedom, offering Spain, where clericofascism in a majority Catholic country had survived, as the ideal model.[32]

But even though Ottaviani and his allies, in a once dramatic set of events, nearly derailed it, Vatican II finally adopted a declaration on religious freedom, the most high-profile and visible part of its work, significantly framed as a necessary consequence of its first principle, the dignity of the human person.[33] If one asks why this startling change occurred when it did, fewer than fifty years ago, the geopolitical context of the Cold War has to be a significant part of the answer. The text of the declaration makes clear that it now seemed that endorsement of the principle of religious freedom undermined global secularism more than risked it. "Men of the present day want to profess their religion freely in private and in public," the Declaration states, before turning this novel Catholic view against the Soviet Union. "[But] there are forms of government under which, despite constitutional recognition of the freedom of religious worship, the public authorities themselves strive to deter the citizens from professing their religion and make life particularly difficult and dangerous for religious bodies."[34] Once denounced by a reactionary church, religious liberty found itself reappropriated. Once tasked in Catholic political thought as a catalyst of secularism, religious freedom found itself recuperated as a crucial tool to stave secularism off.

This point suggests that the most general way to interpret the incorporation of religious freedom as a vital antisecularist principle in Catholicism is to connect it to the formation of Cold War Christianity generally, in which America became the model of the promotion of religion precisely through its commitment to disestablishment and the ideal of religious freedom. For the transformation of Catholicism enabling its embrace of religious freedom was also its Americanization, as defenders and critics of the transformation well understood at the time.

For Catholics, the American situation had been a chief example of the "hypothesis," not a generally defensible model of the relation between a tolerant state and religious truth, from the first papal encyclical on the American church, Leo XIII's *Longinqua Oceani* (1895). After 1945, American Catholics joined their Protestant brethren in promoting religious liberty as the constitution's "first freedom," warning sternly against its interpretation in mistakenly secularist ways by the US Supreme Court of the day.[35] In spite of those high court decisions, Catholics such as Maritain promoted America on the grounds that it showed how religious freedom promoted rather than undermined Christian life. *Everson v. Board of Education*, the Supreme Court's decision radically altering establishment clause jurisprudence interpreting the First Amendment to the US Constitution, may have referred to a national tradition of imposing a "wall of separation" between church and state; but Maritain knew that the deepest truth of American history was that disestablishment of Christianity was the key to its conquest of social life.[36]

In the nineteenth century, Catholic thinker Alexis de Tocqueville's attitude toward Protestant America was that it had figured out, by disestablishing the church, how to make Christianity more publicly powerful than ever. His message to Catholic reactionaries at home who denounced America as godless was that they needed to know how strong Christianity can become precisely among those who have given up the campaign to capture the state. ("I shall wait until they come back from a visit to America," Tocqueville wrote of his reactionary opponents, noting that his fellow Catholics in the United States were if anything more favorable than Protestants toward religious freedom American-style.)[37] Maritain, who had once denounced America too, spent World War II there, forging alliances with theologians such as John Courtney Murray who followed him in marginalizing the thesis/hypothesis model. Murray, under Maritain's influence, became the most pivotal figure in Vatican II's work on religious freedom.[38]

Ultimately, even as the Universal Declaration was finalized, the idea of human rights as a set international legal principles, including one guaranteeing religious freedom, survived nowhere in the cacophony of world ideology, except in what became their Western European homeland, in an era of Christian political and social dominance based on a reformulated conservatism. Dulles may have inspired some Europeans but soon made rather clear, as Dwight Eisenhower's secretary of state, that the United States no longer stood for the internationalization of human rights as a diplomatic and legal matter. Meanwhile, if Western Europeans turned to human rights and experimented with federalism, it was on the basis of newly ascendant Christian parties that experienced unprecedented success and whose statesmen and party apparatuses connected across borders to establish a decades-long dominance.[39] Just as ecumenical Protestantism drove the transatlantic ascent and internationalization of religious freedom, transnational Catholicism undergirded its Europeanization—and provided the deepest foundations of the European human rights regime.

As Marco Duranti and others are beginning to show, the origins of the European Convention reflect a striking degree of influence of Christians critical of secularism, indeed far more than in the case of the Universal Declaration itself.[40] In retrospective appraisals, the Universal Declaration and the European Convention are frequently seen as complementary projects, since they are animated by the same norms. Or else, they are treated as successor enterprises, after the United Nations' failed move to make hard law spurred the origins of a principled community's insistence on enforcement mechanisms. The reality is wholly different. While attracting an eclectic group of supporters, the European Convention involved a stark departure from the welfarist premises of the Universal Declaration, led by those interested in using Europeanization as a way to combat domestic socialism, in an era when the popular and ideological appeal of social democratic ideals and communist ones were rising to new heights. Meanwhile, mechanisms for enforcement were made close to inaccessible; and they were not used for decades, and then mostly after being updated (the European Court of Human Rights set in motion by the treaty decided its first religious freedom case, for instance, in 1993).[41] The European Convention's purposes were, in the beginning, didactic and expressive. As social and economic rights still prominent in the Universal Declaration were dropped, the right of religious freedom—along with that of private property—surged as among the central symbols of what made Western Europe distinct from the encroaching communist foe.

Especially after the communist takeover of Czechoslovakia, and then the internments of Beran and Mindszenty, much of the rhetoric turned on how the Convention would symbolize the essence of Western civilization against eastern criminality (and its local avatars). "All over Europe, Socialism is proving no defence against Communism's attack on the triple European heritage of Christianity, mental freedom and even-handed justice," David Maxwell-Fyfe, conservative British politician (and lead British prosecutor at the Nuremberg trials) declared in 1948, in defense of the Convention project. Anxious not to be outmaneuvered, Labour Party politicians in Great Britain, whether they had any interest in Christianity or not, went along with the Europeanization and "spiritual union" that Winston Churchill and his fellow conservatives felt necessary to combat communism. (For its part, the Left in France simply blocked the ratification of the Convention for more than twenty years, in part out of concern that it was primarily a weapon of the local Right.)[42]

More generally, Christian Democracy was the single most defining feature of the post–World War II European political settlement, of which the European Convention was—as prior chapters have already suggested—an obvious if initially peripheral feature. Soon enough, the Cold War featured a saturation of politics by Christianity in noncommunist Europe as much as transatlantically in a common project uniting "Western" politicians and churches. Indeed, in certain respects, Western Europeans went far further in muddying the line between publicly dominant Christianity and political life than Americans have ever done. After all, if not only having explicitly Christian political parties but having them continentally dominant for most of postwar European history is not a blurring of the divide between religion and politics, what is?[43] From the 1940s through the 1960s, a time of growing religiosity and great public presence of Christianity across Europe by several metrics, this blending included the novel promotion in European and Christian history of "human dignity" and "human rights," notably the international right of religious freedom.

The drafting of Article 9 of the European Convention deserves a different brand of scrutiny to capture the impact of these forces than the doctrinal analysis it has received so far.[44] But it is clear that, given who was in the room, the formulation and passage of the provision was largely uncontroversial, as the treaty took over Article 9(1) essentially verbatim from the Universal Declaration's Article 18, and what debate there was focused on Article 9(2)'s restrictions. The main speakers such as Maxwell-Fyfe and Mouvement républicain populaire (Christian Democrat) representative Pierre-Henri Teitgen were entirely "overt about the role they saw for the *Christian* religion in assisting with the development of human rights," simply equating Western Europe with Christian civilization in many speeches.[45] Whatever persisting debate there is about the "original intent" behind various clauses—as in most such cases—there is none at all about this general point.[46] Evidence teems in the *travaux préparatoires* of the European Convention that a good number of delegates imagined religious freedom as the keystone right, one for which Europe must stand up most vigorously now against the persecutory spirit of political secularism: "We must make it clear that our concepts of human dignity and human rights are something different from what we see in Eastern Europe," the Irish delegate William Norton remarked. "An effort is being made there to put out the light of the Church—not only of one church of almost all churches. . . . We here in this Council of Europe can be a rallying base and a beacon light to men and women struggling against persecution of that kind."[47]

After a certain point in the negotiations, Article 9(2) came to be annexed to the general vision the drafters adopted for the entire treaty, which was widely called the "democratic minimum" approach. Hence as an omnibus provision in Article 9(2), the considerations that might lead to the abridgement of the right of freedom of religion were ones "necessary in a democratic society," the phrase whose interpretation continues to be at stake in the current case law.[48] But the most striking event of the original negotiations for the history of religious freedom even more conclusively shows how mistaken it would be to attribute secularism to the treaty. Turkey, the sole non-Christian power involved, proposed that the treaty explicitly make the democratic minimum a secularist one, anticipating Islamist threats. In response, the Western European states unceremoniously rebuffed the proposal to have Article 9(2) mention religion as a potential threat to the democratic minimum. In the late 1940s, it was not the Western Europeans who were the secularists. It is fascinating and instructive—and perhaps the most revealing piece of evidence for my proposal here—that the result the court reached in *Refah Partisi* fifty years later as a matter of judicial interpretation of the European Convention was one the drafters of the treaty explicitly declined to take up during its formulation.[49]

As noted earlier, there was no case law involving Article 9's right of religious freedom before our own time. However, this absence did not simply follow from the fact that there was so little European Convention case law of any kind. For there is one early Article 9 decision suggesting strongly that "secularism" was not a significant aim of its parties or interpreters. Upholding and importing the German constitutional court's new doctrine of "militant democracy"—a homegrown version of the democratic minimum approach enforced against enemies of the constitution—the first European Commission Article 9 decision (1957) was one allowing the Federal Republic's communist party ban to proceed.[50] That party's announced platform was to scuttle the liberal regime in place, the commissioners concluded; and if so, then the preservation of the democratic character of the regime allowed the Article 9 rights invoked by party members to be overridden.[51] That the first decision in which European Convention Article 9 rights were restricted in the name of the preservation of democracy had nothing to do with religious freedom provides more evidence for the novelty of current interpretations. Doctrinally, put bluntly, one template for the current Muslim headscarf decisions was drawn up in policing the threat of secularism rather than of religion. Whatever one thinks of the expansive concern about extremist political views on a postfascist continent facing down a communist enemy (or indeed in Turkey today where Islamism continues to be prominent), the migration of the Article 9(2)'s "democratic" rationale for abridging rights from political to religious freedom and from a perceived threat revolving around ideology to one linked to religion is anything but a natural or logical extension of early views.[52] At the very least, such an evolution cannot be ascribed to the original secularism of the treaty—whose negotiation and first use were on behalf of a Christian Europe against secularism. The European human rights regime enforced the democratic minimum beginning long ago, but no one would have seen secularism as essential to that minimum until recently.

Though the template for their later judicial interpretation was drawn up early, Article 9's religious freedom clauses in particular were a dead letter for more than four decades, as if born in a time before the current conditions for their uses, and potential abuses, were even conceivable. What happened in between the two eras? The answer is straightforward: to a wholly remarkable and unanticipated extent, Western European Christianity collapsed.

Along with it, the original rationale for the international and European priority of religious freedom, indeed the very meaning of the principle, had to change. It is this transformation together with unprecedented Muslim immigration, emotional disputes over whether Turkey counted as a European country, and 9/11's ramifications across the Atlantic that did most to set the stage for the contemporary politics of religious freedom, including in the European Court of Human Rights.[53]

Conclusion

It is only in very recent times, with the collapse of European Christianity since the 1960s, that it became possible for the ideal of religious freedom to become so closely associated with secularism in the continent's human rights regime and beyond. There certainly were secularists in modern history, but it seems graphically clear that through the Cold War—and particularly in the internationalization and Europeanization of religious freedom—they were not in the driver's seat. Instead, the ideal of religious freedom originated in, and long remained tethered to, the self-conscious attempt to preserve an explicitly and pervasively Christian society—most especially, after a certain point, against the frightening threat of secularism. Though European secularism now attracts criticism for its covert Christianity, most often the ideal of religious freedom served the project of overt Christianity—which left secularism a frequently embattled ideal.

In America today, religious freedom is the core of a continuing consensus and even a new tool after the passing of a more liberal age of politics to mark the limits of government and to rebut the sway of otherwise applicable norms of nondiscrimination.[54] This very fact makes the persistence in Western Europe of assumptions from the age of Christian human rights so striking and disappointing. There is no point in shielding the European Court from the criticism it has properly attracted in its religious freedom cases. But it is important that the story of explicitly "Christian human rights" helps explain how the court's doctrines were forged, even if they are now applied for the sake of secularism. Clearly, a democratic minimum required in a democratic society should not simply provide high principles for a bias against Islam, even in self-declared secularist countries, especially when Christian practices are given a pass.[55]

In a provocative recent book, Ran Hirschl has coined the phrase "constitutional theocracy" to describe legal regimes that distinguish between political and religious authority but nonetheless allow religious norms to pervade public life.[56] It is a good description of much of modern politics, including—with due allowance for its originally nonconstitutional status—the European human rights regime at the start, with its explicitly Christian ambiance. Strangely, however, Hirschl groups Europe today with the rest of the world in a shocking drift further toward theocracy. From another view, however, it is contemporary Europe's *departure* from "constitutional theocracy" in recent decades that deserves emphasis. The Muslim headscarf cases are so troubling not because European secularism is marginal today but because it is the wrong kind of secularism.

Joseph Weiler looks at the situation somewhat differently. Having warned Europeans at the time of the debate over the abortive European constitution against what he termed a "Christophobic ghettoization" of its Christian heritage, Weiler intervened as an advocate in the *Lautsi* appeal to warn Europe against a worrisome secularist drift.[57] Confusingly, Weiler invoked the United States as an example of a secularist society Europe must not become, going so far as to complain, like some American conservatives, that a profane America in which the "public square" is "naked" has to be avoided at all costs.[58] Yet the real contrast between contemporary Europe and contemporary America, contrary to those who pine for a bygone Europe of more than minimal Christian affiliation and observance, is that Europeans have moved so fundamentally to pioneer—rather starkly against the background of human history so far—an unprecedented form of collective life in which religion has lost its hold. And in this context, the more plausible concern is that Europeans seem tempted to discriminate against Muslims, who are a living presence, than that they risk "ghettoizing" a Christianity that has already departed so much and so quickly. The Muslim headscarf cases are troubling not because Europe should return to the public Christianity it has largely given up but because its version of secularism is discriminatory rather than inclusionary.

For that reason, the argument of this chapter also bears on those who believe the headscarf cases show the limits of secularism. None of the above rules out aspects of the critique of secularism; given the purchase it has gained in recent years in contemporary theoretical consciousness, it provides much of value. But secularism is not the only thing to criticize, and perhaps it is worth criticizing in the name of another kind of secularism. The historiographical implication that follows from its alliance with Christianity in and through the origins of international and regional human rights is that the principle of religious freedom became annexed to an exclusionary secularist agenda not in the mists of time but only yesterday. The theoretical implication of this finding is that since secularism is far from the dominant mode in the trajectory of the principle of religious freedom, both secularism and religious freedom turn out to be considerably more ambiguous and promiscuous than either their current uses or the critiques of those uses suggest. It also means they could have other and new forms. Most of all, if human rights should remain central to collective politics, they would have to come in a version that would finally transcend their Christian incarnation—for in a certain sense, the Muslim headscarf cases show contemporary human rights to be not too secular but not secular enough.

Epilogue

No one interested in where human rights came from can afford to ignore Christianity. In the middle of the twentieth century, in fact, human rights were part and parcel of a Christian moment in political affairs. In European and transatlantic history, it now seems unavoidable to emphasize the Christianity of the time—and since the birth of human rights had such tight links to those locales, it is unsurprising that their initial life was marked so strongly by Christianity's startling ascendancy at the time. It had suffered bouts of secularization, and had little reason for triumphalism given a checkered recent past; but Christianity transcended these facts and enjoyed a moment of acme. Interestingly, it succeeded by blaming disaster on secularization itself and facing down a frightening secularism in the communist East and moved into a golden age across the Atlantic—perhaps its last, at least where Western Europe was concerned.

One of the most important interpretations of twentieth-century history remains Charles Maier's *Recasting Bourgeois Europe*, which originally appeared in 1975 and took as its intellectual problem how a fractious and polarized continent could stabilize in between the world wars. Disaster may have been coming once again, Maier observed, but it was surprising that it did not come before. Indeed, at least some of the foundations of the stabilization of Western Europe after World War II were also owed to what Maier identified as a "conservative achievement" in the 1920s, before Adolf Hitler brought destruction and ruin not merely to his own people but to the entire continent.[1] Why, then, did the aftermath of World War II allow for a more enduring stability than the first time around? In a classic extension of his analysis, Maier explained that the answer to this question would have to turn on what new ingredients were added to interwar acquisitions to allow a more permanent formula of stabilization.[2] This book has argued that human rights were part of that mix but only once restored to their congenitally Christian ambiance.

Maier focused narrowly on economic affairs to locate the truly decisive novelty: after the "Malthusian" circumstances of the interwar period, the opening to markets beyond Europe and especially transatlantic trade afforded lasting success.[3] In the decades since, historians have found few reasons to revise Maier's account. But elements that complete and complicate his picture require more emphasis, especially since the economy never stands alone, independent of geopolitics and culture. What, for example, might the fact that empire was going strong in the interwar period imply and that Western Europeans struggled to retain it as the embers of World War II were cooling? It bears stressing that nothing about the Christian invention of human dignity and rights chronicled in this book ruled out the endurance of empire for a long time; as Aimé Césaire observed in his definitive 1950 indictment of European "pseudo-humanism," with only slight exaggeration, "not one established writer, not one academic, not one crusader for law and religion, not one 'defender of the human person'" yet opposed colonialism in principle.[4]

But far beyond the resumption of empire, Christian personalism specifically and religious politics generally need to be painted onto Maier's canvas to make it fully depict the postwar situation. Religious belief and its diverse political invocations were a central feature of postwar Western European democracy, determining much about its identity and helping account for its survival. Christian human rights made their place in the political world as part of the restabilization of bourgeois Europe after World War II, and it was their fate to figure in the dynamic of recasting that Maier originally identified and that finally provided the stability that regimes long lacked: the "containment of the left," the construction of a form of moderate capitalism turning on interest groups, and above all, the move from a conservative maintenance of middle-class rule that was willing to give up democracy if necessary to one that embraced it at all cost. It was not incidental that all these developments occurred under the auspices of Christian politics. More broadly, these developments saw the rise of an influential Cold War liberalism fundamentally marked by Christian belief, and which was therefore fearful of threats, anxious about sin, and fatalistic about human possibilities.

That Maier could overlook publicly dominant Christianity reflected assumptions that were common until recently. Tony Judt's epoch-making *Postwar*, though written much later, provides another example of a treatment of the era that barely mentions religion.[5] But perhaps because of the temper of our own age, the omission is now being rectified as the historiography of postwar Western Europe and the transatlantic space, as well as the broader history of international affairs, is renovated to incorporate religious factors. Today, it is clearer to historians than ever before that, without the success of Christian Democracy across Western Europe (in the circumstances of a transatlantic Christian commitment to Cold War struggle), it is very hard to imagine the restabilization Maier originally chronicled. In the hands of scholars such as the great pioneer Martin Conway and current historians such as Giuliana Chamedes, James Chappel, Maria Mitchell, Jan-Werner Mueller, and Andrew Preston, Christianity's ascendancy both spiritually and politically after World War II has become central.[6] In the end, Christian human rights are a footnote to that story.

Aside from providing insight into the past conditions of reconstruction and restabilization after World War II, can the story of Christian human rights illuminate the present? After all, so many of the circumstances of that lost golden age of Christian hegemony and victory that Christian human rights reflected have passed. Christian Democracy, though institutionally going strong, has been shaken everywhere it once ruled for so long, and its ideology is no longer the same—for some observers, no longer identifiably Christian—in our day.[7] There are surely unsuspected legacies, and this book's portrait of the strange inheritance of the postwar Christian defense of "democracy" against enemies in policing Muslims today is only intended to scratch the surface. Camille Robcis, among others, has documented further legacies, notably in conservative campaigns against same-sex marriage in contemporary European debates—in which invocations of humanity and dignity turn out to be little more than powerful moral talismans against free association.[8]

But the truth is that the history of human rights eventually became largely untethered from the profoundly Christian moment in world affairs that helped birth the principles between the 1930s and 1940s. Signs of this were already apparent in the 1970s. There was serious Christian participation in local and global coalitions in Eastern Europe and Latin America that finally made human rights famous, in their new invocation by an inspired transnational alliance of activists exhausted by maximal political dreams and seeking minimalist moral reform in the face of totalitarian and authoritarian states. But the more spectacular development was the embrace of "human rights" as a new slogan and program by the left in an age of crisis. There is no reason, if all this is true, to think that a secret Christian legacy haunts many or most aspects of human rights regimes that have in fact been built or mobilizations in which advocates currently engage. The shocking secularization of the European continent a quarter century after the transwar era on which this book has focused, which strangely coincided with the true takeoff of human rights mobilization, permits no other conclusion.

It may be more interesting, therefore, to conclude this book with some brief reflections on Christianity not as the *source* of contemporary human rights, with its specific record and persisting quandaries, but as one of the most successful moral movements in the history of human affairs—and which therefore provides many precedents for reflection on how the human rights movement might develop in the future. The blip in world history of the human rights movement so far pales in comparison to the sheer longevity of Christianity, which therefore offers a rich basis for reflection. The millennial history of Christianity is indeed a precious resource for anyone who speculates about the prospects of moral advocacy of any kind.

Christianity is the global faith that many would like human rights to become. Whatever its earlier expansion, in fact, Christianity's era of true globalization began in earnest after World War II, when human rights—even Christian human rights—remained local and inconspicuous. Recent developments in Africa and Latin America, symbolized by the election of Francis I as pope, have made Christianity what it had never been: a religion of the global south.[9] The trajectory of human rights, despite its rise over the past few decades, has enjoyed only a modest breakthrough, judged by the standard of the massive boom of Catholicism and Protestantism (and perhaps Pentecostalism most notably) over the same period.

By comparison to the history of Christianity, both ancient and recent, human rights have a long way to go. In the age this book chronicles, human rights were barely a global idea, and to the extent they had any presence outside the transatlantic Christian homeland, it was assured by Christians such as Charles Malik and Carlos Romulo, along with Latin Americans. This book has not covered the latter, but they were probably the most numerous representatives of Christian human rights at the time, and Latin America's own intricate history of the intersection of Catholic belief and reactionary politics both before and after World War II beckons as terrain for kindred inquiries.[10] Otherwise, human rights remained a discreet faith, and even today to a remarkable extent they are chiefly a transatlantic or even European one, just as Christianity still was fifty years ago.

Messengers from elite networks across borders who promote human rights have cooperated in delocalized ideological transmission and practical solidarity, following the model of tribunes of Christian good news from the time of St. Paul's epistles. Yet for all their hard work, the secular gospel of human rights has experienced nothing like Christian success. The brokered penetration of human rights into diverse locales around the world, what scholars often call the process of "vernacularization," is barely begun and rather unimpressive compared to the Christian record, whether long term or recent. The Universal Declaration of Human Rights may have been industriously translated into nearly as many languages as the Christian Bible but has not been as widely read. However much governments learn to pay it lip service, human rights are so far limited, and perhaps already halted, in their spread as a vocabulary of identification or even a language of advocacy. Empirical studies demonstrate that human rights have not yet become a grassroots idiom, let alone a popular cause.[11]

The most likely reason for this comparative restriction of human rights both to specific locales and superficial penetration within them is not merely lack of time but also that Christians took it upon themselves to induce affiliation though a much larger range of techniques. But no one converts to human rights. If this faith has prophets, they write reports and file lawsuits, and so enjoy only the charisma of the bureaucrat. The cause has judges to its name but no priests for interpersonal succor and local institutionalization. Believers in human rights do not study breviaries or learn catechisms. There is no such thing as prayer in human rights, and devotion to its values is not made beautiful through liturgy nor routinized through emotional rituals—even if Amnesty International, the trendsetting nongovernmental organization, emerged with a few "post-Christian" accoutrements such as votive candles for the suffering.[12] From a more disabused and mercenary perspective, Christianity provided Julien Sorel, in Stendhal's memorable novel *The Red and the Black*, an exit from provincial stultification for the promotion of his talent; human rights today, it is increasingly clear, also offer preprofessional paths for the young engaged in resume building. But unlike Christianity, human rights do not give much of a chance for spiritual transfiguration for the rare authentic seeker of transcendence. Or, if there are knights of faith in the world of human rights, it boasts no churches or cathedrals and has inspired none of the great art that has been Christianity's most impressive contribution to human affairs. And one doubts that human rights will ever move true believers to self-sacrifice or even martyrdom, giving themselves as witnesses to the truth of their faith. Secular nationalism found ways to win that level of devotion from its followers, but secular post- and supranationalism so far has not.

Yet if Christianity today illustrates how a long fuse and more pervasive techniques can lead advocacy toward a belated global explosion, its impressive spread always faced and still confronts severe limits that may teach human rights even more. Its norms diffused only to the point where they met apparently impervious barriers. Its incursions into lands whose denizens fought back—rather than perished of European diseases or in the face of massive force, as after the American conquest—have left Christianity less global than its most ambitious partisans wanted it to become, even today when it spans much of the world. Not all peoples have proved willing to trade in their belief system for a new one. Christianity's borders with Islam, most notably, have been intermittently bloody, and ill-conceived crusades old and new have less promoted affiliation than prompted backlash.

For a long time, further, Christianity also faced the secularist enemy of communism, one that was far from willing to find a productive home for religious faith in the modern state, and perhaps alliance with it, as occurred in American and eventually Western European history, as this book has illustrated. Communism in Eastern Europe persecuted Christians but never extinguished Christianity; yet communism's fall has not blotted out the global memory of the sort of radical secularism that treats religion as the opiate of the masses—even if with the decline of Christianity on the European continent it can sometimes seem as if communism was beaten only to the benefit of its secularism, not to preserve the faith it brazenly challenged.

Christianity thus stands out not only as a model of success but also of limitation and even reversal. The difficulty that Christianity faced of breaching every last frontier, and the loss of many of its historically most devoted followers in its old homeland, is a cautionary lesson for any universalizing moral creed. Of course, it could be early days for human rights. Doubting the significance of Christianity a mere few decades after Jesus's death would look embarrassingly premature now. Or it could be that human rights are already facing some of the same limits as Christianity has long confronted and cannot seem to overcome. The news easily reaches some hospitable climates, but other places offer only harsh and alien terrain. Or it could be that the message is the wrong one.

But perhaps the most fascinating barrier to the victory of human rights someday that the analogy with Christianity allows entertaining is not out in the world but in the hearts of men and women. Part of the failure that Christianity has long faced on this front is institutional: for its internal critics, its institutions have always betrayed the genius of the founder and have propagated the one true faith not merely in ways that were not heard, but that did not penetrate, washing over souls like water over rocks left dry inside. In Alfred Loisy's immortal complaint, "Jesus Christ preached the coming of the Kingdom of God; unfortunately, it is the Church that arrived."[13] The message was right, but the medium failed.

Or did men and women? For the fear is hardly just institutional. Those who have been the true conscience of the Christian movement over time give voice to this heartrending lament. For all the time the clock has run and the trappings of external and global success Christianity has achieved, Jesus's moral teaching has never been internalized by those who hear it daily and profess it most fervently. It is everywhere. But it is not clear how much difference it has made. More caustic opponents of Jesus's

Sermon of the Mount, to be sure, could insist that it had indeed transformed human beings completely. Moralist François de La Rochefoucauld alleged that it had succeeded fabulously—in making men hypocrites. (For the even more acerbic thinker Friedrich Nietzsche, it bred a race of slaves.) Though human rights today also attract occasional scorn of this kind, the Christian analogy remains interesting for those who admire the core values and uplifting promise of a gospel that humanity hears but fails to obey. The prophetic vision (Ezekiel 36:26) that hearts of stone would someday give way to hearts of flesh, which Jesus's movement was supposed to fulfill, remains a promissory note—a few saints aside. What if people learn the truth—and spurn it?

The vision of the human rights movement remains open and unredeemed too, which its most subtle champions and most acid critics increasingly agree means it must face the same anxiety as the most careful and committed Christians have always harbored. Today, in a rerun of Christian introspection, a debate rages among measurement experts about whether human rights make any difference. Disturbingly, it appears that the current faith changes our minds, or at least our rhetoric, with its pieties passing the lips of statesmen daily; but our behavior remains too often unaffected by the principles, with states—and their leaders and populations—failing to suppress their sins in direct response.[14] Human rights activism has transformed the nature of idealism to an impressive extent over a short space of time but has left the world more similar than one might hope.

As in their Christian avatar, therefore, the profoundest limits of human rights in the future may be not so much geographical and cultural as internal and behavioral. If anything, Christianity's awe-inspiring victories in the world over time, from the conversion of the Roman Empire to the evangelization of the New World, could make its defeats when it comes to the soul even more glaring. The analogy suggests that if human rights do not change the conduct of states, organizations, and individuals, their worth will ultimately be open to doubt, sooner or later. And yet their partisans—unlike most Christians—cannot take refuge in opacity and mysticism in response to failure.

After the passing of the age of Christian human rights in the middle of the twentieth century, their promotion has become a secular cause, and it will not satisfy anyone to say, complacently and fideistically, that human rights are providential, with the plan of their fulfillment all the more extraordinary for working through surreptitious mechanisms or in mysterious ways. The old religions have cast aspersion on sinning and called attention to suffering. But they also helped believers reconcile themselves to the endurance and even permanence of both. Human rights cannot, and should not, offer such reconciliation. Unless it is just a new faith, human rights cannot stop short of the elimination of sinning and suffering, if not sooner then later, and in this world, since they do not promise another.

As founder of human rights law Louis Henkin once recorded, the principles are not intended to be comparable to those of the old religions and "do not provide warmth, belonging, fitting, significance, do not exclude the need for love, friendship, family, charity, sympathy, devotion, sanctity, or for expiation, atonement, forgiveness."[15] Yet precisely because human rights focus solely on the most basic demands here and now, the justification of the regimes and movements that aim to provide them also depends more fully on their worldly success. If the human rights movement does not improve states—or even the hearts of the men and women that Christianity at its most ambitious and inspiring promised to transform—it will demand replacement, in the name of its own ideals or some better ones.

N o t e s

Introduction

1 Pius XII, "The Internal Order of States and People" (Christmas Message for 1942), in Vincent Yzermans, ed., *Major Addresses*, 2 vols. (St. Paul, MN: North Central Publishing, 1961), 2:60 (emphasis added). For richer study of this message in context, see Giuliana Chamedes, "Pius XII, Rights Talk, and the Dawn of the Religious Cold War," in Devin O. Pendas, ed., *Religion and Human Rights* (New York: Routledge, forthcoming).

2 Pius XII, "Democracy and a Lasting Peace" (Christmas Message for 1944), in Yzermans, ed., *Major Addresses*, 2:78–89.

3 See John Witte Jr. and Frank Alexander, eds., *Christianity and Human Rights: An Introduction* (New York: Cambridge University Press, 2010).

4 John Paul II, *Ecclesia in Europa* (Vatican City: Libreria Editrice Vaticana, 2003).

5 For a focus on Jesus himself, see Nicholas Wolterstorff, *Justice: Rights and Wrongs* (Princeton: Princeton University Press, 2010); on the Reformation, see John Witte Jr., *The Reformation of Rights: Law, Religion and Human Rights in Early Modern Calvinism* (Cambridge, UK: Cambridge University Press, 2008).

6 Samuel Moyn, *The Last Utopia: Human Rights in History* (Cambridge, MA: Harvard University Press, 2010); compare David Little, "Critical Reflections on *The Last Utopia: Human Rights in History*," in *Essays on Religion and Human Rights: Ground to Stand On* (Cambridge, UK: Cambridge University Press, 2015), chap. 2.

7 Eric Hobsbawm and Terence Ranger, eds., *The Invention of Tradition* (New York: Cambridge University Press, 1983).

8 Extant large-scale treatments of the Christianity and human rights have sectarian versions of the general flaws of teleology, tunnel vision, and triumphalism in human rights history. For examples, see Philippe de la Chappelle, *La Déclaration universelle des droits de l'homme et le catholicisme*, pref. René Cassin (Paris: Persée, 1967); Jozef Punt, *Die Idee der Menschenrechte: Ihre geschichtliche Entwicklung und ihre Rezeption durch die moderne katholische Sozialverkündigung* (Paderborn: F. Schöningh, 1987); Alexander Saberschinsky, *Die Begründung universeller Menschenrechte* (Paderborn: F. Schöningh, 2002); and more recently a huge recent wave in English that includes Thomas D. Williams, *Who Is My Neighbor?: Personalism and the Foundations of Human Rights* (Washington, DC: Catholic University of America Press, 2005).

9 See, for example, Jeremy Waldron, *God, Locke, and Equality: Christian Foundations in Locke's Political Thought* (Cambridge, UK: Cambridge University Press, 2002) and compare Moyn, "Did Christianity Create Liberalism?," *Boston Review* 40, no. 1 (January/February 2015): 50–55.

10 The literature on the entanglement of Christians with the failure of liberalism in Europe, including many of its darkest chapters, is too long to cite, but the phrase is from Richard Steigmann-Gall, *The Holy Reich: Nazi Conceptions of Christianity, 1919–1945* (Cambridge, UK: Cambridge University Press, 2004).

11 We need not go so far as to say that liberalism had not existed before the era of the world wars to conclude that the reshuffling of its commitments transformed it fundamentally, in the face of the socialist and communist left and in a complex interaction with conservatism, which was also changing as far-right politics were destroyed. See Duncan Bell, "What Is Liberalism?," *Political Theory* 42, no. 6 (December 2014): 682–715 and Edmund Fawcett, *Liberalism: The Life of an Idea* (Princeton, NJ: Princeton University Press, 2014); and for the Christian origins of the idea of "totalitarianism," see James Chappel, "The Catholic Origins of Totalitarianism Theory," *Modern Intellectual History* 8, no. 3 (November 2011): 561–90.

12 See, for example, Pedro Ramos Pinto, "Housing and Citizenship: Building Social Rights in Twentieth-Century Portugal," *Contemporary European History* 18, no. 2 (May 2009): 199–215.

13 See, for example, Johannes Morsink, *The Universal Declaration of Human Rights: Origins, Drafting, and Intent* (Philadelphia: University of Pennsylvania Press, 2000) or A. W. B. Simpson, *Human Rights and the End of Empire: Britain and the Genesis of the European Convention* (New York: Oxford University Press, 2001).

14 Mary Ann Glendon, *A World Made New: Eleanor Roosevelt and the Universal Declaration of Human Rights* (New York: Random House, 2001); John Nurser, *For All Peoples and Nations: The Ecumenical Church and Human Rights* (Washington, DC: Georgetown University Press, 2005).

15 Mark Mazower, "The Strange Triumph of Human Rights," *Historical Journal* 47, no. 2 (June 2004): 379–98. An even broader perspective than a focus on Christian discourse affords would show that perhaps the largest imperative to which human rights were an answer in the 1940s was a welfarist revision of citizenship; I pursue this argument in future work.

16 Arno Mayer, *Why Did the Heavens Not Darken?: The Final Solution in History* (New York: Pantheon Books, 1988), 465.

17 See, for example, Susan Zuccotti, *Under His Very Windows: The Vatican and the Holocaust in Italy* (New Haven, CT: Yale University Press, 2002); Peter C. Kent, *The Lonely Cold War of Pope Pius XII: The Roman Catholic Church and the Division of Europe, 1943–1950* (Montreal: McGill-Queen's University Press, 2012); Giuliana Chamedes, "The Vatican and the Reshaping of the European International Order after the First World War," *Historical Journal* 56, no. 4 (December 2013): 955–76; Chamedes, "The Vatican and the Making of the Atlantic Order, 1920–1960" (PhD diss., Columbia University, 2013).

18 Mary Ann Glendon, "Catholicism and Human Rights," in James L. Heft, ed., *Believing Scholars: Ten Catholic Intellectuals* (New York: Fordham University Press, 2005) or Glendon, "The Influence of Catholic Social Doctrine on Human Rights," in Roland Minnerath, Ombretta Fumagalli Carulli, and Vittorio Possenti, eds., *Catholic Social Doctrine and Human Rights* (Vatican City: Pontifical Academy of Social Sciences, 2010), 67–82.

19 Philip Nord, *France's New Deal: From the Thirties to the Postwar Era* (Princeton, NJ: Princeton University Press, 2010), 12–13. With a similar periodization as mine, see Étienne Fouilloux, *Les chrétiens français entre crise et libération 1937–1947* (Paris: Seuil, 1997).

20 Martin Conway, "The Rise and Fall of Western Europe's Democratic Age, 1945–1973," *Contemporary European History* 13, no. 1 (February 2004): 67–88; Wolfram Kaiser, *Christian Democracy and the Origins of the European Union* (Cambridge, UK: Cambridge University Press, 2007).

21 As for the pope himself, Christian Democratic parties were initially threatening, and he permanently kept some distance from them even in staunch support of the Cold War West; see Robert A. Ventresca, *Soldier of Christ: The Life of Pope Pius XII* (Cambridge, MA: Harvard University Press, 2013), 244–49.

22 John Rawls, *A Brief Inquiry into the Meaning of Sin and Faith*, ed. Thomas Nagel (Cambridge, MA: Harvard University Press, 2009), 128.

23 For bitter interconfessional tension in the Nazi era, in spite of common ideological and enacted anti-Semitism, see Doris L. Bergen, "Catholics, Protestantism, and Christian Antisemitism in Nazi Germany," *Central European History* 27, no. 3 (September 1994): 329–48. On German Christian Democracy, the leading study is Maria Mitchell, *The Origins of Christian Democracy: Politics and Confession in Modern Germany* (Ann Arbor: University of Michigan Press, 2012).

24 See Geoff Eley, "When Europe Was New: Liberation and the Making of the Postwar," in Monica Riera and Gavin Schaffer, eds., *The Lasting War: Society and Identity in Britain, France and Germany after 1945* (Houndmills, UK: Palgrave, 2008), 17–43. The *Stunde Null* theme is now standard in popular accounts such as Ian Buruma, *Zero Hour: A History of 1945* (New York: Penguin, 2013).

25 According to the encyclical, "The public authority of the world community must likewise have as its special aim the recognition, respect, safeguarding and promotion of the rights of the human person. . . . A clear proof of the farsightedness of [the United Nations] is provided by the Universal Declaration of Human Rights." John XXIII, *Peace on Earth (Pacem in Terris)* (Washington, DC: USCCB Publishing, 2003), 57.

26 See Daniele Menozzi, "Una dichiarazione cattolica dei diritti umani?: Un dibattito all'indomani della seconda guerra mondiale," in

Annette Becker, Frédéric Gugelot, Denis Pelletier, and Nathalie Viet-Depaule, eds., *Écrire l'histoire du christianisme contemporain: Autour de l'œuvre d'Étienne Fouilloux* (Paris: Karthala, 2013).

27 See Moyn, *The Last Utopia*, esp. 144–46, 166–67, which gives full attention to the participation of Christians in general and Catholics in particular in the coalitional projects that gave birth to contemporary human rights politics, notably in several Latin American states. On the World Council of Churches and human rights in the postwar era, see, for example, Christian Albers, "Der ÖRK und die Menschenrechte im Kontext von Kaltem Krieg und Dekolonisierung," in Katharina Kunter and Annegreth Schilling, eds., *Globalisierung der Kirchen: Der Ökumenische Rat der Kirchen und die Entdeckung der Dritten Welt in den 1960er und 1970er Jahren* (Göttingen: Vandenhoeck und Ruprecht, 2014). Some good early surveys before the deluge that usefully register how controversial human rights were include Arlene Swidler, ed., *Human Rights in Religious Traditions* (New York: Pilgrim Press, 1982) and Robert Traer, *Faith in Human Rights: Support in Religious Traditions for a Global Struggle* (Washington, DC: Georgetown University Press, 1991).

28 See, for example, Randall Ballmer, *Redeemer: The Life of Jimmy Carter* (New York: Basic Books, 2014), chap. 8.

29 Christopher Clark and Wolfram Kaiser, eds., *Culture Wars: Secular-Catholic Conflict in Nineteenth-Century Europe* (Cambridge, UK: Cambridge University Press, 2009).

30 For a more favorable view of Cold War liberalism, see Jan-Werner Mueller, *Furcht und Freiheit: Ein anderer Liberalismus* (Frankfurt: Suhrkamp, 2015). See also Stathis Gourgouris, *Lessons in Secular Criticism* (New York: Fordham University Press, 2015).

Chapter 1

1 To take one of sundry examples of this conventional wisdom, Thomas Howard writes: "In 1949, with the Holocaust and the Nuremberg trials fresh in mind, the drafters of the new West German constitution, or *Grundgesetz*, included in its opening article the statement that 'the dignity of man is inviolable.'" Thomas A. Howard, *Imago Dei:*

Human Dignity in Ecumenical Perspective (Washington, DC: Catholic University Press, 2013), 1.

2 Samuel Moyn, *The Last Utopia: Human Rights in History* (Cambridge, MA: Harvard University Press, 2010).

3 The belated discovery of dignity on the historically long antecedent ground of rights is attractively taken as a significant problem in Jürgen Habermas, "The Concept of Human Dignity and the Realistic Utopia of Human Rights," in *The Crisis of the European Union: A Response*, trans. Ciaran Cronin (Cambridge, UK: Polity Press, 2012), 71–101. (I reject his solution: to claim it must have been there implicitly all along.)

4 For a vivid portrait in his cohort, see Dzovinar Kévonian, "Les juristes juifs russes en France et l'action internationale dans les années vingt," *Archives juives* 34, no. 2 (2001–2): 72–94. For his legal thought, see Stéphane Pinon, "Les idées constitutionelles de Boris Mirkine-Guetzévitch," in Carlos Miguel Herrera, ed., *Les juristes face au politique: Le droit, la gauche, la doctrine sous la Troisième République*, 2 vols. (Paris: Kimé, 2005), 2:61–123.

5 Boris Mirkine-Guetzévitch, *Les constitutions de l'Europe nouvelle* (Paris: Delagrave, 1928, 1930, 1938) and *Les Constitutions européennes*, 2 vols. (Paris: Presses universitaires de France, 1951). See also his most important theoretical works, *Les nouvelles tendances du Droit constitutionnel* (Paris: Librairie générale de droit et de jurisprudence, 1933, 1936) and *Droit constitutionnel international* (Paris: Sirey, 1933), esp. chap. 6, §2 on international human rights.

6 Mirkine-Guetzévitch and Alphonse Aulard, *Les Déclarations des droits de l'homme: Textes constitutionnels concernant les droits de l'homme et les garanties des libertés individuelles dans tous les pays* (Paris: Payot, 1929); Mirkine-Guetzévitch, *Les nouvelles tendances*, chap. 3. After first making himself Paris's expert in Soviet law, Mirkine-Guetzévitch became a scholar of the French Revolution under the tutelage of the famous historian Aulard, linking it with his work in comparative and international constitutionalism. See Mirkine-Guetzévitch, "L'influence de la Révolution française sur le développement du Droit international dans l'Europe orientale," *Recueil des cours de l'Académie de la Haye* 22 (1928): 295–458.

7 On the Resistance, see Mirkine-Guetzévitch, *Les Constitutions européennes*, chap. 4 and, with Henri Michel, *Les idées politiques et*

sociales de la Résistance (Paris: Presses universitaires de France, 1954). On rights after World War II, see Mirkine-Guetzévitch, *Les Constitutions européennes*, chap. 8. His immediate postwar writings on international human rights are "La protection internationale des droits de l'homme," *Revue politique et parlementaire* (October 1946); "La défense des Droits de l'homme et la Charte des Nations unies," in *La Bataille de la paix: Les chances du féderalisme* (Paris: Editions du Monde nouveau, 1947); and "L'O.N.U. et la doctrine moderne des droits de l'homme," *Revue générale de droit international public* 55 (April–June 1951): 161–98. At the behest of Henri Laugier, he also provided the United Nations's nuclear commission on human rights, charged with drafting the Universal Declaration, with his expertise, editing the first *Annuaire des droits de l'homme* (Lake Success, NY: United Nations, 1946); see René Cassin, "Souvenirs sur B. Mirkine-Guetzévitch," in *Hommage à B. Mirkine-Guetzévitch, 1892–1955* (New York: École libre des hautes études, 1955), 31.

8 See Michel Rosenfeld and András Sajó, eds., *Oxford Handbook of Comparative Constitutional Law* (New York: Oxford University Press, 2012), though the editors do acknowledge that the field "became established as a separate scholarly discipline thanks to the scholarship of Boris Mirkine-Guetzévitch" (5).

9 Ran Hirschl, *Constitutional Theocracy* (Cambridge, MA: Harvard University Press, 2010).

10 Mirkine-Guetzévitch, *Les Constitutions européennes*, 42. See also Mirkine-Guetzévitch, "La constitution espagnole de 1931," *Revue d'histoire politique et constitutionnelle* (1938): 258–64.

11 Samuel Moyn, "Silence and the Shoah," *Times Literary Supplement*, August 7, 2013.

12 See James Q. Whitman, "'Human Dignity' in Europe and the United States: The Social Foundations," *Human Rights Law Journal* 25, no. 1 (April 2004): 17–23; and, on Whitman's themes, see the various essays culminating in Jeremy Waldron, *Dignity, Rank, and Rights*, ed. Meir Dan-Cohen (New York: Oxford University Press, 2012). For further remarks on Whitman's historical claims, see note 59.

13 The most important of these is a subsidiary article in the Mexican Constitution of 1917 that already shows the importance of Catholic social thought. For a valuable survey of different uses of human dignity in chiefly philosophical sources, see Michael Rosen, *Dignity: Its History and Meaning* (Cambridge, MA: Harvard University Press,

2012); but it dwells neither on precisely when various meanings were culturally, politically, or legally salient nor on why the competition between different conceptions went in one direction or another over modern history.

14 For the best survey on these years, see Tom Buchanan and Martin Conway, eds., *Political Catholicism in Europe, 1918–1965* (Oxford: Oxford University Press, 1996).

15 Mirkine-Guetzévitch, "Le néo-absolutisme corporatif (Autriche et Portugal)," *L'Année politique et économique*, October 1934, 251–72.

16 See *Fundamental Laws of the State: The Spanish Constitution* (Madrid: S[ervicio] I[nformativo] E[spañol], 1967).

17 See James Chappel, "Slaying the Leviathan: Catholicism and the Rebirth of European Conservatism, 1920–1950" (PhD diss., Columbia University, 2012).

18 Michael Oakeshott, ed., *The Social and Political Doctrines of Contemporary Europe* (New York: Macmillan, 1939).

19 Joseph Vialatoux, "Dignité du groupe? Ou de la personne humaine?: Physique et métaphysique de l'ordre des valeurs," in *La Personne humaine en péril* (Lyon: Chronique Sociale de France, 1937). On Vialatoux, see Emmanuel Gabelieri, "Catholicisme social et 'métaphysique en action': La pensée de J. Vialatoux," *Théophilyon* 10, no. 1 (January 2005): 9–43.

20 Vialatoux, "Dignité," 123, 132–33.

21 On the encyclical in the larger context of the Church's anticommunist politics, see Giuliana Chamedes, "The Vatican and the Making of the Atlantic Order, 1920–1960" (PhD diss., Columbia University, 2013), chap. 6.

22 See Dermot Keogh and Andrew J. McCarthy, *The Making of the Irish Constitution 1937: Bunreacht na hÉireann* (Cork: Mercier Press, 1997), striking for its inattention to the preamble generally. See also V. T. H. Delaney, "The Constitution of Ireland: Its Origins and Development," *University of Toronto Law Journal* 12, no. 1 (1957–58): 1–26.

23 Fearghal McGarry, *Irish Politics and the Spanish Civil War* (Cork: Cork University Press, 1999), esp. chap. 4.

24 Leo Kohn, *The Constitution of the Irish Free State* (London: Allen and Unwin, 1932); for de Valera's views, see Ronan Fanning, "Mr. De Valera Drafts a Constitution," in Brian Farrell, ed., *De Valera's Constitution and Ours* (Dublin: Gill and Macmillan, 1988), 34.

25 Perry Anderson, "After Nehru," *London Review of Books*, August 2, 2012.

26 Dermot Keogh, "Church, State, and Society," in Farrell, ed., *De Valera's Constitution*, 104.

27 Oakeshott, *Social and Political Doctrines*, 72–77.

28 Noel Browne, "Church and State in Modern Ireland," in Tim Murphy and Patrick Twomey, eds., *Ireland's Evolving Constitution, 1937–97: Collected Essays* (Oxford: Oxford University Press, 1998), 46–47.

29 This paragraph relies on Maria Luddy, "A 'Sinister and Retrogressive' Proposal: Irish Women's Opposition to the 1937 Draft Constitution," *Transactions of the Royal Historical Society* 15 (December 2005): 175–95. We are not far here from the Universal Declaration of Human Rights, Art. 16(3): "The family is the natural and fundamental group unit of society and is entitled to protection by society and the State." It is true that Ireland never took up the fully maternalist turn of other places where Catholic social thought was enacted as authoritarian policy in the era. For comparison's sake, see Francine Muel-Dreyfus, *Vichy and the Eternal Feminine: A Contribution to the Political Sociology of Gender*, trans. Kathleen A. Johnson (Durham, NC: Duke University Press, 2001), esp. part 3. For how de Valera and others squared these views with the immediately preceding provision (Art. 40(1)) on equality, with its allusion to equality of "human persons" drawn from contemporary Catholic social thought, see Oran Doyle, *Constitutional Equality Law* (Dublin: Thomson Roundhall, 2004), esp. 56–60.

30 I rely largely here on the new archival compilation, Gerard Hogan, ed., *The Origins of the Irish Constitution 1928–1941* (Dublin: Royal Irish Academy, 2012), along with the Royal Irish Academy website at http://www.ria.ie/research/oic.aspx for further documents.

31 For the original absence and later rise in enforceability of preambular language, see Teresa Iglesias, "The Dignity of the Individual in the Irish Constitution: The Importance of the Preamble," *Studies* 89, no. 353 (Spring 2000): 19–34.

32 Hogan, *The Origins*, 247 (Document 58, October 18, 1936).

33 For his views in the early 1930s, which occasionally referenced dignity, see Edward Cahill, *The Framework of a Christian State: An Introduction to Social Science* (Dublin, 1932), 278–82, 288, 455–56, as well as the translation by Dennis Fahey of Blackrock College of Auguste Philippe, *The Social Rights of Our Divine Lord Jesus Christ, the King*

(Dublin: M. H. Gill and Son, 1932), both highly critical of "liberalism" in the name of Catholic politics. See also Seán Faughnan, "The Jesuits and the Drafting of the Irish Constitution of 1937," *Irish Historical Studies* 26, no. 101 (May 1988): 79–102.

34 The *Press* was also the paper closest to de Valera's Fianna Fáil, covering the encyclical on its front page: "Deceived into Aiding Communism—These Will Be Its First Victims, Says the Supreme Pontiff," *Irish Press*, March 19, 1937; see also "Holy Father Denounces Communism," *Irish Independent*, March 19, 1937, and "Communism Assailed," *Irish Times*, March 19, 1937.

35 John Cooney, *John Charles McQuaid: Ruler of Catholic Ireland* (Syracuse, NY: Syracuse University Press, 2000), chap. 8, which overstates McQuaid's role generally but rightly gives him special importance with respect to the preamble (96–97). McQuaid also gave de Valera a copy (which he read) of the summary of Catholic social teaching originating from the neo-Scholastic circles around Belgian Cardinal Désiré-Joseph Mercier, which invokes "the eminent dignity of the human person," but this appears to have occurred somewhat earlier, so the preambular changes seem to me best explained by the timing and prominence of the encyclical. See Union internationale d'études sociales, *Le code social: Esquisse d'une synthèse sociale catholique* (Paris: Editions Spes, 1927, 1934), 30; cf. Frank Longford and Thomas O'Neill, *Eamon de Valera* (Boston: Houghton Mifflin, 1971), 296.

36 Hogan, *Origins*, 449 (Document 123, April 3, 1937).

37 Ibid., 462 (Document 135, April 11, 1937).

38 No anti-Semite, unlike a great many Catholics at the time, de Valera was in fact on exceptionally friendly terms with Ireland's chief rabbi through 1936, Isaac Herzog, who once sheltered the future statesman when he was being pursued by authorities as a terrorist. Herzog, who then became the chief rabbi of Palestine (and later Israel), so admired de Valera's religious nationalism—including his 1937 constitution—that he often cited both as potential models for Jews in the face of a then-dominant secular nationalism. See Shulamit Eliash, *The Harp and the Shield of David: Ireland, Zionism and the State of Israel* (New York: Routledge, 2007), 49–70; Dermot Keogh, *Jews in Twentieth-Century Ireland: Refugees, Antisemitism, and the Holocaust* (Cork: Cork University Press, 1998), 77, 110; and, for the latest word on the startling contiguity of Catholicism and racism in the era, John Connelly, *From*

Enemy to Brother: The Revolution in Catholic Teaching on the Jews, 1933–1965 (Cambridge, MA: Harvard University Press, 2012), esp. chaps. 1–3.

39 Hogan, *Origins*, 506 (Document 155, April 22, 1937).

40 *Irish Press*, May 17, 1937, as cited in Dermot Keogh, *The Vatican, the Bishops, and Irish Politics 1919–1939* (Cambridge, UK: Cambridge University Press, 1986), 219.

41 Cf. Arthur W. and Mary C. Bromage, "The Irish Constitution: A Discussion of Its Theoretical Aspects," *Review of Politics* 2, no. 2 (April 1940): 145–66. On natural law, consider Vincent Grogan, "The Constitution and the Natural Law," *Christus Rex* 8 (1954): 201–18; Declan Costello, "The Natural Law and the Irish Constitution," *Studies* 45, no. 180 (Winter 1956): 403–14; and John Maurice Kelly, *Fundamental Rights in the Irish Law and Constitution* (Dublin: Figgis and Co., 1961), esp. 38–45.

42 Jean Fernet, *Aux côtés du maréchal Pétain: Souvenirs (1940–1944)* (Paris: Plon, 1953), 216.

43 Michèle Cointet, *Le conseil national de Vichy: Vie politique et réforme de l'État en régime autoritaire* (Paris: Amateur de livres, 1989), 137–56, citations at 137, 142.

44 Ibid, 412–13; see also Etienne Le Floch, "Les projets de constitution de Vichy (1940–1944)" (PhD diss., University of Paris, 2003), 67–70 (personalism), 101–2 (the Portuguese model).

45 Cointet, *Le conseil*, 301–6, 324–27.

46 Fernet, *Aux côtés*, 219–20. A recent survey of French constitutions notes: "It is amazing to register that, during the very period during which the laws of the French state organized a profound discrimination against people of Jewish origins . . . , the constitutional draft began by a declaration of rights, made up of twelve articles that are perfectly democratic in their inspiration, at least on paper." Michel de Guillenschmidt, *Histoire constitutionnelle de la France depuis 1789* (Paris: Economica, 2000), 102.

47 "Projet de constitution de la République française" (30 janvier 1944), rpt. in Fernet, *Aux côtés*, 287.

48 Robert O. Paxton, *Vichy France: Old Guard and New Order, 1940–1944* (New York: Knopf, 1972), 193n119.

49 Xavier Vallat, "La Constitution voulue par le Maréchal," *Écrits de Paris* 128 (June 1955): 53.

50 See Daniele Lorenzini, *Jacques Maritain e i diritti umani: Fra totalitarismo, antisemitismo, e democrazia (1936–1951)* (Brescia:

Morcelliana, 2012). Incidentally, in wartime exile, Maritain and Mirkine-Guetzévitch became friends in New York City, and the former even claimed at the latter's memorial to have sponsored his conversion. See Maritain, "Ceux qui nous consolent d'appartenir à la race humaine," in *Hommage à B. Mirkine-Guetzévitch*, 99.

51 "Pope Bids Church to Guard Man's Rights," *New York Times*, October 13, 1938.

52 See "Lettre de S. Ém. le Cardinal Pacelli," in *La Personne humaine en péril*, which has a section on the "Natural Dignity of the Person."

53 The story of the French Catholic Resistance and its sudden talk of human rights is told in Renée Bédarida, "Dans la tourmente 1940–1944: Des droits de la personne aux droits de l'homme," in Pierre Colin, ed., *Les catholiques français et l'héritage de 1789* (Paris: Beauchesne, 1989), esp. 206–10. As Bédarida notes, the concrete difficulty for Catholics in the Resistance was working together with the dominant communists whom "human dignity" had meant condemning shortly before.

54 Cited in Patrick McNamara, *A Catholic Cold War: Edmund A. Walsh, S.J., and the Politics of American Anticommunism* (New York: Fordham University Press, 2005), 114.

55 "Basic Principles of Reconstruction" (August 9, 1943), in Peter Hoffmann, ed., *Behind Valkyrie: German Resistance to Hitler (Documents)* (Montreal: McGill-Queen's University Press, 2011), 76–77.

56 Jacques Maritain, "Christian Humanism," *Fortune*, April 1942.

57 Pius XII, "True and False Democracy," in Vincent Yzermans, ed., *Major Addresses*, 2 vols. (St. Paul, MN: North Central Publishing, 1961), 2:88. Pius XII's further comment that "democracy, taken in the broad sense, admits of various forms, and can be realized in monarchies as well as in republics" (80) might suggest a somewhat idiosyncratic understanding of the term, except that political theorists like Maritain agreed that what made a regime democratic was not formal structure but whether the natural law was respected and the common good achieved through it.

58 For the best general account, see Martin Conway, "Democracy in Postwar Western Europe: The Triumph of a Political Model," *European History Quarterly* 32, no. 1 (January 2002), 59–84; see also Jan-Werner Mueller, *Contesting Democracy: Political Ideas in Twentieth-Century Europe* (New Haven, CT: Yale University Press, 2011), chap. 4.

59 The continuity or "transwar" thesis I offer is thus radically different from Whitman's proposal that Nazi concern with honor flowed into post–World War II appeals to human dignity. Allowing a more plausible view about long-term social trends in status to explain specific events and short-term political and legal phenomena it does not fit, Whitman also neglects the rather important fact that the Nazis had no actual discourse of human dignity, where transnational Christians did, and massively so, across the same era. Whitman, "On Nazi 'Honour' and the New European 'Dignity,'" as well as Gerald Neuman's brief rejoinder, "On Fascist Honour and European Dignity: A Sceptical Response," both in Christian Joerges and Navraj Singh Ghaleigh, eds., *Darker Legacies of Law in Europe: The Shadow of National Socialism over Europe and Its Legal Traditions* (Oxford: Hart Publishing, 2003).

60 Charles R. Beitz, "Human Dignity in the Theory of Human Rights: Nothing but a Phrase?," *Philosophy and Public Affairs* 41, no. 3 (Summer 2013): 259–90 at 266; see earlier and very sketchily Christopher McCrudden, "Dignity and the Judicial Interpretation of Rights," *European Journal of International Law* 19, no. 4 (September 2008): 655–724 at 675–78. For further information on Gildersleeve's edit, see my post, "Why Is Dignity in the Charter of the United Nations?," *Humanity* (blog), http://bit.ly/1DEs1Tl. For documentation of Gildersleeve's deep-seated anti-Semitism, defeating initial intuitions about why she might have thought it important to add dignity at the end of World War II, see Stephen H. Norwood, *The Third Reich in the Ivory Tower: Complicity and Conflict on American Campuses* (Cambridge, UK: Cambridge University Press, 2009), 104–5, 130, 236.

61 Beitz, "Human Dignity," 266–67.

62 Carlos P. Romulo, "On Natural Law and International Law," *Virginia Law Review* 35, no. 8 (December 1949): 1053.

63 Verfassung des Freistaates Bayern, December 2, 1946. On Hundhammer's role, and his participation in then-dominant religious appeals to natural law, see Oliver Braun, *Konservatives Existenz in der Moderne: Das politische Weltbild Alois Hundhammers, 1900–1974* (Munich: Hanns-Seidel-Stiftung, 2006), 282–310, 318–20.

64 Notably in the recently decided European Court of Human Rights case of *Lautsi v. Italy* (2011), which deemed state-mandated crucifixes in public school classrooms not in violation of the right to freedom of conscience. See chapter 4.

65 Verfassung des Landes Hessen (December 1, 1946), Art. 3: "Life and health, honor and the dignity of man are inviolable."

66 On the origins of the Grundgesetz provision, see Christoph Goos, *"Innere Freiheit": Eine Rekonstruktion des grundgesetzlichen Würdebegriffs* (Göttingen: Vandenhoeck und Ruprecht, 2011); for a more general picture of the impact of Catholicism on constitutional origins, see Burkhard von Schewick, *Die katholische Kirche und die Entstehung der Verfassungen in Westdeutschland 1945–1950* (Mainz: Matthias-Grunewald-Verlag, 1980). Constitutional documents in Berlin, Hamburg, Lower Saxony, and Schleswig-Holstein all provide examples of drafting by socialist majorities with no reference to dignity. See generally Michaela Hailbronner, *Tradition and Transformation: The Rise of German Constitutionalism* (New York: Oxford University Press, 2015) for a critique of supposing early developments determined the meaning (and therefore global radiance) of West German constitutionalism decades later.

67 Some constitutional proposals of the Resistance also insisted on the need to move beyond nineteenth-century liberalism for the sake of "humanism." As one put it, "The revolution of the 18th century was individualist. That of the 20th century was fated to be totalitarian. We want a humanist revolution. . . . People today want to be free, but also governed." "Projet de constitution (janvier 1944)," in Michel and Mirkine-Guetzévitch, *Les Idées politiques*, 302–3.

68 République française, Constitution du 27 octobre 1946, Préambule. For the MRP's role, see Andrew Shennan, *Rethinking France: Plans for Renewal, 1940–1946* (New York: Oxford University Press, 1989), chaps. 4–5. Compare Stéphanie Hennette-Vauchez, "Human Dignity in French Law," in Roger Brownsword and Dietmar Mieth, eds., *Cambridge Handbook of Human Dignity* (Cambridge, UK: Cambridge University Press, 2014). Also worth a look, though a more complicated case, is the South Korean constitution of 1948, in which dignity figures too.

69 Cited in William Inboden, *Religion and American Foreign Policy, 1945–1960: The Soul of Containment* (Cambridge, UK: Cambridge University Press, 2010), 109, whose discussion offers wide-ranging evidence of human dignity in American Cold War discourse.

70 Mirkine-Guetzévitch, *Les constitutions de l'Europe nouvelle*, 1938 ed., esp. 49–54.

71 Dermot Keogh, *Ireland and Europe, 1919–1948* (Dublin: Rowman and Littlefield, 1988).

72 For the Irish case, see Whyte, *Church and State in Modern Ireland, 1923–1970* (Dublin: Gill and Macmillan, 1971), chap. 11. For Catholicism in the early years of the Basic Law, see Hans Maier, "Katholische Sozial- und Staatslehre und neuere deutsche Staatslehre," *Archiv des öffentlichen Rechts* 93, no. 1 (1968): 1–36, and esp. Frieder Günther, *Denken vom Staat her: Die bundesdeutsche Staatsrechtslehre zwischen Dezision und Integration 1949–1970* (Munich: Oldenbourg, 2004).

73 For a good place to start on this problem, see Oliver Sensen, "Human Dignity in Historical Perspective: The Contemporary and Traditional Paradigms," *European Journal of Political Theory* 10, no. 1 (January 2011): 71–91.

74 For judicial interpretation, see Teresa Iglesias, "The Dignity of the Individual," and especially William Binchy, "Dignity as a Constitutional Concept," in Eoin Carolan and Oran Doyle, eds., *The Irish Constitution: Governance and Values* (Dublin: Round Hall, 2008).

75 Before recently, more generally, the main thinkers of note to explore (let alone advocate) dignity were conservatives. See Aurel Kolnai, "Dignity," *Philosophy* 51, no. 197 (July 1976): 251–71; Robert Spaemann, "Über den Begriff der Menschenwürde," in Ernst-Wolfgang Böckenförde and Robert Spaemann, eds., *Menschenrechte und Menschenwürde: Historische Voraussetzungen, säkulare Gestalt, christliches Verständnis* (Stuttgart: Klett Cotta, 1987); Hans-Georg Gadamer, "Die Menschenwürde auf ihrem Weg von der Antike bis heute," *Humanistische Bildung* 12 (1988): 95–107. Cf. Herbert Spiegelberg's subtle "Human Dignity: A Challenge to Contemporary Philosophy," *World Futures* 9, no. 1–2 (March 1971): 39–64.

76 See, aside from already cited sources, Ronald Dworkin, *Justice for Hedgehogs* (Cambridge, MA: Harvard University Press, 2011); George Kateb, *Human Dignity* (Cambridge, MA: Harvard University Press, 2011); and, most stylishly, Avishai Margalit, *The Decent Society* (Cambridge, MA: Harvard University Press, 1996) and "Human Dignity between Kitsch and Deification," *Hedgehog Review* 9, no. 3 (Fall 2007): 7–19.

77 See Myres S. McDougal, "Perspectives for an International Law of Human Dignity," *Proceedings of the American Society of International Law* 53 (April 1959): 107–36; and esp. Alfred Verdross, "Die Würde des Menschen in der abendländischen Rechtsphilosophie," in Joseph Höffner, Alfred Verdross, and Francisco Vito, eds., *Naturordnung in*

Gesellschaft, Staat, Wirtschaft: Festschrift für Johannes Messner (Innsbruck: Tyrolia-Verlag, 1961); Verdross, "Die Würde des Menschen als Grundlage der Menschenrechte," in *René Cassin: Amicorum Discipulorumque Liber*, 4 vols. (Paris: A. Pédone, 1969); and Verdross, *Die Würde des Menschen und ihr völkerrechtlicher Schutz* (Vienna: Niederösterreichische Pressehaus, 1975). For how Verdross overlooked the differences between his Christian nationalism and National Socialism in 1938, see Anthony Carty, "Alfred Verdross and Othmar Spann: German Romantic Nationalism, National Socialism and International Law," *European Journal of International Law* 6, no. 1 (1995): 78–97.

78 The exploding literature is too vast to cite. Louis Henkin did not yet mention Kant or dignity in *The Rights of Man Today* (Boulder: Westview Press, 1978); the next year, his partner Alice Henkin edited a volume of Aspen Institute proceedings titled *Human Dignity: The Internationalization of Human Rights* (New York: Oceana Publications, 1979) but no contributors mentioned dignity (or invoked Kant, except Judge Charles Wyzanski Jr., who dismissed him as a statist proponent of positive liberty [13]). Just a few years later, see Oscar Schachter's pioneering "Human Dignity as a Normative Concept," *American Journal of International Law* 77, no. 4 (October 1983): 848–54. Most recently, with generally faulty senses of dignity's origins, see Erin Daly, *Dignity Rights: Courts, Constitutions, and the Worth of the Human Person* (Philadelphia: University of Pennsylvania Press, 2012); Christopher McCrudden, ed., *Understanding Human Dignity* (New York: Oxford University Press, 2013); and Aharon Barak, *Human Dignity: The Constitutional Value and the Constitutional Right* (Cambridge, UK: Cambridge University Press, 2015).

Chapter 2

1 On the Institute from its nineteenth-century origins through this period, see most notably Martti Koskenniemi, *The Gentle Civilizer of Nations: The Rise and Fall of International Law* (Cambridge, UK: Cambridge University Press, 2002).

2 Cf. Elizabeth Borgwardt, *A New Deal for the World: America's Vision for Human Rights* (Cambridge, MA: Harvard University Press, 2005).

3 "Les droits fondamentaux de l'homme, base d'une restauration du droit international," *Annuaire de l'Institut de droit international* 41 (1947): 1–13 (travaux préparatoires by Charles de Visscher), 142–90 (discussion), 258–60 (declaration), 153–54 (citation). For the text of the declaration in English, see "Fundamental Rights of Man, as the Basis of a Restoration of International Law," *International Law Quarterly* 2, no. 2 (Summer 1948): 231–32. On de Visscher, see François Rigaux, "An Exemplary Lawyer's Life (1884–1973)," *European Journal of International Law* 11, no. 4 (April 2000): 877–86.

4 See John Hellman, *The Communitarian Third Way: Alexandre Marc's Ordre Nouveau, 1930–2000* (Montreal: McGill-Queen's University Press, 2002).

5 Jan Olof Bengtsson, *The Worldview of Personalism: Origins and Early Development* (New York: Oxford University Press, 2006).

6 On his Parisian period, see Olivier Clément, *Berdiaev: Un philosophe russe en France* (Paris: Desclée de Brouwer, 1991) and Antoine Arjakovsky, *La génération des penseurs religieux de l'émigration russe* (Paris: L'Esprit et la lettre, 2002). On the larger tradition of Russian personalism, see George L. Kline, "Changing Attitudes toward the Individual," in Cyril Black, ed., *The Transformation of Russian Society* (Cambridge, MA: Harvard University Press, 1960).

7 On Scheler's personalism, see Stephen Schneck, *Person and Polis: Max Scheler's Personalism as Political Theory* (Albany: State University of New York Press, 1987), as well as Michael Gubser, *The Far Reaches: Phenomenology, Ethics, and Social Renewal in Central Europe* (Stanford, CA: Stanford University Press, 2014), which offers a picture of phenomenological personalism with many later ramifications in Eastern Europe. Another Jewish convert to Catholicism named Paul-Ludwig Landsberg was Scheler's chief promoter in France and Belgium. See Paul-Louis Landsberg, "Quelques réflexions sur l'idée chrétienne de la personne," *Esprit* (December 1934), rpt. in Landsberg, *Problèmes du personnalisme* (Paris: Éditions du Seuil, 1952).

8 Maritain, *The Person and the Common Good*, trans. John J. Fitzgerald (New York: Scribner, 1947), 13.

9 Cited in Nicolas Kessler, *Histoire politique de la Jeune Droite (1929–1942): Une révolution conservatrice à la française* (Paris: L'Harmattan, 2001), 208; cf. 230–33, 242–49 for more reactionary personalism.

10 On the general scene, the classic is Jean Louis Loubet del Bayle, *Les Non-conformistes des années trente: une tentative de renouvellement de la pensée politique française* (Paris: Éditions du Seuil, 1969). The allegation that these circles were basically fascistic is most familiar from the controversial works of Zeev Sternhell. Zeev Sternhell, *Neither Right nor Left: Fascist Ideology in France*, trans. David Maisel (Berkeley: University of California Press, 1986). For the best overview, see Robert O. Paxton, "The Church, the Republic, and the Fascist Temptation," in Richard J. Wolff and Jörg K. Hoensch, eds., *Catholics, the State, and the European Radical Right, 1919–1945* (Boulder, CO: Social Science Monographs, 1986). See also W. D. Halls, *Politics, Society, and Christianity in Vichy France* (Oxford: Berg, 1995).

11 Bukharin cited in Jochen Hellbeck, *Revolution on My Mind: Writing a Diary under Stalin* (Cambridge, MA: Harvard University Press, 2006), 31. See also Kline, "Changing Attitudes," 624, on the revival of nineteenth-century Russian personalism in this 1930s moment.

12 Emmanuel Mounier, *A Personalist Manifesto*, trans. Monks of St. John's Abbey (New York: Longmans, Green, 1938), 17–18.

13 The texts are most conveniently available in René Rémond, *Les crises du catholicisme en France dans les années trente* (Paris: Seuil, 1996), appendix.

14 Maritain, *Trois réformateurs: Luther—Descartes—Rousseau* (Paris: Plon Nourrit, 1925); in English, *Three Reformers: Luther—Descartes—Rousseau* (New York: Scribner, 1955). Simon to Maritain, September 3, 1941, Yves R. Simon Institute, Mishawaka, Indiana. He continued: "Last winter, our seniors had a debate on the question of whether Thomistic personalism is the true internationalism. As a joke it was proclaimed that all that is idiotic is due to individualism, while all that is beautiful stems from personalism."

15 These claims are contentious in the literature, but there is no space to defend them here.

16 See Sandra Teroni and Wolfgang Klein, eds., *Pour la défense de la culture: les textes du Congrès international des écrivains, Paris 1935* (Dijon: Éditions universitaires de Dijon, 2005).

17 This section summarizes the more detailed analysis in Samuel Moyn, "Jacques Maritain: le origini dei Diritti umani e il pensiero politico cristiano," in Luigi Bonanante and Roberto Papini, eds., *Il dialogo interculturale e diritti umani* (Bologna: Il Mulino, 2008), in English as

"Jacques Maritain, Christian Politics, and the Birth of Human Rights," in Luigi Bonanante, Roberto Papini, and William Sweet, eds., *Intercultural Dialogue and Human Rights* (Washington, DC: Council for Research in Values and Philosophy, 2011), since superseded by Daniele Lorenzini, *Jacques Maritain e i diritti umani: Fra totalitarismo, antisemitismo, e democrazia (1936–1951)* (Brescia: Morcelliana, 2012).

18 J. Bryan Hehir, "Religious Activism for Human Rights: A Christian Case Study," in John Witte Jr. and Johan D. van der Vyver, eds., *Religious Human Rights in Global Perspective: Religious Perspectives* (The Hague: Martinus Nijhoff Publishers, 1996), 101.

19 Cf. Emilio Gentile, *Politics as Religion*, trans. George Staunton (Princeton, NJ: Princeton University Press, 2006), 92–93 and chap. 4. On the popes and Mussolini, see David I. Kertzer, *The Pope and Mussolini: The Secret History of Pius XI and the Rise of Fascism in Europe* (New York: Random House, 2014).

20 Pius XI, Encyclical Letter "Mit brennender Sorge," March 14, 1937, as translated in Georges Passelecq and Bernard Suchecky, *The Hidden Encyclical of Pius XI*, trans. Steven Rendall (New York: Harcourt Brace, 1997), 105.

21 See Xavier de Montclos, "Le discours de Pie XI sur la défense des droits de la personne humaine," in *Achille Ratti, pape Pie XI* (Rome: École française de Rome, 1996), and esp. Fabrice Bouthillon, *La naissance de la Mardité: Une théologie politique à l'âge totalitaire, Pie XI (1922–1939)* (Strasbourg: Presses Universitaires de Strasbourg, 2001). Other works, such as Anthony Rhodes, *The Vatican in the Age of the Dictators* (London: Holt, Rinehart and Winston, 1973), provide helpful context.

22 "Lettre de S. Em. le Cardinal Pacelli," in *La Personne humaine en péril* (Lyon: Chronique Sociale de France, 1937), 5–8.

23 For a variety of contemporary commentaries on the novel surge of the human person after 1936 in statements by Pius XI and XII, see *The Foundations of International Order (Proceedings of the Catholic Congress on International Peace, The Hague, 1938)* (Oxford: Catholic Social Guild,1938); André Saint-Denis, *Pie XI contre les idoles: bolchévisme, racisme-étatisme* (Paris: Plon, 1939); or Lewis Watt, SJ, *Pope Pius XII on World Order* (Oxford: Catholic Social Guild, 1940), chap. 5, "The Dignity of the Human Person."

24 For a general picture of Pius's wartime positions, see Peter C. Kent, "Toward the Reconstitution of Christian Europe: The War Aims

Notes to pp. 76–80

of the Papacy, 1938–1945," in David B. Woolner and Richard B. Kurial, eds., *FDR, the Vatican, and the Roman Catholic Church in America, 1933–1945* (New York: Palgrave Macmillan, 2003).

25 Pius XII, "The Anniversary of Rerum Novarum," *Logos* 5, no. 4 (Fall 2002): 163. Note, however, that these pronouncements were explicitly restricted to the right to use material goods, as befit the occasion.

26 Paul A. Hanebrink, *In Defense of Christian Hungary: Religion, Nationalism, and Antisemitism, 1890–1944* (Ithaca, NY: Cornell University Press, 2006), 170–80; Piotr Kosicki, "Masters in Their Own Home or Defenders of the Human Person?: Wojciech Korfanty, Anti-semitism, and Polish Christian Decmoracy's Illiberal Rights Talk," *Modern Intellectual History*, forthcoming.

27 "Pope Bids Church to Guard Man's Rights," *New York Times*, October 13, 1938.

28 "Pastoral Letter [of the American Catholic Hierarchy] on the Teaching of Democracy," *New York Times*, November 25, 1938.

29 See now Charles Gallagher, SJ, "Promise Unfulfilled? A First Look at the Committee of Catholics for Human Rights," in Devin Pendas, ed., *Religion and Human Rights* (New York: Routledge, forthcoming).

30 See esp. A. W. Brian Simpson, *Human Rights and the End of Empire: Britain and the Genesis of the European Convention* (Oxford: Oxford University Press, 2001), chap. 4; Paul Gordon Lauren, *The Evolution of International Human Rights: Visions Seen*, 2nd ed. (Philadelphia: University of Pennsylvania Press, 2003), chap. 5.

31 Aloisius Muench, "One World in Charity" (1946), rpt. as Appendix C in Suzanne Brown-Fleming, *The Holocaust and the Catholic Conscience: Cardinal Aloisius Muench and the Guilt Question in Postwar Germany* (Notre Dame, IN: Notre Dame University Press, 2006), 154.

32 As, for example, the case of Bishop Klemens von Galen shows. See Beth A. Griech-Poelle, *Bishop von Galen: German Catholicism and National Socialism* (New Haven, CT: Yale University Press, 2002).

33 See the text of the issue in François and Renée Bédarida, eds., *La Résistance spirituelle 1941–1944: Les cahiers clandestins du "Témoignage chrétien"* (Paris: Albin Michel, 2001), 159–86.

34 See the excellent reconstruction by Florian Michel, "Jacques Maritain en Amérique du Nord," *Cahiers Jacques Maritain* 45 (December 2002): 26–86. Some of his earliest connections, in an atmosphere in which American Catholicism considered its own nonstate religiosity the

"hypothesis" in special circumstances rather than a "thesis" or general model, were with Dorothy Day and her Catholic Worker movement. See Mark and Louise Zwick, *The Catholic Worker Movement: Intellectual and Spiritual Origins* (New York: Paulist Press, 2005), chap. 10.

35 Maritain, *A Christian Looks at the Jewish Question* (New York, 1939), 34. Most of material cited here actually originated in another essay on the Jews of 1937 and was inserted in this English translation of a February 1938 Paris lecture for its December 1938 New York delivery. See Maritain, "L'impossible antisémitisme," in Henri Daniel-Rops, ed., *Les Juifs* (Paris: Plon, 1937) and "Les Juifs parmi les nations," *La Vie intellectuelle*, February 1938, both rpt. in Maritain, *L'impossible antisémitisme*, pref. Pierre Vidal-Naquet (Paris: Désclée de Brouwer, 1994), 97–98, 125.

36 "Warns America Sectarianism Is a World Menace: Rejuvenated Democracy Is Urged by Maritain," *Chicago Daily Tribune*, October 25, 1938.

37 Maritain, *Le Crépuscule de la civilisation* (Paris: Editions de l'Arbre, 1941), 78, in English, *The Twilight of Civilization*, trans. Lionel Landry (New York: Sheed and Ward, 1943), 54–55.

38 Cited in Hellman, *Emmanuel Mounier and the New Catholic Left, 1930–1950* (Toronto: University of Toronto Press, 1981), 168. For personalism—including fulsome invocation of Maritain's formulae—at Vichy, see Hellman's writings: "Maritain, Simon, and Vichy's Elite Schools," in Michael D. Torre, ed., *Freedom in the Modern World* (Notre Dame, IN: University of Notre Dame Press, 1989); "Communitarians, Non-conformists, and the Search for a 'New Man' in Vichy France," in Sarah Fishman, Laura Lee Downs, and Ioannis Sinanoglu, eds., *France at War: Vichy and the Historians* (Oxford: Berg, 2000); and *The Knight-Monks of Vichy France: Uriage, 1940–1945* (Montreal: McGill-Queen's University Press, 1994).

39 On this issue, see Hellman's excellent article, "The Anti-Democratic Impulse in Catholicism: Jacques Maritain, Yves Simon, and Charles de Gaulle during World War II," *Journal of Church and State* 33, no. 3 (Summer 1991): 453–71.

40 The earliest publications are "The Natural Law and Human Rights" (Windsor, Ontario, 1942), an award acceptance speech dated January 18, 1942, published as a pamphlet, and "Natural Law and Human Rights," *Dublin Review* 210 (April 1942): 116–24. The book is *Les*

droits de l'homme et la loi naturelle (New York: Éditions de la Maison française, 1942).

41 I cite the English version: Maritain, *The Rights of Man and Natural Law*, trans. Doris Anson (New York: Scribner, 1943), 65.

42 For radically contrasting stories on the origins of rights that nevertheless concur on this point, see Leo Strauss, *Natural Right and History* (Chicago: University of Chicago Press, 1953); Richard Tuck, *Natural Rights Theories: Their Origin and Development* (Cambridge, UK: Cambridge University Press, 1979); and Michel Villey, *Le droit et les droits de l'homme* (Paris: Presses Universitaires de France, 1983).

43 In 1943, Thomist Charles De Koninck published *De la primauté du bien commun contre les personnalistes* (Quebec: Editions de l'Université Laval, 1943) (the title explains the contents); compare here the revival of natural law by Heinrich A. Rommen, author of *Die ewige Wiederkehr des Naturrechts* (Leipzig: Hegner, 1936), an anti-Nazi Catholic who emigrated to the United States in 1938. There, he wrote his mammoth *The State in Catholic Thought* (St. Louis, MO: B. Herder, 1945), in which the concept of rights, though treated positively, is barely integrated and not allowed to compete with the more fundamental ones of natural law and common good (44, 58–59, 277–78, 377–78). However, a good number of his postwar manuscripts, held at Georgetown University where he became a professor, turn frontally to the topic. His study of natural law appears in English as *The Natural Law: A Study in Legal and Social History and Philosophy*, trans. Thomas Hanley (St. Louis, MO: B. Herder, 1947). For two postwar articles, see Rommen, "The Church and Human Rights," in Gurian and M. A. Fitzsimmons, eds., *The Catholic Church in World Affairs* (Notre Dame, IN: Notre Dame University Press, 1954) and "Vers l'internationalisation des droits de l'homme," *World Justice/Justice dans le monde* 1, no. 2 (December 1959): 147–77.

44 Aurel Kolnai, "The Synthesis of Christ and Anti-Christ," *Integrity* 5, no. 11 (August 1951): 41 (see also John Oesterreicher's response in a letter, *Commonweal*, September 14, 1951). Alasdair MacIntyre's *After Virtue: A Study in Moral Theory* (Notre Dame, IN: Notre Dame University Press, 1981), took the position—more plausible historically at least—that medieval natural law did not flow into modern natural rights but broke down to produce them, but MacIntyre remained a marginal dissenter in an era when Pope John Paul II would champion the equation of Catholicism and human rights. For other worries that human rights opens the

door to "liberalism" rather than successfully reformulates natural law, see, for example, James V. Schall, "Human Rights as an Ideological Project," *American Journal of Jurisprudence* 32 (1987): 47–61.

45 Pius XII, "The Internal Order of States and People," in Vincent A. Yzermans, ed., *Major Addresses*, 2 vols. (St. Paul, MN: North Central, 1961). See John A. O'Brien, "The Pope's Way to Peace," *International Conciliation* 44 (October 1944): 647–63 (rights of the human person throughout). In the same papal collection, one may wish to compare the 1958 Christmas message, "The Rights of Man," in Yzermans, ed., *Major Addresses*.

46 John A. Creaveny, "Person and Individual," *The New Scholasticism* 18, no. 3 (July 1943): 247.

47 Christopher Dawson, *The Judgment of the Nations* (New York: Sheed and Ward, 1942), 185–86.

48 William L. Laurence, "Political Theory of Religion Is Hit," *New York Times*, September 17, 1940. Though well informed, Maritain consistently presented France as captured, thus drastically understating the extent and zeal of the collaborationism of some of his countrymen.

49 Maritain to Charles de Gaulle, November 21, 1941, in *Cahiers Jacques Maritain* 16–17 (April 1988): 61. By the next year he urged de Gaulle to champion a "renewed democratic ideal" rooted in personalism. Ibid., 68.

50 Joseph M. Corrigan and G. Barry O'Toole, eds., *Race, Nation, Person: Social Aspects of the Race Problem* (New York: Barnes and Noble, 1944), with chapters like "The Rights of the Human Person vis-à-vis of the State and the Race" and "Catholic Personalism Faces Our Times."

51 See Pius XII, "True and False Democracy," in *Major Addresses*.

52 Richard Pattee, "Human Rights" (June 3, 1945), in George N. Shuster et al., eds., *Problems of the Postwar World: A Catholic Hour Symposium* (Washington, DC: National Council of Catholic Men, 1945), 29.

53 John Eppstein, *Defend these Human Rights! Each Man's Stake in the United Nations—A Catholic View* (New York: America Press, 1948), 5.

54 John Courtney Murray, "The Natural Law," in Robert M. MacIver, ed., *Great Expressions of Human Rights* (New York, 1950), as rpt. in Murray, *We Hold These Truths: Catholic Reflections on the American Proposition* (New York: Harper and Brothers, 1960), 320, alluding to Maritain's claim that Christianity is the "integral" rather than "partial" humanism.

55 De Visscher, "Les droits fondamentaux de l'homme," 158.

56 On Maritain, see Mounier, *Oeuvres*, 4 vols. (Paris: Éditions du Seuil, 1961–63), 4:694; for the declaration, see Mounier, "Faut-il refaire la Déclaration des droits?," *Oeuvres*, 4:96–104. This document was widely read in the process of the abortive and then the final framing of the Fourth Republic's constitution.

57 See esp. Paolo Pombeni, *Il gruppo dossettiano e la fondazione della democrazia italiana (1938–1948)* (Bologna: Il Mulino, 1979) and Olivier Compagnon, *Jacques Maritain et l'Amérique du Sud* (Villeneuve-d'Ascq: Presses universitaires du Septentrion, 2003). Mary Ann Glendon and her student Paolo Carozza have emphasized the personalist foundations of Latin American politicking over the Universal Declaration, but chiefly to demonstrate the compatibility of Catholicism and state-based concern for economic rights that the recent developments in North America have made difficult to perceive. See Glendon, "The Forgotten Crucible: The Latin American Influence on the Universal Human Rights Idea," *Harvard Human Rights Journal* 16 (Spring 2003): 27–40.

58 François de Menthon, "Opening Address (January 17, 1946)," in Michael R. Marrus, ed., *The Nuremberg War Crimes Trial 1945–46: A Documentary History* (Boston: St. Martin's Press, 1997), 89–94; cf. Laurent Ducerf, *François de Menthon: un Catholique au service de la République* (Paris: Cerf, 2006), chap. 10.

59 His most graphic early anti-Semitic comment calls for the "necessary campaign against the Judeo-Masonic peril." Maritain, "A propos de 'la question juive,'" *La vie spirituelle* 4 (July 1921): 305–10, also in *La Documentation catholique* 6, no. 116 (August 1921): 80–82. For his early Holocaust consciousness, see François Azouvi, *Le mythe du grand silence: Auschwitz, les Français, la mémoire* (Paris: Fayard, 2012), 53, 55, 81–83, and for an especially important episode in which Maritain begged the pope after the war to say more about the Jewish fate (without success), Michael R. Marrus, "A Plea Unanswered: Jacques Maritain, Pope Pius XII, and the Holocaust," *Studies in Contemporary Jewry* 11 (2005): 3–11.

60 His UNESCO address is "La Voie de la Paix: Discours prononcé à la séance inaugurale de la IIe Conférence internationale de l'Unesco" (Mexico City, 1947), in English in many places, such as "Possibilities for Co-operation in a Divided World," in Maritain, *The Range of Reason* (New York: Scribner, 1952); for his UNESCO rights inquiry,

see Maritain, ed., *Human Rights: Comments and Interpretation* (New York: Columbia University Press, 1949); see also Maritain, *The Meaning of Human Rights* (Philadelphia: The Brandeis Lawyers Society, 1949) and, for his own fullest views, see Maritain, *Man and the State* (Chicago: University of Chicago Press, 1951).

61 Edward Miller, "The Diplomacy of Personalism: Civilization, Culture, and the Cold War in the Foreign Policy of Ngô Đình Diệm," in Christopher Goscha and Christian Osterman, eds., *Connecting Histories: Decolonization and the Cold War in Southeast Asia, 1945–1962* (Stanford, CA: Stanford University Press, 2009).

62 Cf. Roland Burke, "'The Compelling Dialogue of Freedom': Human Rights at the Bandung Conference,"*Human Rights Quarterly* 28, no. 4 (November 2006): 947–65 or Glenn Mitoma, *Human Rights and the Negotiation of American Power* (Philadelphia: University of Pennsylvania Press, 2013), 11 and chaps. 3–4 for how Malik and Romulo established the "transcultural legitimacy" of human rights, without mentioning their Christian frameworks.

63 Charles Malik, "The Prospect for Freedom" (address at honorary rectorial convocation, University of Dubuque, IA, February 19, 1951), unpaginated.

64 Carlos Romulo, "Natural Law and International Law," *University of Notre Dame Natural Law Institute Proceedings* 3 (1949): 121, 126.

65 See Boris Mirkine-Guetzévitch, *Les constitutions européennes* (Paris: Presses Universitaires de France, 1951), chap. 8 and, for British delay, Charles O. H. Parkinson, *Bills of Rights and Decolonization: The Emergence of Domestic Human Rights Instruments in Britain's Overseas Territories* (Oxford: Oxford University Press, 2007).

66 Wolfram Kaiser, *Christian Democracy and the Origins of the European Union* (Cambridge, UK: Cambridge University Press, 2007). See also the more affirmative and invested views in Roberto Papini, ed., *L'apporto del personalismo alla costruzione dell'Europa* (Milan: Massimo, 1981) and Philippe Chenaux, *De la chrétienté à l'Europe: les Catholiques et l'idée européenne au XXe siècle* (Paris: CLD, 2007), esp. chap. 3, "L'influence du personnalisme dans la construction de l'Europe."

67 Richard Vinen, *Bourgeois Politics in France, 1945–1951* (Cambridge, UK: Cambridge University Press, 1995), 152.

68 See Gerd-Rainer Horn and Emmanuel Gerard, eds., *Left Catholicism: Catholics and Society in Western Europe at the Point of*

Liberation (Leuven: Leuven University Press, 2001), esp. Martin Conway's synthesis, "Left Catholicism in Europe in the 1940s: Elements of an Interpretation," 270–71 and 277–78: "In comparison with the rapid growth of Christian Democracy, the Left Catholic groups must inevitably appear as something of a historical footnote."

69 De Visscher, "Les droits fondamentaux de l'homme," 158.

70 The allusion is to Charles Maier's work on Europe after World War I, to which I return in the epilogue. Conway, "Left Catholicism," 277, 281.

71 For a broader and mostly later study of Christianity and European Union, see Lucian Leustean, *The Ecumenical Movement and the Making of the European Community* (New York: Oxford University Press, 2014).

72 See Simpson, *Human Rights and the End of Empire*, esp. 568–70 ("Saving Western Civilization") and 577–79 ("What Was the Spiritual Union?"), citation at 579.

73 Dianne Kirby, "Divinely Sanctioned: The Anglo-American Cold War Alliance and the Defence of Western Civilization and Christianity, 1945–1948," *Journal of Contemporary History* 35, no. 3 (July 2000): 385–412 and Kirby, ed., *Religion and the Cold War* (New York: Palgrave Macmillan, 2003).

74 Jeanne Morefield, *Covenants without Swords: Idealist Liberalism and the Spirit of Empire* (Princeton, NJ: Princeton University Press, 2005).

75 Bruno Ackermann, *Denis de Rougemont: De la personne à l'Europe* (Lausanne: L'Age de Homme, 2000).

76 See Hans-Manfred Bock, ed., *Entre Locarno et Vichy: les relations culturelles franco-allemandes dans les années 30* (Paris: CNRS éditions, 1993) and Thomas Keller, *Deutsch-französische Dritte-Weg-Diskurse: personalistische Intellektuellendebatte der Zwischenkriegszeit* (Munich: Willhelm Fink, 2001). See also Heinz Hürten, "Der Einfluß Jacques Maritains auf das politische Denken in Deutschland," in Hürten, *Katholiken, Kirche, und Staat als Problem der Historie*, ed. Hubert Gruber (Paderborn: Schöningh, 1994).

77 Many German Catholics in the emigration, like Waldemar Gurian or Heinrich Rommen, did not return. A parallel German story to Maritain's creation of a nonreactionary personalism can be told about Dietrich von Hildebrand, a Scheler disciple who fled Germany

to Austria (where he favored "Austro-fascist" corporatism) before flee-ing to France and then to the United States, where he took up Marit-ain's cause. See Hildebrand, "Der Kampf um die Person," *Die christliche Ständestaat* 6 (January 14, 1934), rpt. in Hildebrand, *Memoiren und Aufsätze gegen den Nationalsozialismus 1933–1938*, ed. Ernst Wenisch (Mainz: Matthias-Grunewald-Verlag, 1994) and "The World Crisis and the Human Personality," *Thought* 16, no. 62 (September 1941): 457–72. James Chappel's work pursues all these developments; on Gurian in par-ticular, see Udi Greenberg, *The Weimar Century: German Emigres and the Ideological Foundations of the Cold War* (Princeton, NJ: Princeton University Press, 2014), chap. 3.

78 Maria Mitchell, "Materialism and Secularism: CDU Politicians and National Socialism, 1945–49," *Journal of Modern History* 67, no. 2 (June 1995): 278–308; Mitchell, "'Antimaterialism' in Early German Christian Democracy," in Thomas Kselman and Joseph A. Buttigieg, eds., *European Christian Democracy: Historical Legacies and Compara-tive Perspectives* (Notre Dame, IN: Notre Dame University Press, 2003); and now Mitchell, *The Origins of Christian Democracy: Politics and Con-fession in Modern Germany* (Ann Arbor: University of Michigan Press, 2012); cf. Konrad Jarausch, *After Hitler: Recivilizing Germans, 1945–1995* (New York: Oxford University Press, 2006).

79 See chapter 1.

80 See Willi Geiger, *Grundrechte und Rechtsprechung* (Munich: Pustet, 1959) and "Die Wandlung der Grundrechte," in Max Imboden, ed., *Gedanke und Gestalt des demokratischen Rechtsstaates* (Vienna: Herder, 1965). Cf. Gerhard Leibholz, Hans Joachim Faller, Paul Mikat, and Hans Reis, eds., *Menschenwürde und freiheitliche Rechtsordnung: Festschrift für Willi Geiger zum 65. Geburtstag* (Tübingen: Mohr, 1974). Also of importance was the Bavarian judge Josef Wintrich, whose personalist formulae the Bundesverfassungsgericht took over; see, for example, *Zur Problematik der Grundrechte* (Cologne: Westdeutscher Verlag, 1957) and Ulrich Becker, *Das "Menschenbild des Grundgesetzes" in der Rechtsprechung des Bundesverfassungsgerichts* (Berlin: Duncker and Humblot, 1996). On Geiger under Nazism, see Ingo Müller, *Hitler's Justice: The Courts of the Third Reich*, trans. Deborah Schneider (Cam-bridge, MA: Harvard University Press, 1992), 218.

81 On human rights in these circles, see Terence Renaud, "How the Churches Conceived of Human Rights: The Personalist Anthropology

of the Protestant Ecumenical Conference at Oxford (1937)," online at http://terencerenaud.com/selected-writings/churches-human-rights/.

82 Bell, "The Church in Relation to International Affairs" (address at Chatham House), *International Affairs* 25, no. 4 (October 1949): 405–14, at 407, 409.

83 Gerhard Leibholz, *Christianity, Politics, and Power* (London: Sheldon Press, 1943), and "Politics and Natural Law," a paper delivered at the conference that gave rise to A. R. Vidler and W. H. Whitehouse, eds., *Natural Law: A Christian Re-consideration* (London: S. C. M. Press, 1946). Both of Leibholz's texts and many others from his émigré years are in Leibholz, *Politics and Law* (Leyden: A. W. Sythoff, 1965), citation at 23. On the postwar career, see Manfred Wiegandt, *Norm und Wirklichkeit: Gerhard Leibholz, 1901–1982: Leben, Werk und Richteramt* (Baden-Baden: Nomos, 1995). For more on Leibholz, see Noah B. Strote, *Nation Builders: Political Dynamics in Germany from Collapse to Reconstruction, 1924–1964* (forthcoming).

84 Frieder Günther, *Denken vom Staat her: Die bundesdeutsche Staatsrechtslehre zwischen Dezision und Integration 1949–1970* (Munich: Oldenbourg Wissenschaftsverlag, 2004), 192 and, for the larger context of rights, 192–96, 202–4. For the view of a contemporary, see Hans Maier, "Katholische Sozial- und Staatslehre und neuere deutsche Staatslehre," *Archiv des öffentlichen Rechts* 93, no. 1 (1968): 1–36.

85 Günter Dürig, "Die Menschenauffassung des Grundgesetzes," *Juristische Rundschau* (1952): 259–63, rpt. in Dürig, *Gesammelte Schriften*, eds. Walter Schmitt Glaeser and Peter Häberle (Berlin: Duncker and Humblot, 1984). For his classic commentary on the Grundgesetz, Art. 1, see Dürig and Theodor Maunz, *Grundgesetz: Kommentar* (Munich: Beck, 1958); cf. Ernst-Wolfgang Böckenförde, "Die Menschenwürde *war* unantastbar," *Frankfurter Allgemeine Zeitung*, September 9, 2003.

86 "A strong personalist and communitarian philosophy pervades this conception of the human person," the leading Anglophone authority on German constitutional jurisprudence confirms. Donald P. Kommers, *The Constitutional Jurisprudence of the Federal Republic of Germany*, new ed. (Raleigh, NC: Duke University Press, 1997), 304.

87 Cf. Mark Mazower, "The Strange Triumph of Human Rights, 1930–1950," *Historical Journal* 47, no. 2 (June 2004): 379–98.

88 For graphic evidence of the sheer difficulty of defending individualism in law in the 1940s, see Marcel Waline, *L'individualisme et le droit* (Paris: Domat-Monchrestien, 1945).

89 This decline, which ought to be shocking, remains essentially unexplained, but see Callum Brown, *The Death of Christian Britain: Understanding Secularization, 1800–2000* (New York: Routledge, 2001) and Mark Edward Ruff, *Wayward Flock: Catholic Youth in Postwar West Germany* (Chapel Hill: University of North Carolina Press, 2005).

90 The literature here is large, but see Karol Wojtyła, "Thomistic Personalism" (1961), "On the Dignity of the Human Person" (1964), and other essays in *Person and Community: Selected Essays (Catholic Thought from Lublin)*, trans. Theresa Sandok (New York: Peter Lang, 1993); cf. Avery Cardinal Dulles, "John Paul II and the Mystery of the Human Person," *America*, February 2, 2004, rpt. in Dulles, *Church and Society: The Laurence A. McGinley Lectures, 1988–2007* (New York: Fordham University Press, 2008), as well as Gubser, *The Far Reaches*, esp. chap. 9. Cf. Jens David Ohlin, "Is the Concept of the Person Necessary for Human Rights?," *Columbia Law Review* 105, no. 1 (January 2005): 209–49.

Chapter 3

1 Gerhard Ritter, "Ursprung und Wesen der Menschenrechte," *Historische Zeitschrift* 169, no. 2 (August 1949): 233–63. It is republished, with a few minor differences, in Ritter's *Lebendige Vergangenheit: Beiträge zur historisch-politischen Selbstbesinnung* (Munich: Oldenbourg, 1958) and also in Roman Schnur, ed., *Zur Geschichte der Erklärung der Menschenrechte* (Darmstadt: Darmstadt Wissenschaftlichte Buchgesellschaft, 1972). I cite the original in this chapter.

2 There had been prior work, some cited below, on the revolutionary-era concept of "the rights of man." The same year Ritter gave his lecture, a more peripheral historian, Fritz Hartung, published his documentary compilation *Die Entwicklung der Menschen- und Bürgerrechte von 1776–1946* (Berlin: Wissenschaftliche Editionsgesellschaft, 1948), and other similar books appeared in Germany, such as Arthur Hossbach, *Die Menschenrechte* (Braunschweig:

G. Westermann, 1948) and Alfred Voigt, *Geschichte der Grundrechte* (Stuttgart: Spemann, 1948). In English, international lawyer Hersch Lauterpacht offered historical arguments about human rights in the course of his failed advocacy for their role in international law. Lauterpacht, *International Law and Human Rights* (London: Stevens, 1950).

3 Alice K. Conklin, "Colonialism and Human Rights, A Contradiction in Terms? The Case of France and West Africa, 1895–1914," *American Historical Review* 103, no. 2 (April 1998): 419–42; Linda K. Kerber, "We Are All Historians of Human Rights," *AHA Perspectives*, October 2006.

4 This chapter places human rights in the more general, now established picture of "reorientation" of German conservatism proposed by a classic work such as Jerry Z. Muller, *The Other God That Failed: Hans Freyer and the Deradicalization of German Conservatism* (Princeton, NJ: Princeton University Press, 1987), esp. chap. 9 and usefully summarized in Jan Eckel, *Geist der Zeit: Deutsche Geisteswissenschaften seit 1870* (Göttingen: Vandenhoeck und Ruprecht, 2008), chap. 4, "Entradikalisierung und lange Umorientierung."

5 I have benefited very much from the main study, Christoph Cornelißen, *Gerhard Ritter: Geschichtswissenschaft und Politik im 20. Jahrhundert* (Düsseldorf: Droste, 2001). I have not cited Ritter's books and articles specifically except where they come in for some discussion or other; for a full bibliography of his writings, see Klaus Schwabe and Rolf Reichardt, eds., *Gerhard Ritter: Ein politischer Historiker in seinen Briefen* (Boppard am Rhein: Boldt, 1984), Appendix III.

6 Though it provides indispensable help in understanding Ritter's interest in human rights, the accumulated literature has neglected this episode in his career; see esp. Christoph Cornelißen, *Gerhard Ritter: Geschichtswissenschaft und Politik im 20. Jahrhundert* (Düsseldorf: Droste Verlag, 2001). When his study was reissued after the Nazi seizure of power, he changed its title from "Luther: Person and Symbol" to "Luther the German": Ritter, *Luther: Gestalt und Symbol* (Munich: F. Bruckmann, 1925); Ritter, *Luther der Deutsche* (Munich: Bruckmann, 1933).

7 Nicolas Berg, *Der Holocaust und die westdeutschen Historiker: Erforschung und Erinnerung* (Göttingen: Wallstein, 2003), chap. 2.2; compare Cornelißen, *Gerhard Ritter*, 239, as well as Henryk Olszewski, *Zwischen Begeisterung und Widerstand: Deutsche Hochschullehrer und*

der Nationalsozialismus (Posen: Instytut Zachodni, 1989), 111–30, for the most critical account. Ritter, *Friedrich der Große: ein historisches Profil* (Leipzig: Quelle und Mayer, 1936), in English as *Frederick the Great: A Historical Profile*, trans. Peter Paret (Berkeley: University of California Press, 1968); Ritter, *Carl Goerdeler und die deutsche Widerstandsbewegung* (Stuttgart: Deutsche Verlags-Anstalt, 1955), in English as *The German Resistance: Carl Goerdeler's Struggle against Tyranny*, trans. R. T. Clark (New York: Praeger, 1958).

8 Fritz Fischer, *Griff nach der Weltmacht: die Kriegszielpolitik des kaiserlichen Deutschland 1914–1918* (Düsseldorf: Droste, 1961), in English as *Germany's Aims in the First World War* (New York: W. W. Norton, 1967); Ritter, *Staatskunst und Kriegshandwerk: das Problem des "Militarismus" in Deutschland*, 4 vols. (Munich: Oldenbourg, 1954–68), in English as *The Sword and the Scepter: The Problem of Militarism in Germany*, 4 vols. (Coral Gables: University of Miami Press, 1969–73); V. R. Berghahn, review in *English Historical Review* 90, no. 356 (July 1975): 680; see also John A. Moses, *The Politics of Illusion: The Fischer Controversy in German Historiography* (London: Prior, 1975).

9 Ritter, "Ursprung," 233.

10 Ibid.

11 Ibid., 234.

12 Ibid.

13 Ibid.

14 Ibid.

15 Ibid., 235.

16 Ibid.

17 See Ernst Troeltsch, "Das stoisch-christliche Naturrecht und das moderne profane Naturrecht," *Verhandlungen des ersten deutschen Soziologentages vom 19.-22. Oktober 1910 in Frankfurt a.-M.* (Tübingen: Mohr Siebeck, 1911), rpt. in *Historische Zeitschrift* 106, no. 2 (1911): 237–67; in English as "Stoic-Christian Natural Law and Modern Profane Natural Law," in Christopher Adair-Toteff, ed., *Sociological Beginnings: The First Conference of the German Society for Sociology* (Liverpool: Liverpool University Press, 2006), as well as in Troeltsch, *Religion in History*, trans. James Luther Adams and Walter E. Bense (Minneapolis, MN: Fortress Press, 1991).

18 Ritter, "Ursprung," 236.

19 Ibid., 237.

20 For background, see Duncan Kelly, "Revisiting the Rights of Man: Georg Jellinek on Rights and the State," *Law and History Review* 22, no. 3 (Fall 2004): 493–530.

21 Ritter, "Ursprung," 240.

22 Ibid., 243.

23 Ibid., 245.

24 Ibid., 247.

25 Ibid., 248.

26 Ibid., 254.

27 Ibid.

28 Ibid., 256.

29 Ibid., 259.

30 Ibid., 260.

31 Ibid., 261.

32 Ibid., 262.

33 Ritter, "Die Menschenrechte und das Christentum," *Zeitwende* 21, no. 1 (July 1949): 1–12.

34 Compare Heinz Hürten, "Der Topos vom christlichen Abendland in Literatur und Publizistik nach den beiden Weltkriegen," in Hubert Gruber, ed., *Katholiken, Kirche, und Staat als Problem der Historie* (Paderborn: Schöningh, 1994); with Axel Schildt, *Zwischen Abendland und Amerika: Studien zur westdeutschen Ideenlandschaft der 50er Jahre* (Munich: Oldenbourg, 1999). See also Stephen Brockmann, "Germany as Occident at the Zero Hour," *German Studies Review* 25, no. 3 (October 2002): 477–96.

35 Ritter, "Untergang und Wiedererweckung der abendländischen Idee: eine Zeitbetrachtung von 1942," *Neubau* 2, no. 7 (October 1947): 290–97 and 2, no. 8 (November 1947): 342–50.

36 Klaus Schwabe, "Change and Continuity in German Historiography from 1933 into the Early 1950s: Gerhard Ritter (1888–1967)," in Hartmut Lehmann and James van Horn Melton, eds., *Paths of Continuity: Central European Historiography from the 1930s to the 1950s* (Cambridge, UK: Cambridge University Press, 1994), 89–90; cf. Schwabe, "Der Weg in die Opposition: Der Historiker Gerhard Ritter und der Freiburger Kreis," in Eckhard John, Bernd Martin, and Martin Mück, eds., *Die Freiburger Universität in der Zeit des Nationalsozialismus* (Freiburg: Ploetz, 1991). It should be noted that while this circle's wartime memoranda, in which Ritter had a major hand, invoke natural

law and Christian order, they do not include human rights language. See Klaus Schwabe and Rolf Reichardt, eds., *Gerhard Ritter: Ein politischer Historiker in seinen Briefen* (Boppard am Rhein: Boldt, 1984), Appendix II, and Helmut Thielicke, ed., *In der Stunde Null: Die Denkschrift des Freiburger "Bonhoeffer Kreises"* (Tübingen: Mohr, 1979).

37 Ritter, "Luthertum, katholisches und humanistisches Weltbild," *Zeitwende* 18, no. 2 (1946–7): 65–84; in English as "Lutheranism, Catholicism, and the Humanistic View of Life," in *Archiv für Reformationsgeschichte* 44, no. 2 (1953): 145–60.

38 Ritter, "Luthertum," 69–71; "Lutheranism," 148–49. On the Lutheran legacy of abstention from politics, see also Ritter, "Luther und die politische Erziehung der Deutschen," *Zeitwende* 18, nos. 10–11 (April/May 1947): 592–609. For similar ideas throughout German and European Catholicism at the time, compare Damian van Melis, "'Strengthened and Purified through Ordeal by Fire': Ecclesiastical Triumphalism in the Ruins," in Richard Bessel and Dirk Schumann, eds., *Life after Death: Approaches to a Cultural and Social History of Europe in the 1940s and 1950s* (Cambridge, UK: Cambridge University Press, 2003).

39 Ritter, "Luthertum," 71–73; "Lutheranism," 148–51.

40 No good history of the ecumenical movement exists, but documents and its own self-study provide useful information: G. K. A. Bell (Bishop of Chichester), ed., *Documents on Christian Unity*, 4 vols. (London: Oxford University Press, 1920–58) and Ruth Rouse and Stephen Charles Neill, *A History of the Ecumenical Movement 1517–1948* (London: Westminster Press, 1954), esp. chap. 16 on the origins of the World Council of Churches by its general secretary, Willem Adolf Visser 't Hooft.

41 See Commission to Study the Bases of a Just and Durable Peace, *Six Pillars of Peace* (New York: Federal Council of the Churches of Christ in America, 1943), 72–80. Surprisingly, the otherwise well-informed Ritter seems to have been unaware of FCC activist Frederick Nolde's participation in 1944–45 at San Francisco in adding human rights to the United Nations Charter or his work after. See Nolde, *Free and Equal: Human Rights in Ecumenical Perspective* (Geneva: World Council of Churches, 1968), for his memoirs. Compare John Nurser, *For All Peoples and All Nations: The Ecumenical Church and Human Rights* (Washington, DC: Georgetown University Press, 2005). For a more evenhanded view of human rights within the overall ecumenical

agenda, see Edward Duff, *The Social Thought of the World Council of Churches* (London: Longmans, Green, 1956).

42 For all this, the crucial source is Ritter, "Die englisch-amerikanischen Kirchen und die Friedensfrage," *Zeitwende* 19 (1947–48): 459–70, citation at 469. For the letter, dated July 29, 1947, see Schwabe and Reichardt, *Gerhard Ritter*, 439n1. For Dulles and Nolde at Amsterdam, see Dulles, "The Christian Citizen in a Changing World," and Nolde, "Freedom of Religion and Related Human Rights," in World Council of Churches, *Man's Disorder and God's Design*, vol. 4, *The Church and the International Disorder* (London: S. C. M. Press, 1948), 73–189.

43 Ritter, "Lutheranism," 158 (not in the German original).

44 The wartime third edition (1943) was a serious revision, changing the subtitle to *Gestalt und Tat* and the dedication from his wife to his son Berthold who fell in the Wehrmacht in Russia on Christmas Eve 1941; the fourth (1947) retooled the introduction and last chapter on the legacy, with the fifth (1949) and sixth (1959) editions altering the latter slightly; the sixth serves as the basis of the English translation, *Luther: His Life and Work*, trans. John Riches (New York: Harper and Row, 1963). He kept the famous "eternal German" tag, however, through the 1947 edition (238).

45 Ritter, *Luther* (1925), 154; (1942), 242; and English, 218.

46 Ritter, "Lutheranism," 156–59 (not in the German original). In a recent book, Konrad Jarausch has canvassed the means (the reorientation of the politics of religion aside) by which Germans were brought "back from perpetrating unspeakable crimes to a sincere commitment to human rights." To do so, he explains, is to examine how a rapprochement with "the West" and "civilization" took place over the decades. The difficulty with this framework, however, is that *every one* of the positive terms toward which Germans are supposed to have headed in this progressive trajectory was already part of their immediate postwar conservative discourse, as the case of Gerhard Ritter clearly shows—human rights included. Konrad Jarausch, *After Hitler: Recivilizing Germans* (New York: Oxford University Press, 2006), vii.

47 Maritain, "Christian Humanism," *Fortune*, April 1942. See also Maritain, *Les droits de l'homme et la loi naturelle* (New York: Editions de La Maison Française, 1942), in English as *The Rights of Man and Natural*

Law, trans. Doris C. Anson (New York: Scribner, 1943), and many post-war writings.

48 Schwabe and Reichardt, *Gerhard Ritter*, 439.

49 Wilhelm Grewe, review of Hartung and others, *Archiv des öffentlichen Rechts* 74 (1948): 508.

50 Of course, unlike Ritter, Talmon saw revolution as a "messianic" transformation of religion rather than a departure from it. Jacob Talmon, *The Origins of Totalitarian Democracy* (London: Secker and Warburg, 1952), 150; cf. 35–36, 91, 156–57 (property versus social rights), or 203 (terroristic rights from revolutionary Gracchus Babeuf on). Compare Leo Strauss, *Natural Right and History* (Chicago: University of Chicago Press, 1952), also fearful of the ambiguity of originally hedonist rights and in which Rousseau points ahead to baleful twentieth-century developments.

51 Bell, *Christianity and World Order* (Harmondsworth: Penguin, 1940), 104.

52 Bell, "The Church in Relation to International Affairs" (address at Chatham House), *International Affairs* 25, no. 4 (October 1949): 407, 409.

53 Emil Brunner, "Das Menschenbild und die Menschenrechte," *Universitas* 2, no. 3 (March 1947): 269–74 and 2, no. 4 (April 1947): 385–91 at 269.

54 Charles Malik, "The Universal Declaration of Human Rights," in Nolde, *Free and Equal*, 10.

55 Edward Said, *Out of Place* (New York: Knopf, 1999), 265.

56 See UNESCO, *Human Rights: Comments and Interpretations*, intro. Maritain (New York: Columbia University Press, 1949); and R. M. MacIver, ed., *Great Expressions of Human Rights* (New York: Harper, 1950), with chiefly religious authors and contents, including famed American Catholic natural law theorist John Courtney Murray's appropriation of rights as part of praise for American traditions of fusing religious liberty and moral community.

57 See Marco Duranti, *The European Project and the Conservative Origins of Human Rights* (New York: Oxford University Press, forthcoming).

58 See UN Gen. Ass. Res. 272 (III) (1949) and, later, Res. 294 (IV) (1949) and Res. 385 (V) (1950); see also chapter 4 of this volume.

59 Judith N. Shklar, *After Utopia: The Decline of Political Faith* (Princeton, NJ: Princeton University Press, 1957), 174.

60 Friedrich Meinecke, *Die Idee der Staatsräson in der neueren Geschichte* (Munich: Oldenbourg, 1924), in English as *Machiavellism: The Doctrine of Raison d'État and Its Place in Modern History*, trans. Douglas Scott (New Haven, CT: Yale University Press, 1957); and *Ranke und Burckhardt: ein Vortrag, gehalten in der Deutschen Akademie der Wissenschaften zu Berlin* (Berlin: Akademie-Verlag, 1948), in English as "Ranke and Burckhardt," in Hans Kohn, ed., *German History: Some New German Views* (Boston: Beacon Press, 1954). Compare H. R. Trevor-Roper, "Jacob Burckhardt," *Proceedings of the British Academy* 70 (1984): 359–78; Lionel Gossman, *Basel in the Age of Burckhardt: A Study in Unseasonable Ideas* (Chicago: University of Chicago Press, 2000), chap. 15; and Gossman, "Jacob Burckhardt, Cold War Liberal?," *Journal of Modern History* 74, no. 3 (September 2002): 538–72.

61 Ritter, *Machtstaat und Utopie: Vom Streit um die Dämonie der Macht seit Machiavelli und Morus* (Munich: Oldenbourg, 1940). The postwar editions, beginning in 1947, were titled *Die Dämonie der Macht: Betrachtungen über Geschichte und Wesen des Machtproblem im politischen Denken der Neuzeit* (Munich: Leibniz Verlag, 1948); the English version, *The Corrupting Influence of Power*, trans. F. C. Pick (Hadleigh: Tower Bridge, 1952), is based on this edition.

62 For the original comment, see Ritter, *Machtstaat* (1940), 9, and in all editions except the English one; cf. 146–47n13, 169–70n24. For the postwar comment, see Ritter, *Dämonie*, 164; *The Corrupting Influence*, 182. In the notes that follow, I cite the 1940 *Machtstaat* unless there is reason to do otherwise.

63 Thomas Morus, *Utopia*, trans. Ritter (Berlin: R. Hobbing, 1922); see also Hermann Oncken, "Die Utopie des T. Morus und das Machtproblem in der Staatslehre," *Sitzungsberichte der Heidelberger Akademie der Wissenschaften* (Philosophisch-historische Klasse) 13, no. 2 (1922): 1–25, rpt. in Oncken, *Nation und Geschichte: Reden und Aufsätze* (Berlin: G. Grote'sche, 1935).

64 The text can be read as an early version of Robert Kagan's recent *Of Paradise and Power: America, Europe, and the New World Order* (New York: Knopf, 2003), only in this story, Germans were from Mars and Anglo-Americans from Venus, and the antagonistic structure of their relationship meant that the humanitarians, instead of tacitly

depending on the Machiavellians for their protection (as Kagan supposes Europeans now do), also fight wars, even as they pretend to be activated by universal principles.

65 Ritter, *Machtstaat*, 30 and *The Corrupting Influence*, 23; *Dämonie*, 36 and *The Corrupting Influence*, 25. In jail in 1944–45, Ritter wrote "Machiavelli und der Ursprung des modernen Nationalismus," in *Vom sittlichen Problem der Macht* (Bern: A. Francke, 1948).

66 Ritter, *Machtstaat*, 60, 65; *The Corrupting Influence*, 59, 65.

67 Ibid., 79; *The Corrupting Influence*, 80–81.

68 Carl Schmitt, *The Concept of the Political*, trans. George Schwab (Chicago: University of Chicago Press, 1996, 2007), 54.

69 Ritter, *Machtstaat*, 32 (citing Schmitt, as the postwar edition does); *The Corrupting Influence*, 26–27.

70 See Ritter, "Vom Doppelsinn des Politischen," *Deutsche Rundschau* 68 (January 1942): 6–10 and *Machtstaat* (1943 ed.), Appendix; then *Dämonie*, chap. 5, "Versuch einer theoretischen Überwindung des Gegensatzes," in the English version as "The Contrast Resolved." See also Cornelißen, *Gerhard Ritter*, chap. VI.3 and Ritter, "The German Professor and the Third Reich," *Review of Politics* 8, no. 2 (April 1946): 246, along with his English-language preface, for his own self-interpretation.

71 Ritter, *Machtstaat*, 118–21; *The Corrupting Influence*, 131–33.

72 Ritter, *Europa und die deutsche Frage: Betrachtungen über die geschichtliche Eigenart des deutschen Staatsdenkens* (Munich: Münchner Verlag, 1948), republished as Ritter, *Das deutsche Problem: Grundfragen deutschen Staatslebens gestern und heute* (Munich: Oldenbourg, 1962), on which the English version is based, *The German Problem: Basic Questions of German Political Life, Past and Present*, trans. Sigurd Burckhardt (Columbus: Ohio State University Press, 1965). For a later English summary of Ritter's attempt to blame Nazism on democracy, see his "The Historical Foundations of the Rise of National-Socialism," in International Council for Philosophy and Humanistic Studies, *The Third Reich: A Study* (New York: Praeger, 1955). For context, see Jean Solchany, *Comprendre le nazisme dans l'Allemagne des années zéro (1945–1949)* (Paris: Presses universitaires de France, 1997), and, for historians specifically, Solchany, "Le nazisme: déviance allemande ou mal de la modernité? La réflexion des historiens dans l'Allemagne des années zéro (1945–1949)," *Vingtième siècle* 34, no. 2 (April 1992): 145–56.

73 "Current Periodicals," *Times Literary Supplement*, March 31, 1950.

74 Geoffrey Barraclough, "The *Historische Zeitschrift*," *Times Literary Supplement*, April 14, 1950. Barraclough had been impressed by reading before publication an essay by Johann Albrecht von Rantzau, "Individualitätsprinzip, Staatsverherrlichung und deutsche Geschichtsschreibung," *Die Sammlung* 5 (May 1950): 284–99, in English as "The Glorification of the State in German Historical Writing," in Kohn, ed., *German History*, which indicts Ritter's inability to break from the German conception of history.

75 Letter of April 4, 1950, in Schwabe and Reichardt, *Gerhard Ritter*, 461. For further correspondence between the two, see ibid., 463 n.11. For Ritter's public reply, see "Letters to the Editor," *Times Literary Supplement*, May 12, 1950.

76 See Ritter, "Die englisch-amerikanischen Kirchen," 460–61; Ritter, "Christentum und Geschichte: Zu Herbert Butterfields christlicher Geschichtsbetrachtung," *Zeitwende* 24, no. 2 (August 1952): 139–51, esp. 145; and Schwabe and Reichardt, *Gerhard Ritter*, 515–16. The emergence of Christian realism as a transnational event deserves its own historian, but for now, see Heather A. Warren, *Theologians of a New World Order: Reinhold Niebuhr and the Christian Realists* (New York: Oxford University Press, 1997).

77 Barack H. Obama, "Nobel Lecture," Oslo, Norway, December 10, 2009.

78 Ritter, "Luthertum," 73; "Lutheranism," 151.

Chapter 4

1 Belgin Dogru v. France, App. No. 27058/05, 49 Eur. H.R. Rep. 179 (2008), at ¶¶ 5–9.

2 Dahlab v. Switzerland, Eur. Ct. H.R. 449 (2001); Leyla Şahin v. Turkey, 44 Eur. H.R. Rep. 5 (2007). For the European Court on the French religious symbol law of 2004, see also Aktas v. France, App. No. 43563/08; Bayrak v. France, App. No. 14308/08; Gamaleddyn v. France, App. No. 18527/08; Ghazal v. France, App. No. 29134/08; J. Singh v. France, App. No. 25463/08; and R. Singh v. France, App. No 27561/08

(2009) (these last cases also involved Sikh boys wearing a *keski*, or turban, to school). Lautsi v. Italy, App. No. 30814/06 (2009) (Chamber); Lautsi v. Italy, App. No. 30814/06 (2011) (Grand Chamber).

3 See chapter 1.

4 Emmanuel Decaux, "Chronique d'une jurisprudence annoncée: laïcité française et liberté religieuse devant la Cour européenne des droits de l'homme," *Revue trimestrielle des droits de l'homme* 82 (2010): 251–68.

5 *Şahin* (Tulkens, J., dissenting), esp. ¶ 10.

6 John Rawls, *Political Liberalism* (New York: Columbia University Press, 1993).

7 Gil Anidjar, "Secularism," *Critical Inquiry* 33, no. 1 (Autumn 2006): 52–77, for one statement—though I do not assume that it is representative of the "critique of secularism" in general; and Peter G. Danchin, "Islam in the Secular *Nomos* of the European Court of Human Rights," *Michigan Journal of International Law* 32, no. 4 (Winter 2011): 663–747, for application to recent cases.

8 Joan Wallach Scott, *The Politics of the Veil* (Princeton, NJ: Princeton University Press, 2007), 92. See also Leora Auslander, "Bavarian Crucifixes and French Headscarves: Religious Signs and the Postmodern European State," *Cultural Dynamics* 12, no. 3 (November 2000): 283–309.

9 Convention for the Protection of Human Rights and Fundamental Freedoms, March 20, 1952, 213 U.N.T.S. 222 (European Convention of Human Rights in what follows).

10 Gay News Ltd. v. United Kingdom, App. No. 8710/79, 5 Eur. H.R. Rep. 123 (1982); Choudhury v. United Kingdom, App. No. 17439/90, 12 Hum. Rts. L.J. 172 (1991); Otto-Preminger-Institut v. Austria, 295 Eur. Ct. H.R. (ser. A) (1994); Wingrove v. United Kingdom, 23 Eur. Ct. H.R. 1937 (1996).

11 La Ligue des Musulmans de Suisse v. Switzerland, App. No. 66274/09 (2011); Ouardiri v. Switzerland, App. No. 65840/09 (2011).

12 *Dogru*, ¶ 62.

13 S.A.S. v. France, App. No. 43835/11 (2014) (Grand Chamber), ¶ 82.

14 Ibid., ¶ 122.

15 Refah Partisi (No. 2) v. Turkey, 37 Eur. H.R. Rep. 1 (2003) (Grand Chamber), esp. ¶ 93. Though the court focused on Article 11's right to assembly, it made clear that its permissive attitude toward a secularist democratic minimum covered the other rights, including

Article 9's protection of the right to manifest religion. For its citation, see, for example, *S.A.S.*, ¶ 127.

16 See William B. Husband, *"Godless Communists": Atheism and Society in Soviet Russia, 1917–1932* (DeKalb: Northern Illinois University Press, 2000) and Daniel Peris, *Storming the Heavens: The Soviet League of the Militant Godless* (Ithaca, NY: Cornell University Press, 1998).

17 Gene Zubovich, "The Global Gospel: Protestant Internationalism and American Liberalism" (PhD diss., University of California-Berkeley, 2014).

18 Cf. Andrew Preston, "The Spirit of Democracy: Religious Liberty and American Anti-Communism during the Cold War," in Duncan Bell and Joel Isaac, eds., *Uncertain Empire: American History and the Idea of the Cold War* (New York: Oxford University Press, 2012); for larger contexts, see Preston, *Sword of the Spirit, Shield of Faith: Religion in American War and Diplomacy* (New York: Knopf, 2012) and Anna Su, *Exporting Freedom: Religious Liberty and American Power* (Cambridge, MA: Harvard University Press, 2015).

19 Commission to Study the Bases of a Just and Durable Peace, *Six Pillars of Peace* (New York: Federal Council of the Churches of Christ in America, 1943), 72–81; and Moyn, *The Last Utopia: Human Rights in History* (Cambridge, MA: Harvard University Press, 2010), chap. 2, for larger context.

20 M. Searle Bates, *Religious Liberty: An Inquiry* (New York: Harper and Bros., 1945).

21 H. G. Wood, *Religious Liberty To-Day* (Cambridge, UK: Cambridge University Press, 1949), which spends most of its time reviewing violations behind the Iron Curtain (chap. 4) before turning to a "failure of left-wing intellectuals" for failing to see that their socialism was driving them into the arms of intolerant communism.

22 Jane Dailey, "Of Theory and Practice: The Sacralization of Civil Rights in the United States," paper delivered at "Does Human Rights Have a History?" conference, University of Chicago, April 11, 2015.

23 David Sehat, *The Myth of American Religious Freedom* (New York: Oxford University Press, 2011), chap. 11. For Dulles and Nolde at Amsterdam, see the last chapter of this book. Compare also John Stuart, "Mission, Ecumenism, and Human Rights: 'Religious Liberty' in Egypt, 1919–1956," *Church History* 83, no. 1 (March 2014): 110–34.

24 Katherine Healon Gaston, "The Genesis of America's Judeo-Christian Moment: Secularism, Totalitarianism, and the Redefinition of Democracy" (PhD diss., University of California-Berkeley, 2008); Kevin M. Schulz, *Tri-Faith America: How Catholics and Jews Held Postwar America to Its Protestant Promise* (New York: Oxford University Press, 2011); David Hollinger, *After Cloven Tongues of Fire: Protestant Liberalism in Modern American History* (Princeton, NJ: Princeton University Press, 2013).

25 See William Inboden, *Religion and American Foreign Policy, 1945–1960: The Soul of Containment* (New York: Oxford University Press, 2010) on presidential rhetoric and diplomacy; Jason W. Stevens, *God-Fearing and Free: A Spiritual History of America's Cold War* (Cambridge, MA: Harvard University Press, 2010) on culture; and Jonathan P. Herzog, *The Spiritual-Industrial Complex: America's Religious Battle against Communism in the Early Cold War* (New York: Oxford University Press, 2011). See also now Kevin Kruse, *One Nation under God: How Corporate America Invented Christian America* (New York: Basic Books, 2015).

26 See UN Gen. Ass. Res. 272 (III) (1949) and, later, Res. 294 (IV) (1949) and Res. 385 (V) (1950). Cf. Cornelis D. de Jong, *The Freedom of Thought, Conscience, and Religion or Belief in the United Nations (1946–1992)* (Antwerp: Intersentia, 2000).

27 Mark Mazower, "The Strange Triumph of Human Rights," *Historical Journal* 47, no. 2 (June 2004): 379–98.

28 Linde Lindqvist, "Shrines and Souls: The Reinvention of Religious Liberty and the University Declaration of Human Rights" (PhD diss., University of Lund, 2014), chaps. 3–4, emphasizing Malik's debts to Harvard idealist philosopher William Ernest Hocking and Nolde's interest in missionary work; see also Lindqvist, "The Politics of Article 18: Religious Liberty in the Universal Declaration of Human Rights," *Humanity* 4, no. 3 (Fall 2013): 429–47.

29 Cited in Lindqvist, "Shrines and Souls," 86. See also, for example, U.N. Doc. A/C.3/SR.127–128. For a contemporary and, I assume, independent revival of this once commonplace Soviet position, see Brian Leiter, "Why Tolerate Religion?," *Constitutional Commentary* 25, no. 1 (Spring 2008): 1–28 and Leiter, *Why Tolerate Religion?* (Princeton, NJ: Princeton University Press, 2012). See also Micah J. Schwartzman,

"What If Religion Isn't Special?," *University of Chicago Law Review* 79, no. 4 (Fall 2012): 1351–427.

30 Brendan Simms and D. J. B. Trim, eds., *Humanitarian Intervention: A History* (Cambridge, UK: Cambridge University Press, 2011), chaps. 2–3.

31 For doctrinal details, see Malcolm D. Evans, *Religious Liberty and International Law in Europe* (Cambridge, UK: Cambridge University Press, 1997), chaps. 2–6.

32 See Carlos Santamaria, "L'Église et les libertés dans l'histoire," in *L'Église et la liberté* (Paris: P. Horay, 1952) and, for commentary, A. F. Carrillo de Albornoz, *Roman Catholicism and Religious Liberty* (Geneva: World Council of Churches, 1959).

33 Ottaviani and his faction succeeded in postponing consideration of the declaration in 1964, which caused a major international uproar. Robert C. Doty, "1,000 Bishops Balk at Moves to Drop a Vote on Liberty," *New York Times*, November 20, 1964; Doty, "1,000 Bishops Fail in Plea to Pontiff on Liberty Draft," *New York Times*, November 21, 1964. The pope then sided against the reactionaries the next year, saving the proposal. Doty, "Italian [Cardinal Ottaviani] Assails Church Liberty," *New York Times*, September 18, 1965; Doty, "Pope Intervenes on Liberty Text, Backs Liberals," *New York Times*, September 22, 1965, John Cogley, "Freedom of Religion: Vatican Decree Supplants Ancient Doctrine that 'Error Has No Rights,'" *New York Times*, December 8, 1965.

34 "Dignitatis humanae (Declaration on Religious Freedom)," in Austin Flannery, OP, ed., *Vatican Council II: The Conciliar and Post-Conciliar Documents* (Northport, MN: Costello, 1975), 811–12.

35 See Wilfred Parsons, SJ, *The First Freedom: Considerations on Church and State in America* (New York: D. X. McMullen, 1948).

36 330 U.S. 1 (1947). See Philip Hamburger, *Separation of Church and State* (Cambridge, MA: Harvard University Press, 2002), esp. 454–63.

37 Alexis de Tocqueville, *Democracy in America*, trans. George Lawrence (New York: Harper and Row, 1966), 294.

38 John Courtney Murray, "Freedom of Religion," *Theological Studies* 6, no. 1 (March 1945): 85–113; John Cogley, "'The American Schema': Vatican Text on Religious Liberty Derives from U.S. Tradition," *New York Times*, October 27, 1965; Murray, *The Problem of Religious Freedom* (Westminster, MD: Newman Press, 1965); Murray, ed.,

Religious Liberty: An End and a Beginning (New York: Macmillan, 1966); John McGreevy, *Catholicism and American Freedom* (New York: W. W. Norton, 2003), chap. 7, "Democracy, Religious Freedom, and the *Nouvelle Théologie*." It was on this basis that later American Catholics, such as Father Robert Drinan, could champion religious freedom as "a new global right." See Drinan, *Can God and Caesar Coexist?: Balancing Religious Freedom and International Law* (New Haven, CT: Yale University Press, 2004).

39 Wolfram Kaiser, *Christian Democracy and the Origins of the European Union* (Cambridge, UK: Cambridge University Press, 2007).

40 See Marco Duranti, "Conservatives and the European Convention on Human Rights," in Norbert Frei and Annette Weinke, eds., *Toward a New Moral World Order: Menschenreschtspolitik und Völkerrecht seit 1945* (Weimar: Wallstein Verlag, 2013) and *The European Project and the Conservative Origins of Human Rights* (New York: Oxford University Press, forthcoming). On the Cold War framework, see earlier literature including Antonin Cohen and Mikael Rask Madsen, "Cold War Law: Legal Entrepreneurs and the Emergence of a European Legal Field (1945–1965)," in Volkmar Gessner and David Nelken, eds., *European Ways of Law: Towards a European Sociology of Law* (Oxford: Hart, 2007).

41 Kokkinakis v. Greece, App. No. 14307/88, 260 Eur. Ct. H.R. (ser. A) (1993).

42 Citation from Duranti, "Curbing Labour's Totalitarian Temptation: European Human Rights Law and British Postwar Politics," *Humanity* 3, no. 1 (Winter 2012): 370.

43 Cf. James Q. Whitman, "Separating Church and State: The Atlantic Divide," *Historical Reflections/Réflexions historiques* 34, no. 3 (Winter 2008): 86–104.

44 For a start, see Evans, *Religious Liberty and International Law in Europe*, chap. 10.

45 Carolyn Evans, "Religious Freedom in European Human Rights Law: The Search for a Guiding Conception," in Mark W. Janis and Carolyn Evans, eds., *Religion and International Law* (The Hague: Martinus Nijhoff Publishers, 1999), 388.

46 By a founding figure, see Polys Modinos, "La Convention Européenne des Droits de l'Homme: ses origines, ses objectifs, sa réalisation," *Annuaire Européenne* 1 (1955): 141–72. Recently, see Danny Nicol, "Original Intent and the European Convention on Human Rights," *Public*

Law (April 2005): 152–72, or Ed Bates, *The Evolution of the European Convention on Human Rights: From Its Inception to the Creation of a Permanent Court of Human Rights* (Oxford: Oxford University Press, 2011), which does view the Convention as "safeguard against totalitarianism" but does not mention how religion or religious freedom figured in this project.

47 Council of Europe, *Collected Edition of the "Travaux Préparatoires,"* 5 vols. (The Hague: M. Nijhoff, 1975), 1:130.

48 Compare similar phrases in the treaty's Preamble as well as Arts. 6, 8, 10, and 12.

49 Compare Carolyn Evans, *Freedom of Religion under the European Convention of Human Rights* (New York: Oxford University Press, 2001), 42–44.

50 For its interwar origins at the hands of Karl Loewenstein, see now Udi Greenberg, *The Weimar Century: German Emigres and the Ideological Foundations of the Cold War* (Princeton, NJ: Princeton University Press, 2014), chap. 4, and "Militant Democracy and Human Rights," *New German Critique*, forthcoming.

51 Kommunistische Partei Deutschlands c. Allemagne, European Commission, Requête N° 250/257 (1957). For the only discussion I have found on militant democracy in the European Court of Human Rights, see Sven Eiffler, "Die 'wehrhafte Demokratie' in der Rechtsprechung des Europäischen Gerichtshofs für Menschenrechte," *Kritische Justiz* 36, no. 2 (Spring 2003): 218–25, but this does not focus on its legacy in the Muslim headscarf cases.

52 Indeed, after the Cold War, the court was willing to find an Article 11 freedom of assembly violation in the Turkish suppression of a communist party (Article 9 claims were not reached): United Communist Party of Turkey and Others v. Turkey, App. No. 19392/92 (1992) (Grand Chamber).

53 For a good summary of debates about the nature and causes of Europe's religious change, see Hugh McLeod, *The Religious Crisis of the 1960s* (New York: Oxford University Press, 2007), esp. chap. 1. For a comparative study of Catholic countries, see Jean-Louis Ormières, *L'Europe désenchantée: La fin de l'Europe chrétienne? France, Belgique, Espagne, Italie, Portugal* (Paris: Fayard, 2005).

54 These currently raging debates are beyond the scope of this book, but see Moyn, "Religious Freedom between Truth and Tactic," in

Winnifred Fallers Sullivan, Elizabeth Shakman Hurd, Saba Mahmood, and Peter G. Danchin, eds., *Politics of Religious Freedom* (Chicago: University of Chicago Press, 2015), as well as Douglas NeJaime and Reva B. Siegel, "Conscience Wars: Complicity-Based Conscience Claims in Religion and Politics," *Yale Law Journal* 124, no. 7 (May 2015): 2516–91.

55 Promisingly, in spite of the more recent S.A.S. v. France case, the European Court has now found an Article 9 violation in a headscarf case from Turkey in which the applicants merely wanted to wear religious attire in a public square rather than in an institutional setting in which its precedents might have led it to demand "neutrality" of the sort enforced in *Dahlab*, *Şahin*, and *Dogru*. Affaire Ahmet Arslan et autres c. Turquie, App. No. 41135/98 (2010), esp. ¶¶ 44–52, for its "democratic society" analysis.

56 Ran Hirschl, *Constitutional Theocracy* (Cambridge, MA: Harvard University Press, 2010).

57 J. H. H. Weiler, *Un'Europa cristiana: Un saggio esplorativo* (Milan: Rizzoli, 2003), Part I as well as 116–21 for a "Christian historiography of European integration" radically different from the one I have suggested here. For some reason, only a small portion of this book has been published in English, as Weiler, "A Christian Europe?: Europe and Christianity: Rules of Commitment," *European View* 6 (2007): 143–50.

58 A transcription of Weiler's oral pleadings as lawyer representing various intervening states can be found at http://bit.ly/1BHb9VP. The rhetoric of the pleadings originates in Richard John Neuhaus, *The Naked Public Square* (New York: Eerdmans, 1984). See also Pasquale Annichino, "Winning the Battle by Losing the War: The Lautsi Case and the Holy Alliance between American Conservative Evangelicals, the Russian Orthodox Church and the Vatican to Reshape European Identity," *Religion and Human Rights* 6, no. 2 (2011): 213–19.

Epilogue

1 Charles S. Maier, *Recasting Bourgeois Europe: Stabilization in France, Germany, and Italy in the Decade after World War I* (Princeton, NJ: Princeton University Press, 1975).

2 Charles S. Maier, "The Two Postwar Eras and the Conditions for Stability in Twentieth-Century Western Europe," *American Historical Review* 86, no. 2 (April 1981): 327–52.

3 Ibid., 349–50. Maier did credit "the new Christian Democratic parties" as "the major force preventing ideological repolarization" either to the far left or far right (332).

4 Aimé Césaire, *Discourse on Colonialism*, trans. Joan Pinkham (New York: Monthly Review Press, 1972), 17; but compare Udi Greenberg, *Days of Fire: Protestants, Decolonization, and European Integration* (forthcoming).

5 Tony Judt, *Postwar: A History of Europe since 1945* (New York: Penguin, 2005). By contrast to others, one of the founders of modern European intellectual history in the United States, Stuart Hughes, often made room for Christian thought in his books, and his account of French Catholicism during the same years that mine covers is still valuable: H. Stuart Hughes, *The Obstructed Path: French Social Thought in the Years of Desperation* (New York: Harper and Row, 1966), chap. 3.

6 Their works are all cited elsewhere in this book.

7 See, for example, Jan-Werner Mueller, "The End of Christian Democracy," *Foreign Affairs*, July 15, 2014.

8 Camille Robcis, "Catholics, the 'Theory of Gender,' and the Turn to the Human in France: A New Dreyfus Affair?," *Journal of Modern History*, forthcoming.

9 See, for example, Philip Jenkins, *The Next Christendom: The Coming of Global Christianity*, 3rd ed. (New York: Oxford University Press, 2011).

10 Surprisingly, Kathryn Sikkink does not even mention Catholicism in her otherwise illuminating recent essay, "Latin American Countries as Norm Protagonists of the Idea of International Human Rights," *Global Governance* 20, no. 3 (July 2014): 389–404.

11 James Ron, David Crow, and Shannon Golden, "The Struggle for a Truly Global Human Rights Movement," *Open Democracy,* June 18, 2013.

12 Stephen Hopgood, *Keepers of the Flame: Understanding Amnesty International* (Ithaca, NY: Cornell University Press, 2006), esp. chap. 3.

13 Alfred Firmin Loisy, *L'Évangile et l'Église*, 3rd ed. (Paris, 1904), 155.

14 This literature was initiated by Oona Hathaway, "Do Human Rights Treaties Make a Difference?," *Yale Law Journal* 111, no. 8 (June 2002): 1935–2042, and I have some comments on it in Moyn, "Do Human Rights Treaties Make Enough of a Difference?," in Costas Douzinas and Conor Gearty, eds., *Cambridge Companion to Human Rights Law* (Cambridge, UK: Cambridge University Press, 2012). See also Eric Posner, *The Twilight of Human Rights Law* (New York: Oxford University Press, 2014).

15 Louis Henkin, *The Age of Rights* (New York, 1990), 186, and "Religion and Human Rights," *Journal of Religious Ethics* 26, no. 2 (Fall 1998): 229–39 at 239.

Index

Index

Gide, André, 74

Gildersleeve, Virginia, 55, 195n.60

Gilson, Étienne, 80

Glendon, Mary Ann, 12, 14, 206n.57

Goerdeler, Carl, 106

Gossman, Lionel, 128–29

Great Britain, 40, 84, 88, 94–95, 97, 110, 129, 133–34, 150, 154, 159–60

Grewe, Wilhelm, 123

Gurian, Waldemar, 208–9n.77

Habermas, Jürgen, 188n.3

Hanebrink, Paul, 77

hedonism. *See* utilitarianism

Hegel, G.W.F., 53

Hellman, John, 69, 203n.38

Henkin, Louis, 180, 198n.78

Herzog, Isaac, Rabbi, 192–93n.38

Hildebrand, Dietrich von, 208–9n.77

Hirschl, Ran, 31, 165

Hitler, Adolf, 10, 53, 80–81, 106, 117, 130, 170

Hocking, William Ernest, 223n.28

Holocaust, the, 1–2, 11, 13–14, 26, 32, 57, 67, 79–80, 90, 96, 103–4, 187n.1, 206n.59

Holocaust memory, 32, 90, 205n.59

Howard, Thomas A., 187–88n.1

Hughes, H. Stuart, 228n.5

human dignity. *See* dignity, human

human person. *See* personalism

Hundhammer, Alois, 57

individual, versus person. *See* personalism

individualism. *See* personalism

Institute for International Law (*Institut de droit international*), 65–66

International Court of Justice, 66

Ireland, 15, 25–63, 161, 191n.29

Irish Christian Front, 40

Islam, 14, 19–20, 138–42, 144–45, 165, 177

Israel, 41, 192–93n.38

Italy, 1, 57, 137–38, 155, 195n.64

Jarausch, Konrad, 216n.46

Jellinek, Georg, 111

Jesus Christ, 6, 10, 15, 25, 109, 178–79

John XXIII, Pope, 22

John Paul II, Pope, 5, 100, 204–5n.44

Joint Commission on Religious Liberty, 149–50

"Judeo-Christianity," 24, 150–51

Judt, Tony, 171

Kagan, Robert, 218–19n.64

Kant, Immanuel, 26–27, 98–99, 198n.78

Kantianism, 27, 62–63, 98–99. *See also* autonomy

Kaiser, Wolfram, 16, 92

Kelsen, Hans, 57, 63

Keogh, Dermot, 39, 42, 60

Index

Index

Stendhal (Henri Beyle), 176
Sternhell, Zeev, 200n.10
Stoicism, 109–10, 112, 115, 213n.17
Strauss, Leo, 217n.50

Talmon, Jacob L., 123–24, 217n.50
Teitgen, Pierre-Henri, 94
Témoignage chrétien (French resistance group), 80
thesis-hypothesis, Catholic theory of American religious freedom, 155–57, 202–3n.34
Thomas Aquinas, 68, 83, 109
Thomism, *See* Scholasticism
Times Literary Supplement, 133–34
Tocqueville, Alexis de, 33, 85, 157
totalitarianism, 3, 8–10, 15, 17–18, 32, 37, 53, 59, 63, 74–75, 78, 84–86, 97, 108, 114–15, 120–23, 126, 133, 173, 184n.11, 196n.67, 225–26n.46
transwar chronology, 15, 16, 22–23, 183, 205n.59
Treblinka, 1
Treitschke, Heinrich von, 53
Trevor-Roper, Hugh, 128
Troeltsch, Ernst, 109
Truman, Harry S, 59
Tulkens, Françoise, 138
Turkey, 142–44, 147, 162–64, 227n.55

Union of Soviet Socialist Republics (USSR). *See* Soviet Union

United Kingdom. *See* Great Britain
United Nations, 12, 14, 26, 56, 66–67, 79, 91–92, 111, 115, 126, 151–53, 158, 186n.25, 188–89n.7
United Nations Charter (1945), 26, 30, 39–40, 55–56, 65, 149, 215–16n.41
United Nations Educational, Scientific and Cultural Organization (UNESCO), 90–91
United States Supreme Court, 151, 157
utilitarianism, 10, 63, 87, 112, 122
Universal Declaration of Human Rights (1948), 12, 16, 26, 30, 51–52, 56–57, 92, 99, 101, 115, 126, 149, 151–53, 158–59, 161, 175, 188–89n.7, 206n.57; familialism of, 191n.29

Vallat, Xavier, 51
Vatican II, 155, 157, 224n.33
Verdross, Alfred, 62–63, 197–98n.77
Vialatoux, Joseph, 36–37
Vichy. *See* France
Vidler, Alec, 97
Vinen, Richard, 93
Visscher, Charles de, 66, 88–89, 93
Voice for Human Rights, 78–79

Waldron, Jeremy, 189n.12
Walsh, Edmund A., 52–53
Walshe, Joseph, 47–48

Index

Weiler, J.H.H., 165–66, 227n.57

West, the, 18–19, 70, 85, 91, 95, 107–9, 113–21, 125, 127, 151, 154, 160, 216n.46

West Germany. *See* Germany

Whitman, James Q., 189n.12, 195n.59, 225n.43

Wintrich, Josef, 96

Wojtyła, Karol. *See* John Paul II

World Council of Churches (WCC), 17, 119–20, 134, 150, 187n.27, 215–16nn.40–41

Wyzanski, Charles, Jr., 198n.78

Young Right (*Jeune Droite*), 70

Acknowledgments

When I first traveled to the Jacques Maritain Center at the University of Notre Dame in July 2007, interested in how the greatest philosopher of human rights of the 1940s came to his views, I did not know where I was going. Many years later, this book is the unexpected result.

Not long after my visit, I decided that it made more sense to study the history of human rights not as *intellectual* history but as *ideological* history—there were too few thinkers, of too little merit, to proceed otherwise, so long as the publicistic and even propagandist aspects of the idea mattered more than philosophical finesse or legal doctrine. In the 1940s, and even in the 1970s, human rights remained more political slogan than they were either theory or law—both of which human rights have finally become in our day. While I made room for Christian human rights in my overall account of how the larger idea made its way to its current popularity, I ultimately subordinated them to a story of postponement. If Christianity provided an incubator without which human rights might not even have survived the 1940s, it was not in the guise of Christian human rights that they have triumphed since the 1970s, in spite of some unsuspected legacies.

Acknowledgments

It was only when I was given the chance to deliver the Mellon Distinguished Lectures at the University of Pennsylvania in fall 2014, under the auspices of Penn Press, that I realized that I had enough material to return to my old choice—not to undo it but rather to emphasize a part of the whole on its own and for its own sake that took only a small place in my overall scheme. I am exceptionally grateful to Peter Agree for so generously extending the invitation, Eric Halpern for superintending Penn Press with such professionalism, and above all Damon Linker— who subsequently became the omnicompetent editor of this book—for being such a wonderful host and interlocutor during my visit. Needless to say, warm thanks are due the Andrew W. Mellon Foundation for funding the enterprise (as well as subventing the publication of this book). The lectures were attended with generosity by a stalwart crew of Philadelphia listeners to whom I am very appreciative, often for their over-the-top introductions or helpful questions, and who included William Burke-White, Antonio Feros, Sarah Barringer Gordon, Peter Holquist, Jeffrey Kallberg, Amy Kaplan, Stephanie McCurry, Benjamin Nathans, Vanessa Ogle, Sophie Rosenfeld, Jonathan Steinberg, John Tresch, and Beth Wenger.

For the original grant to visit the Maritain Center, I am grateful to John O'Callaghan (and to Thomas Kselman, John McGreevy, and Anthony O. Simon, who were so welcoming at the time). Chapter 3 was written at the Institute for Advanced Study, in Princeton, New Jersey, where librarian Karen Downing gathered up crucial pieces of far-flung evidence, and with support from the American Council of Learned Societies Frederick Burkhardt Fellowship for Recently Tenured Scholars program and the John

Acknowledgments

Simon Guggenheim Foundation fellows program as well as good advice from Jan Eckel, Paul Hanebrink, and Jerry Z. Muller. I appreciated postpublication correspondence with Klaus Schwabe concerning his teacher, notably when it came to the propriety of the label "conservative"—a term I continue to use advisedly, in part because Cold War liberalism had so many contiguities with a rethought conservatism. Robert O. Paxton, my admired former colleague, provided counsel on the evanescent Vichy constitution.

I benefited from presenting chapter 1 at the University of Oxford and before my then-future colleagues at Harvard Law School, chapter 2 in the Yale University legal history series, chapter 3 at Columbia University's Deutsches Haus, and chapter 4 before the Yale Law School faculty and at conferences in Venice on "the politics of religious freedom" organized under the auspices of the Henry R. Luce Foundation project of the same name, and in Paris at an event on a similar theme that Jean L. Cohen, Yasmine Ergas, and I co-organized. I first formulated some of the thoughts in the epilogue on the analogy between the Christian and human rights movements at two different symposia that Eric Posner and Jack Snyder organized. When the chapters appeared as essays in various places, I owed the invitation to contribute—and often welcome assistance and criticism—to Nehal Bhuta, Jean L. Cohen, Peter Danchin, Stefan-Ludwig Hoffmann, Elizabeth Shakman Hurd, Cécile Laborde, Saba Mahmood, Christopher McCrudden, and Winnifred Fallers Sullivan, while Robert Schneider of the *American Historical Review* ran one of the other chapters through his notoriously tortuous review process.

I am grateful for permission to reprint and rework from earlier sources. Chapter 1: "The Secret History of

Constitutional Dignity," in Christopher McCrudden, ed., *Understanding Human Dignity* (Oxford University Press for the British Academy, 2013); chapter 2: "Personalism, Community, and the Origins of Human Rights," in Stefan-Ludwig Hoffmann, ed., *Human Rights in the Twentieth Century* (Cambridge University Press, 2011); chapter 3: *American Historical Review* 116, no. 1 (February 2011): 58–79; and chapter 4: "From Communist to Muslim: Religious Liberty in European Human Rights Law," *South Atlantic Quarterly* 113, no. 1 (Winter 2013): 63–86, and in different form as "Religious Freedom and the Fate of Secularism," in Jean L. Cohen and Cécile Laborde, eds., *Religion, Secularism, and Constitutional Democracy* (Columbia University Press, 2015). All the chapters have been significantly transformed and supersede their original versions. The *Yale Human Rights and Development Law Journal* published a much expanded version of chapter 1 under the same title (17, no. 1 [2014]) that takes up several matters about the contemporary fate of the concept that I have left out here. Similarly, portions of chapter 4 find their place in an otherwise excluded longer treatment of religious freedom since medieval times in a forthcoming volume of the Collected Courses of the Academy of European Law. Roberto Papini solicited a piece specifically about Maritain, which I have not included either, but a few passages from it found their way into chapter 2.

Since my first and superficial exploration of this topic, I am happy to say, it has been built upon and superseded in most respects by a series of extraordinary young scholars. These include Giuliana Chamedes, James Chappel, Marco Duranti, Udi Greenberg, Piotr Kosicki, Linde Lindqvist, Justin Reynolds, Noah Strote, and Anna Su. Several of them are former students, and it has been a treat for them to transform themselves so quickly into teachers of mine, by whom I am thrilled to be left behind. I have not tried to update my chapters more than superficially to reflect their tremendous ongoing insights, though their publishing contributions are already taking the debate around Christian politics between the 1930s and 1940s (of which Christian human rights proper were in the end a minor feature primarily of interest today) in fascinating new directions. James and Justin, in particular, gave me some good advice on the introduction, while Udi sent me an illuminating document from the German resistance. I also crossed paths several times with John Connelly, whose fine work on Catholic racism during the same period mine covers was helpful, like his committed personal counsel. Oran Doyle generously advised on details of Irish law. Josef Ansorge provided critical assistance with chapter 1; Sanford Diehl and Michaela Hailbronner helped too. In preparing the lectures for publication, I relied heavily on Saptarishi Bandopadhyay and Rachel Craft, while Ethan Kisch made the index. Kyriaki Tsaganis turned in a thorough copyedit, and John Hubbard designed a lovely cover based on a painting by Catholic modernist (and Maritain associate) Georges Rouault, whose heirs generously approved.

Keen reports for the press allowed me to introduce extra clarification, though I did not always follow their recommendations for more caution. Martin Conway wrote a truly helpful one and helped me strengthen my framing; his fingerprints are all over the introduction. Jan-Werner Mueller weighed in later with characteristically robust advice. In spring and summer 2015, the Social Science Research Council hosted a forum on some of these materials on "The Immanent Frame," its lively blog, and I replied to a series of insightful critics, who deserve thanks too, whatever their skepticism about my arguments. Their interventions amount to early reviews of this book. I am thankful to Daniel Steinmetz-Jenkins for serving as the impresario of the proceedings.

I owe most to my loving partner, Alisa, and our wonderful children, Lily and Madeleine. But the dedication for the book goes out to two close friends, Julian Bourg and Paul Hanebrink, conspirators since grad school and grade school, respectively. In the meantime, they have become two of our leading historians and have been models of insight and rigor who set examples to which I always aspire. Along the way, both friends have talked with me for all those years about lots of things, including Christianity in general (especially Julian) and in the twentieth century (especially Paul)—and together taught me much of what I know about it. Paul gave me indispensable advice on this book, from early days to the last drafts. I am grateful to them both.